Lumsden of the Guides

EARLY DAYS
JOHN AND HARRY LUMSDEN

Lumsden of the Guides

The Life and Campaigns of the Founder
of the Corps of Guides—An Elite Regiment
of the Indian Army

Sir Peter S. Lumsden

LEONAUR

Lumsden of the Guides
The Life and Campaigns of the Founder
of the Corps of Guides—An Elite Regiment
of the Indian Army
by Sir Peter S. Lumsden

First published under the title
Lumsden of the Guides

Leonaur is an imprint of Oakpast Ltd

Copyright in this form © 2011 Oakpast Ltd

ISBN: 978-0-85706-611-4 (hardcover)
ISBN: 978-0-85706-612-1 (softcover)

http://www.leonaur.com

Publisher's Notes

Contents

DEDICATED
BY PERMISSION
TO
FIELD-MARSHAL HIS ROYAL HIGHNESS
THE PRINCE OF WALES,
K.G., K.T., K.P., G.M.B., G.C.S.I.,
G.C.M.G., G.C.I.E., G.C.V.O.,
HONORARY COLONEL
THE QUEEN'S OWN CORPS OF GUIDES.

Preface

In compiling the following sketch of the life of Sir Harry Lumsden, it has been our endeavour, as much as possible, to let him and his associates speak for themselves. Probably, however, no one could have been less conscious than Lumsden that he was leaving behind him any material from which even an outline of his career could be obtained. It was not till after his death that a search at Belhelvie resulted in the discovery that his mother had carefully preserved the full and interesting letters which her son had written to his parents during his Indian career. These letters are produced almost in their entirety. They reveal their author's character with singular felicity from boyhood onwards. Indeed, it may truly be said, "These letters are Harry Lumsden."

In addition to letters, we have some anecdotes specially recorded for the late Colonel Sir Henry Yule, R.E., together with many rough pencil notes, too fragmentary to be produced as they stand. Full use, however, of these notes has been made, and portions of the narrative have been based on them, the original phraseology being as far as possible adhered to.

From Lumsden's official diaries we have quoted in full detail the description of the march of the Mission from Peshawur to Candahar, as given in chapter 15. The account of the life of the Mission at Candahar, and the constitution of the Afghan army as described in chapters 16 and 17, is founded on the diaries. Where original material has failed we have not hesitated to quote from notes and writings by Sir F. R. Pollock, Sir Henry Daly, the Rev. T. P. Hughes, Colonel J. Peyton, Colonel H. C. E. Ward, and from the published lives of Sir Harry's contemporaries Sir Henry and Sir John Lawrence, Lord Clyde, John Nicholson, also from Trotter's *India*, Paget and Mason's *Narrative of North-West Frontier Expeditions*, and from the early *Regimental History of the Guides*. A remarkable series of letters written by Herbert Edwardes,

Commissioner of Peshawur, to Lumsden at Candahar, describing the progress of the Indian Mutiny of 1857-58, is given almost in full in chapters 18-24.

We are indebted to Mrs. J. T. Walker for permitting the original drawings in her album of the Amir Dost Muhammad Khan and of the village of Akora from the pencil of the late Colonel W. Fane to be copied for this work; and also to the authorities of the South Kensington Museum for the copy of the portrait of Resaldar Futteh Khan, of the Guides, by W. Carpenter, and to the many associates and old friends of Harry Lumsden for the use of their notes and personal memoranda.

It will be noticed that we have taken care to avoid overloading the text with genealogical details, which might hinder the flow of the early part of the narrative. Those of our readers who would learn more of the history of the ancient Scottish family of Lumsden will find a full account thereof in an excellent book by Lieutenant-Colonel H. W. Lumsden, R.A., entitled, *Memorials of the Families of Lumsdaine, Lumisden, or Lumsden*, printed under the auspices of Mr. David Douglas, of Edinburgh.

A word or two of explanation is perhaps necessary in regard to the manner in which we have transcribed Oriental names. No very hard and fast line has been followed. Where custom has clearly sanctioned a popular mode of spelling, as, for instance, Delhi, Cawnpore, Cabul, etc., we have followed custom in our text; where we have had—or thought we had—a *tabula rasa*, we have followed the Jonesian system more or less closely, *e.g.*, Afridi, Yusafzai, Muhammad. For the most part we have allowed Oriental names to stand as we have found them in the original letters and books quoted; occasionally, however, in order to prevent the confusion which might arise from the very varied ways of spelling such names of common occurrence as Afridi, Abazai, Yusafzai, we have tried to make the spelling uniform throughout, as we thought it possible that a reader coming across Eusafzie, Yoosufzye, and Yusafzai, might well be puzzled to know whether these names represented three different places, or only one place. We have employed accents as sparingly as possible, only inserting them when we thought a reasonable doubt might arise as to whether a vowel was long or short.

CHAPTER 1

Harry Lumsden's Boyhood
and Education

Harry Burnett Lumsden first saw the light during a storm in the
Bay of Bengal, on board the East India Company's ship *Rose*, on the
12th November, 1821. His father, Lieutenant Thomas Lumsden, fourth
son of Hary[1] Lumsden of Belhelvie Lodge, Aberdeenshire, haying entered the Bengal Artillery in 1808, went home on leave in 1819, married Hay, daughter of John Burnett of Elrick, an estate not far from
Belhelvie, and was returning to India with his wife in the following
year, when their eldest son was born. Thomas Lumsden had already,
before his marriage, been marked amongst his brother officers as one
above the crowd. He had served with the Horse Artillery at the siege
of Hatrass and at the capture of Kalunga in 1817, and in the two suc-
ceeding years in the Pindari campaigns under the Marquis of Hastings,
by whom his services were specially brought to notice. His homeward
journey in 1820 was of a type not very usual in the early part of the
century. Instead of taking the ordinary sea route, *via* the Cape of Good
Hope, Thomas Lumsden accompanied his distinguished cousin, Matthew Lumsden, Professor of Persian and Arabic in Calcutta, on a difficult overland expedition through Persia, Armenia, Georgia, Russia,
Austria, and France to England.

The travellers were overtaken by a snowstorm in the Caucasus,
during which Thomas Lumsden lost a valuable gold watch. Several
years later, however, Matthew Lumsden made a second journey over
the same route, and greatly to his surprise was presented with his
cousin's watch by certain monks, who stated that it had been found on

---

1. *Sic* An old Scottish mode of spelling Harry.

a mountain path. The watch has now become an heirloom in the family, and has been inscribed with the appropriate motto *Nil desperandum.* Lieutenant Lumsden, having rejoined the headquarters of the Bengal Artillery, was promoted to be captain in the following year, 1822, and was appointed to the command of the 1st Troop 1st Brigade Bengal Horse Artillery. With that troop he was employed in 1825, in the first Burmese war, and was present throughout every siege and action. The despatches of that campaign bear testimony to the good service of Captain Lumsden, the attention of Government "being specially attracted to his gallant conduct" in continuing, while badly wounded, to direct his guns during the attack on Napade on December 25th.

On the conclusion of peace three officers were specially chosen to convey the ratification of the treaty to the golden fort at Amerapura, *viz*., Captain Thomas Lumsden, Lieutenant Henry Havelock,[2] Deputy Assistant Quartermaster-General, and Assistant Surgeon George Knox. Honours were not in those days very liberally conferred on officers of the East India Company's forces; but on the accession of Her Majesty the Queen, Thomas Lumsden (then a colonel in the army) was appointed a Companion of the Bath.

Captain Lumsden continued in command of the same troop of Horse Artillery till he obtained his majority in 1832. He was then appointed to the charge of the gun-carriage agency at Futtehgurh, which he retained until he retired from the service in 1842. He died at Belhelvie Lodge in 1873, the father of six sons and five daughters.

In 1827 young Harry Lumsden had been sent home and placed in charge of his grandmother at Belhelvie, and under the guardianship of his father's brother, Henry Lumsden of Tilwhilly and Auchindoir, Aberdeenshire. The boy's first school was the Bellevue Academy, in Aberdeen, then conducted by the Rev. George Tulloch and his wife—a French lady, familiarly known to her husband's many pupils as "*Madame*," The rudiments of education were well taught by Mr. Tulloch and his assistants, discipline being rigidly enforced by a liberal use of the rod. Harry was much liked, both by masters and boys. He had a happy facility for languages, which he combined with great power of application. He was gifted with a good temper, a happy disposition, great originality, and aptness. From boyhood to old age he gave his whole might to his pursuits, whether of work or play. His love of nature was intense—animals were his friends, field sports his passion. The mountains, the rivers, the glens of Aberdeenshire, and the birds and beasts

2. Afterwards General Sir Henry Havelock.

and fishes which dwelt therein, kindled his enthusiasm while he was a mere child.

From Bellevue, Harry Lumsden went to Mr. Dawes' well-known school at Bromley, in Kent; and at the age of sixteen years and three months was nominated to a direct Indian cadetship by Mr. John Shepherd—himself an Aberdeenshire man—one of the directors in Leadenhall Street Lumsden's service dated from the 1st March, 1838, and in the same year he was gazetted to the 59th Bengal Native Infantry, at Moradabad, as an ensign, and marched with his regiment to Loodiana in the cold weather of 1839-40. On arrival in India he spent some time with his parents, Major and Mrs. Lumsden, at Futtehgurh, doing duty with the 34th Native Infantry stationed there. Major Lumsden, knowing his son to be an apt learner, and, at the same time, more than a keen sportsman, took every opportunity to urge the importance of passing examinations in the native languages without delay. Harry obeyed his father to some purpose, and in a comparatively short time qualified himself for high appointments by obtaining the interpreter's and quartermaster's certificates; but he did not neglect his regimental duties.

The 59th was one of the best corps in the native army. He regarded it as his home, and he rapidly became a great favourite both of officers and men. A mark of affection given to him by his companions at this time was the happily-chosen name of "Joe," by which he was familiarly known during the rest of his life. No precise reason can be assigned for the choice, though various guesses might be made. But we may be sure that the merry, bright fellow who was called "Joe" Lumsden by his intimate friends owed the pet name, which he fully accepted, to the kindly feelings with which he was always regarded. In December, 1841, Lumsden was unexpectedly appointed to act as interpreter and quartermaster to the 33rd Native Infantry, then marching to Peshawur to form part of the army proceeding, under the command of General Sir George Pollock, to avenge our disasters in Afghanistan.[3] Of some of the events of the later part of the year 1842 we have his own accounts in letters which have been preserved.

Gundamuk, 6th September, 1842.

We are all here at last, after great bother with camels having run away and died on the road from overwork. Last night I was up all night, making arrangements for a wing of our regiment to

---

3. See Appendix C.

remain and collect grain for the force. We were to have gone to Soorkháb this morning. When everything was ready, out comes an order that we are not to advance today; so I might have had sleep last night. However, one thing is sure, that if any part of the regiment goes on, the Colonel will go with it; and if he goes, his staff cannot be left, so I must see Cabul, anyhow. Many of our poor fellows are dreadfully disgusted with the idea of having to remain behind with the wing.

Futteh Jung[4] is now in our camp, having escaped from confinement The prisoners have been carried to Bamean, but one of the chiefs has made a bargain with the General to make them over to us on payment of money.

The people of Cabul are quite disgusted with Akbar, but his name has such a charm now that not one of them has resolution enough to stand against him, though he is murdering hundreds every day.

Futteh Jung thinks that we shall be able to get as much provisions in Cabul as we can desire to bring us back; if only we can once get there, and the advance is to be made tomorrow. Nott has gained a decisive victory over the enemy before Ghuzni, and taken four guns from them. The particulars have not reached us yet, but we are assured that that grand fort has again fallen into our hands. This time we must, I think, send it up to the clouds.

Henry Lawrence has had the greatest difficulty in making the Seikhs—who, from the beginning, have not had their hearts in this business—to come up here to the post He has at last succeeded, but they will not stay here one day unless we leave an artillery battery with them, so Larkins has been told off to remain. . . .

The next letter was written six weeks afterwards, also from Gundamuk, but in the interval the army had advanced to and returned from Cabul.

Camp Gundamuk, 20th October.

Here we are again—safe and sound, thank God—after having gone through some trouble, a little privation, and no end of fighting, and at last retrieved the honour of our country by the

4. Son and successor of Shah Shuja.

destruction of the enemy's army wherever we could find them, ravaging the country all around us for miles, drawing off their sheep, and finishing the campaign by making a bonfire of the capital I think the Afghan nation will rue for generations to come that they ever thought of the treachery by which our last army was cut up, but which we, thank God, have avenged in a most satisfactory manner.

We started from this on the 8th *ultimo*, and did not see a man the first day, and also got over the second march very well, only having a few shots fired at us, one of which, however, brought down my charger—*as dead as a stone*. We received orders on the 10th to make a march to join headquarters at Tezeen, which we did; and next day Colonel Richmond, who commanded the rear guard, ordered me to stay with him and carry orders, so I was done out of going with the advance. But as soon as the column and baggage had got into the mouth of the Tezeen Pass our work commenced.

The enemy's artillery and cavalry came down the valley, and opened a well-directed fire on the rear guard from a distance of some 1200 yards. The first round shot they sent at us went within two feet of my horse's legs, and sent our doctor, who was leaning on a *dooly*,[5] spinning, breaking the *dooly* to pieces, whilst the next shot killed a *sowar's* horse.

When the enemy's cavalry had advanced about half-way towards us I went with an order to the officer commanding the 3rd Dragoons (Major Bond) to retire before the enemy, and when they should come well out from the hills to charge.

The moment the Dragoons retired the enemy came out in thousands, horse and foot, thinking our cavalry were repulsed.

The Dragoons retired until joined by the 1st Bengal Cavalry and by Tait's Horse, who, on being formed up, received the order to charge. Every horse shot round, and off went the whole line, boot to boot, as hard as four legs could take them.

In a flash our Cavalry were through the broken enemy like lightning, back again, and through them again. We could see nothing of the actual fighting part of the business, only here and there the glimmer of a sabre through the dust; but the number of Afghan horses without riders galloping over the plain spoke their own tale, and testified to the masterly manner in which

5. Litter.

15

our Cavalry were being handled, and the success of the operation. This lasted for about a quarter of an hour, when the 1st Bengal Cavalry returned, showing their crimsoned blades and one of the enemy's standards, which Goad had captured from Khuda Bux Khan (Chief of Tezeen).

After this, as the enemy's guns were bothering, Lawrence replied from guns with the Seikh force. God only knows what damage he did, but the enemy's guns were silenced in four shots.

By this time the baggage had moved well into the hills, and we had to protect it, so could not afford to waste time, or we should have captured them all.

On entering the pass we were received with a heavy fire from the heights on the right. The colonel sent me to bring up one company, which I did, and went with it to the top of the hill. I pointed out to the party a *sungur* (or breastwork) they were to occupy, and as soon as I got down again was sent off with another company of the 35th N.I. to the left. Shortly after I was again sent up to the same company, and was giving poor Norton the order to push on to the next hill when he fell at my horse's feet, shot through the mouth.

Two *sepoys* were also hit, one of whom I took down the hill on my horse.

We gave the Afghans a great mauling, not giving them time to carry off their dead and wounded. We carried most of the sungurs (breastworks) with the bayonet, showing to the world that *sepoys* can and will use that weapon, when required to do so, with coolness and effect.

The Colonel told me I had rendered great assistance during the day, and that he was greatly pleased with the way I had carried out his orders. Was not that something to make your firstborn hold up his head?

From this point, so far as we were concerned, we had nothing more to do. We pushed on to Cabul, which we have totally destroyed.

The flag of England was hoisted on the Bala Hissar on the day we arrived, under a salute, and shortly afterwards some troops were sent to destroy the *bazaar*.

Just fancy, the first European article I found in Cabul was the letter-book of the 1st Troop 1st Brigade Bengal Horse Artillery, with your handwriting. I seized it, but it was taken from my *syce*[6] in the town, before we returned from blowing up the *bazaar.*[7]

On the return march to India we had a day's fight in the Jugdulluk Pass, and served the enemy out. Alexander's battery gave shells beautifully planted. One of the Bombay guns broke down, and could not be used after the first shot. Ours are the gun-carriages to be depended upon; not one of the troops up here has broken anything, not even started a spoke.

We arrived here yesterday afternoon, and learned that we are to have a medal and six months' *batta.* What fun it will be peacocking about with my own regiment, where no other officer has anything of the sort!

You must excuse my not having written to you from Cabul, as every post was sent with the General's despatches, and married men alone were able to send small communications. Never mind, they will not make me on that account marry a bit sooner; but now that young hopeful is to have a medal, there may be some hope of his being able to pick up a sound and quiet creature one day.

Camp Attok, 16th November, 1842.

We are at Attok, on the home side of the Indus, once more. The General has given out in orders that we are not to halt if it can be avoided. Ferozepore will see us about the 13th *proximo.* Report has it that we are to be received with all sorts of triumphal arches and parades. I hope to goodness they will not take the trouble, for our men have been worked quite enough, without having to go through all sorts of *tumasha*[8] when they get home.

I have a great mind to send in a letter and try if I cannot get the acting quartermastership of my own corps, now that Hyslop is acting in the commissariat. It would be a great thing to get back to the 59th now that this war is over. Quartermaster's work is not after my sort, and I should so rejoice to return to my own corps and take charge of my own company. I have at

---

6. Groom.
7. Harry Lumsden and John Nicholson met for the first time in the city of Cabul. They found themselves together in a tough corner, from which they emerged with difficulty. This was the beginning of a very close friendship, which grew stronger and stronger, till Nicholson fell, fifteen years later, in the hour of victory at Delhi
8. Show or display.

times during this campaign, as quartermaster, been a good deal bothered. Officers who want camels do not realize that they are not to be found under every stone. Again, the difficulty of looking after every *bunniah*[9] with as much care as if he was a lady's Sunday nightcap, whilst other natives go to the commanding officer and tell him they have not seen *atta*[10] for a week, though in reality they may have just devoured half a *seer*[11] apiece of it, but think they might hold more. These are a few of the everyday trials that a quartermaster on service has, when perhaps he has spent the night in going and writing and rewriting to the commissariat about camels for the morning's march, and discovering towards daybreak that carriage is not to be had even for the sick and wounded. Is not this a pleasure?

I would rather be Harry Burnett Lumsden, Lieutenant, 59th N.I., than acting-quartermaster to the Queen. I should be delighted to return to my corps, but I am afraid you might not approve of it, and I do not know exactly how to do so without giving offence to this regiment.

If you see no harm in my returning to my own regiment, do let me know how on earth it is to be brought about; I'll be off at Ferozepore. I am thinking of sending home for a regular good gun, with 500 *rupees* of *batta*, which, I believe, will secure a first-rate one. I have got a charger, a grey Cabul horse, about 14-3, who stands fire beautifully. He is only five years old. I must have a charger, and shall not probably be able to get a better.

---

9. Trader.
10. Flour.
11. Seer=2 lbs.

ATTOCK, ON THE INDUS, 1852

CHAPTER 2

With 59th at Loodiana

Lumsden crossed the Sutlej with General Pollock's force on the 19th December, 1842, and was present with the rest of the Grand Army concentrated at Ferozepore under the commander-in-chief, Sir Jasper Nicolls. Early in 1843 he rejoined his own corps, the 59th Native Infantry, at Loodiana, and his days there were often recalled by him as amongst the happiest of his life. He spent much time in reading, he studied his profession, and he had full opportunity of indulging his passion for sport. His associates, both European and native, were congenial to him. He delighted to wander, either alone or with a companion, in the jungles and in the villages of the Sikhs of the Cis-Sutlej states, or of the Juts on the northern banks of the river. He thus rapidly acquired a knowledge of the language and customs of these people which proved of great value to himself and to the Government in after years. An incident in Lumsden's life at this period has been related by himself, and may be quoted in his own words.

While an ensign in the 59th N.I. I had my first official introduction to Henry Lawrence, then political assistant in charge of Ferozepore, and as the story is rather an interesting one, it may well be recorded here:—

Barrett, the vet of Alexander's troop of horse artillery, and I had obtained leave for a fortnight's shooting along the banks of the Sutlej. As the country was considered not altogether settled, we were allowed an escort of a corporal and four men of my regiment as a baggage guard. We had fair sport, and were enjoying our trip as only youngsters can do who are just entering on the threshold of sporting life, with all its spring and freshness, and had got to within two marches of the cantonments of Ferozepore, when the following incident occurred. Our custom was to rise early, have breakfast, and, sending on all our tents and servants, to shoot leisurely, on to our next encamping ground, which we generally reached about four or five in the afternoon. We had got over half our day's work, when we heard the sound of drums in the village ahead, and saw a mob of people coming in our direction.

Concluding that it must be a marriage or some Seikh festival, we agreed to go and see the fun, and, giving our guns to our attendants, mounted our horses, and rode on by ourselves to meet the party, which did not at first show any signs of discontent, but let us ride in the midst of them in the most friendly way; but as soon as we began to move on with them, we were both knocked off our horses by blows on the back from iron clubs, and before we could recover our feet we were seized by the wrists by two men on each side, and marched off to a fort in the village, where we were put into a room and made a sort of public show of, hundreds of people coming to see us, examine our clothes, etc.

After a short time, what was my astonishment to find my own groom appear in this mob of sightseers, and hustle me into a corner in the most insolent manner, declaring in loud tones that at last he would be avenged for some wrong which I had never previously heard of.

When he had pushed me a little out of the way of observation, he put a pencil, with a scrap of paper rolled round it, into my hand, and vanished, only to return and go through the same manoeuvre half an hour later, during which time I had contrived to amuse the mob at the door, while Barrett pretended to sulk in a corner, and wrote on the paper "We are prisoners, badly treated, and don't know what for; come and help us, quickly." This I gave to the groom, who vanished immediately. About 4 p.m. we were taken out into the open, and told we should be executed in ten minutes for the murder of a man we were said to have shot. We repudiated all knowledge of the matter, but to no purpose, and things looked very ugly indeed for about an hour, opinion evidently swaying from side to side between immediate execution and further inquiry.

All of a sudden something occurred which completely changed the state of affairs; for we were not only taken back to the fort, but soon found ourselves released, our servants collected, camp arranged, and abundance of provisions brought in for man and beast. The headman of the village arrived with presents and all sorts of apologies for the apparent harsh reception of us, which they now protested was absolutely necessary to quiet the indignation of the mob, on account of the son of the high priest having been shot dead by one of our soldiers.

Our servants, however, told us that they too had been plundered and ill-treated, until one of them, in a rage, let out that my groom was well on his way to Ferozepore, and that Henry Lawrence must know all about it by this time.

These were the magical words which had saved our lives as well as opened our prison doors.

At 10 p.m. Henry Lawrence himself turned up, accompanied by about 20 *sowars* and a lot of camel riders; and the result of the investigations, made then and there, proved beyond all doubt that the inhabitants of this notoriously bad village were a gang who had long plundered on the Ferozepore and Loodiana high-road, and on the morning of our adventure some of them, headed by the son of the headman, had attempted to plunder my bed, which was carried on the heads of two *coolies*, as usual, and escorted by a young Rajput soldier, who, seeing that the attacking party was too strong for him to resist, crept into a bush, and as soon as a good opportunity offered fired into the group round the bed, substituting a handful of stones for ball over the ordinary charge of powder, with the result that the gang bolted, leaving their leader dead beside the bed—a most damning proof against the whole village.

Lawrence ordered an immediate parade of all the inhabitants, and securing such of them as we could point out as most prominent actors in the business, took them to Ferozepore on the camels he had brought with him. Our depositions, as well as those of our servants necessary in the case, were taken in writing, and Lawrence was back in Ferozepore by 10 o'clock next morning.

Two years later, while Lumsden was serving with his regiment at Meerut, came the mustering in hot haste of the army of India on the left bank of the Sutlej. Ranjit Singh having died, the Sikhs, freed from his iron hand, refused to be controlled by his feeble successors, and determined to measure their strength with the British and native soldiers of the East India Company. They accordingly advanced towards the British frontier, and crossed the Sutlej in December, 1845, with an army of 60,000 men and 150 guns. On the 18th December the battle of Mudki was fought, the Sikhs being defeated with heavy loss. Three days afterwards followed the closely-contested fight of Ferozshahr. On the 22nd January the Sikhs were again defeated at Aliwal, and finally, on the 10th February, the campaign was brought to an end by the capture and total defeat of the enemy at Sobraon. Of this last great battle we have a stirring account in a letter from Harry Lumsden to his father.

Camp Lahore, 26th February, 1846.

Now for the battle of Sobraon, which you will be able to understand by looking at the accompanying sketch of our position. The whole army moved out on the morning of the 10th February with as little noise as possible, and took up our places in the line of attack before sunrise, with the exception of General Dicks' division, which was taken up to within two thousand yards of the right face of the enemy's entrenched position, and kept under cover of a dry *nullah*[1] in readiness to storm as soon as our guns had silenced the enemy's fire. Exactly at seven o'clock in the morning the Seikhs were saluted by a salvo from our heavy gun batteries, near the tower in front of Rhodawalla, which they instantly returned, with interest, from every battery along their front The cannonade thus commenced was carried on with the greatest spirit on both sides for upwards of three hours, the enemy serving their guns with wonderful rapidity and precision, knocking our Horse Artillery (which had gone out to the front very boldly, and given them several rounds of grape) back to the line in no time.

In about half an hour more the commander-in-chief, seeing that our Horse Artillery could not silence the enemy's guns, sent down an order for the storming division to advance. We instantly formed up—H.M. 10th Foot on the right, then the 43rd N.I. and 59th N.I. in the centre, with H.M. 53rd Foot on the left of the line of stormers, covered by Fordyce's troop of Horse Artillery on our right, and supported by the rest of the division as a reserve.

---

1. Ravine.

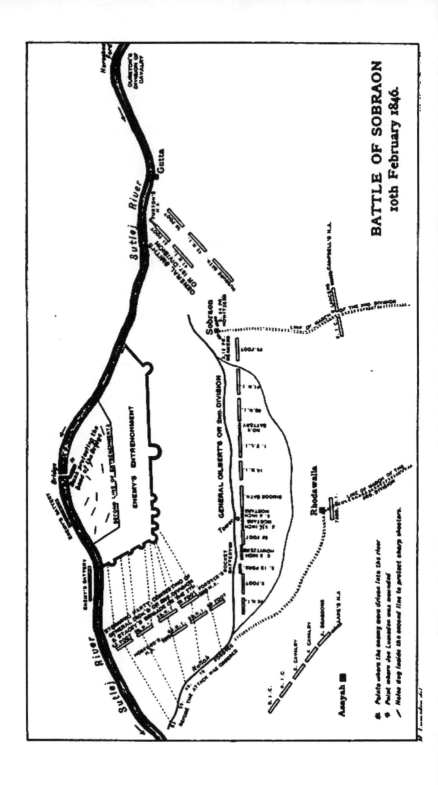

BATTLE OF SOBRAON
10th February 1846.

The instant we moved out of our cover in the *nullah* we were saluted with an awful discharge of well-directed shot, which did great mischief in our line; and this sort of amusement the enemy kept up for us with great effect until we reached within 800 yards of their batteries, when our troop of Horse Artillery gave them a few shells, while the Infantry closed up their half-broken line, and once more moved forward to the charge. The enemy now changed their round shot for quilted grape, which caused even greater loss than the former, but could not stop our men, who were by this time driven half mad with seeing so many of their companions killed around them, and having reached within 200 yards of the entrenchments we gave the Seikhs the benefit of a round of musketry from the whole line, and, with three cheers, regularly raced into the trenches with the bayonet, killing all the gunners on the spot, and driving the whole line of the Seikh infantry from the right of their entrenchment into the river, where they were shot down like so many ducks. We now cut away two of the centre boats from their bridge across the Sutlej, thereby cutting off all hope from the rest of the enemy, who, ignorant of our success on their right, were quietly keeping up a heavy fire on the whole of Smith's and Gilbert's divisions, which were now advancing in line.

The enemy had just succeeded in repelling an attack made on them in front by our European regiment and two Goorkah battalions, which they almost cut to pieces with grape, when, to their horror, they saw the whole of our division drawn up inside their own second line of entrenchments exactly in their rear. When turning from their guns, they made an attempt to escape by their left flank, but were instantly charged in front and rear at the same time, and bayoneted almost to a man. Some five or six regiments reached the river, but finding the bridge cut were obliged to try the ford, under a fire of two troops of Horse Artillery and about ten regiments of infantry, and, as you may fancy, were rather roughly handled.

The enemy's cavalry, which had only once shown themselves for about ten minutes, on our left flank, as we stormed the trenches and then drew off towards their left, now came in for their share of punishment, and finding their situation getting rather hot for them, also made for the bridge.

It was in getting my own company together at the head of the bridge, to give these worthies a suitable reception, that I received my wound. I had just got the boys in line, and was looking out to prevent them throwing away their fire by taking long shots, when I was shot through the foot by some desperate rascal, who had got into one of the boats in the bridge; but I was so excited at the time that I scarcely knew that I was hit, and sat on my charger, who was also shot through the leg about the same time, until the cavalry were driven into the river, after which I felt very sick, and would have fallen off my horse had not an officer of the 10th Foot, seeing that I was wounded, given me a glass of brandy, which refreshed me very much, and enabled me to do my duty until the action was over.

My foot got so swollen that I was obliged to get one of the men to cut the boot and stocking off, and found that a musket ball had entered on the top of the little toe, and come out half way down the foot. When I got home I was obliged to have the wound opened from end to end, and all sorts of queer-looking little bones taken out This, I was told, was the only chance of saving the foot, so I was obliged to submit, like a good boy, though, I must confess, it was anything but agreeable at the time. However, our M.D. tells me that the wound is wonderfully well, and will not make me the least lame; on the contrary, I shall now be able to put on a much more fashionable boot If you hear of an old boy wishing for a cure for corns, just recommend him to have a musket shot sent through them.

Our regiment, which went into this action with 450 bayonets, lost 73 killed and wounded, and is considered the most fortunate corps in the brigade, if not in the whole army, so you may fancy what nice warm work it was. I am happy to say that I am the only one out of seven officers present with the corps who got hit.

General Dick was killed at the head of our division in the storm, and Brigadier Stacey hit by a grape shot Our colonel also had his charger shot under him, so that all our commanders were down on the ground about the same time. As soon as the action was over, Lord Gough came down to our brigade and paid both the 43rd and our regiment the highest compliment he could have done; for he told us that he had always had a very good opinion of native troops, but he would never have hoped to have seen them go through such a fire in the style they had done, the two corps actually racing to be the first in the trenches. He went up to the *jemadar* of my company who had carried the regimental colours, and shook hands with him, which delighted the *sepoys* very much, and they cheered him all down the line.

We took and destroyed in this action seventy-two guns of all sizes, and so utterly ruined all the aspirations of the Seikhs, that in three days after we were in Lahore, with the Union Jack flying over the fallen empire of the proud Seikhs.

Everything is now arranged, and it is reported that we shall all be back in our respective cantonments by the 18th of next month.

CHAPTER 3

After the Sutlej Campaign

The 59th did return to cantonments, but meanwhile events had occurred which very materially affected young Lumsden's career.

"Broadfoot is killed and you are required forthwith," was the summons received on the evening of the 6th January, 1846, by Major Henry Lawrence, the Governor-General's agent at Nepal. Lawrence at once set out to join the headquarters of the army on the Sutlej. He arrived in time for the battle of Sobraon, where, as an Artillery officer, he was continuously employed in carrying orders, or assisting in the working of the guns on the field. In earlier days, Henry Lawrence and Thomas Lumsden, both Artillery officers, had been associated together in the regiment, and had maintained a close friendship. In the Afghan war, Lawrence had kept his eye on young Harry, the son of his friend, and had noted him as a chip of the old block, not to be lost sight of Indeed, it was a well-known custom of Henry Lawrence to keep notes of the names of promising men. When at messes or assemblies, where the merits of officers were discussed, he would take out his note-book and forthwith make entries of men described by their comrades as good and true.[1]

After Sobraon the British army marched unopposed to Lahore, where terms of peace were dictated. Those terms were, briefly, the cession in full sovereignty to the British Government of the territory lying between the Sutlej and Beas Rivers, and the payment of a war indemnity of one and a half million sterling. The Lahore Government, however, was unable to pay this sum, or even to give satisfactory security for the payment of one million. It was therefore arranged that all the hill country between the Beas and the Indus, including Cashmere

---

1. I have seen him do it—P. S. L.

and Huzara, should be ceded, [2] Simultaneously a treaty was executed with Maharaja Gulab Singh, of Jamu, by which the English made over to him in sovereignty, in consideration of a payment of three-quarters of a million sterling, the Cashmere territory ceded by the Lahore Government It was also arranged that a British Resident should be established at Lahore, and that a British force should remain there for a time to aid in the construction of a satisfactory administration.

The first agent of the Governor-General was Henry Lawrence, on whom it forthwith devolved to choose assistants on whom he could rely in his most difficult task of administration and control. Harry Lumsden's name was amongst those chosen. Others were George Lawrence, Macgregor, James Abbott, Herbert Edwardes, John Nicholson, Reynell Taylor, Arthur Cocks, Hodson, Richard Pollock, Lewin Bowring, Henry Coxe, and Melvill—a staff described in after days by Lawrence himself as "men such as you will seldom see anywhere, but when collected together worth double and treble the number taken at haphazard. Each was a good man, the most were excellent officers."

Harry Lumsden joined his new appointment as assistant to the Resident at Lahore, but was sent almost immediately to take part in the collection of supplies and the making of a road for the advance of General Wheeler's column on Kot Kangra. In the month of May, 1846, Lumsden rendered valuable service by securing a position from which our guns could entirely command that fortress, the garrison of which capitulated practically without resistance. Lumsden then remained for three months in civil charge of the Kangra district, but on the 8th August we find him again writing from Loodiana—

You must not be the least surprised at seeing my letters addressed from almost any station in the Punjab, for I am sure to be sent all over the country. Lawrence and his first assistant Edwardes are both ill at Simla, and the Government have considered it necessary, under the existing state of things at Lahore, to order Lawrence's brother John (the commissioner) to take his place, and superintend the movements of the *durbar*.

Lawrence wrote to me to move down with all possible haste and take Edwardes' place under his brother, so off I set, and rode the distance from Kangra in four days. . . . I am quite delighted at being ordered down to Lahore at this particular time, as in case of a row with the Khálsa-Jee (Seikhs) I shall be just in the

---

2. See Hunter's *Imperial Gazeteer of India.*

right box to see everything, and may with a little luck contrive to draw a prize; for I begin to think that luck is all in these matters, when I see old officers getting all sorts of honours for making a mess of every fight they get their heads into, and sacrificing men for want of knowledge and judgement. I begin to lose faith in all despatches, as, when matters take a disagreeable turn, it seems to me that some officers do not hesitate to draw on their imaginations.

I had a month and a half of as hard work at Kangra as any Christian could well be called upon to get through, having to work from morning until after dark in *kutcherry* to keep the business of the office from falling into arrears, and after dinner to make up rather heavy treasury accounts. None of the English clerks appointed to the office had arrived, so I was left to my own wits and resources. As you know, I do not mind any amount of work, but office work and confinement within doors is not my speciality; I would always rather ride twenty miles than write a note. I have, however, made over the office all right to that good man Lake,[3] who has taken my place at Kangra.

Old Brigadier Wheeler, after his return to Jullundur from Kangra, sent two most handsome letters about my services in assisting his division along the road, both to Grant, the adjutant-general (a 59th N.I. man), and to the commander-in-chief, and also made most flattering mention of my name in his orders to the division on breaking up the force, which, if it does not do me some good, cannot possibly do any harm.

Jullundur, 10th September, 1846.

Since my last letter I have, as you may see, been again wandering, having received an intimation from Lawrence that my services might be required in the political line at Lahore or elsewhere. I got my carriage together, and had no sooner done so than the order arrived from Simla for me to make all haste to meet the commissioner, John Lawrence, at Loodiana, on his way to Lahore. I started at once for Loodiana, where I spent three days with little Dunsford of my own corps, who was acting brigade major. From Loodiana we went by water to Ferozepore, and put up with Lawrence's sister for three days, and then rode two stages out towards Lahore during the night, where we met the

---

3. Afterwards Major-General Edward Lake, Financial Commissioner of the Punjab.

old *Ranee's Belati*[4] carriage, with four gun-horses in it, to take the commissioner in state; and, sure enough, if pace could do so, we should feel highly honoured, for no sooner were the men on the horses than whip and spur were put in requisition, and kept hard at work for six miles, when a fresh brace of nags were standing, all ready, and in like manner galloped their tails off. For a wonder we were conveyed all safe to Lahore.

During my short stay there I was initiated into all the mysteries of Grand *Durbars* and the like, introduced to Lai Sing, the Prime Minister, young Dulip Sing, and a large bundle of clothes, placed on a chair and called the *Maharanee*, out of which, now and then, might be seen a pair of feet and a remarkably pretty little hand. When the bundle was addressed, even in the most flowery Persian, the reply was always in a grinding sort of sound, strongly resembling that produced in the process of grinding coffee. However, the bundle, although she will not show her eyes, evidently has good ones, and shows her taste in the choice of her *wazir*, Lai Sing. I have seldom seen a better-looking man than Lai Sing. He is, I should say, about thirty years of age, strongly built, tall, and very soldier-like, though as cunning as a fox; talks in a bland, kind tone, which would lead anyone who did not know him to suppose he could not hurt a fly, though he would just as soon cut a man's windpipe as look at him.

Every one of the *sirdars* hate him, and make no secret of their dislike, but say with the greatest coolness that Lai Sing's life is not worth two hours' purchase after the withdrawal of the British troops from Lahore, which, according to present understanding, we are bound to do in October. Should this withdrawal take place, the unfortunate Punjab will have once more to witness those fearful scenes of murder and confusion for which the Seikh court has of late been so remarkable, and we shall assuredly have to return and annex the country. I cannot help thinking how much better it would be for all parties if we could only, for the sake of humanity, divest ourselves of a little of that mock modesty the political assumes when acting towards other states, and tell the local authorities at once, that if they cannot undertake to keep all quiet, we must assume the government.

In such a case we might grant the little *rajah* and the royal fam-

4. European.

ily a handsome pension; but "No," Government says, "we have made over the country to you, and you must keep it or fall." The former they cannot do, and the latter will inevitably be brought about by the secret pistol or sword.

To see all the chiefs in *durbar* one would say that he had never seen greater friends; but hear each man converse in private. There is not one of them who is not looking out anxiously for the time when, by our withdrawal from the scene, he may seize the opportunity of opening his neighbour's throat. I am sorry that, from Edwardes having returned from Simla, I may have to go back to Kot Kangra, as I am quite convinced in my own mind that before six months we shall have either a permanent Resident and assistants at Lahore, or the whole country under our rule. In either case there will be some scope for a youngster.

Lumsden, however, did not return to Kangra. A more interesting field of work lay before him. He had the good fortune to be selected to accompany Colonel Henry Lawrence in an expedition to Cashmere.

In July, 1846, the Maharaja Gulab Singh, escorted by a body of his own troops and accompanied by Arthur Broome and John Nicholson, crossed the mountains from Jamu to take possession of his new kingdom of Cashmere.[5]

We had not been many days in the valley, (wrote Nicholson), before we learnt that the Governor (Sheikh Imam-ud-din) had made up his mind to drive Gulab Singh's small force out of the valley, and seize us. We had great difficulty in effecting our escape, which we did just in time to avoid capture.

Marching off by one of the southern passes, Broome and Nicholson rejoined the Maharaja at Jamu about September 20th. Meanwhile Gulab Singh's troops in the Cashmere valley had been heavily defeated by the insurgent forces. The survivors threw themselves into the fort of Hari Purbut, where they might hold out until relief should come.

The report of the outbreak found Lord Hardinge at Simla, where Colonel Henry Lawrence also was taking a little rest after many months of hard and incessant labour. Both of them saw the need for prompt and vigorous action. Wheeler's brigade in Jullundur was or-

---

5. Trotter's *Life of John Nicholson*.

dered off at once to protect Jamu, while Henry Lawrence, hurrying back to Lahore, marched towards the scene of danger at the head of some ten thousand of those very Sikhs who had fought against us at Ferozshahr and Sobraon. He had reason to believe that the rebellious governor Sheikh Imam-ud-din had been egged on by the treacherous *wazir*, Lai Sing; and John Lawrence, who took his brother's place at Lahore, was instructed to seize and imprison the traitor in the event of harm befalling the British Resident.

Then, for the first time, was seen the extraordinary spectacle, to use Lawrence's own words, "of half a dozen foreigners taking up a lately-subdued mutinous army through as difficult a country as there is in the world, to put the chief formerly their commander, now in their minds a rebel, in possession of the brightest gem of their land."

Fortune on this occasion stood by the brave. By the end of October Imam-ud-dm had ridden across the mountains and yielded himself up to the safe keeping of Herbert Edwardes, who on the 1st November conducted his penitent captive to the tent of Colonel Lawrence.[6]

The conduct of the Sikh troops, (said Lord Hardinge), under the same officers who led them so lately in their invasion of our provinces, now employed in carrying out the conditions of the treaty of Lahore, and, perhaps, the least palatable part of those conditions, under the instructions of British officers, cannot but command admiration.

Lieutenant Lumsden accompanied the force, his political position with which can be judged from a copy of a letter from Edwardes, dated:

Camp Segowlie, 17th October, 1846.
(8 o'clock p.m.)

My dear Lumsden,—Tej Sing, in the civilest manner in the world, has declined a meeting with the *Maharajah* at Dhun-deesur. His plea is ill-health, but if he is well enough to march at all he is well enough to come to meet the *Maharajah*. However, that is not the point If he was really ill, it would not do at the present moment to decline a meeting. The report of a split in the camp would go abroad immediately, and do great mischief. Tej Sing has not come thus far about his own business; he has come about Goolab Sing's, and G. S. thinks it necessary to meet

---

6. Edwardes' and Merivale's *Life of Sir Henry Lawrence.*

and concert future measures.

Please tell him, therefore, he must come, and make him name his time, and stick to it. It would never do to bring the *Maharajah* to Dhundeesur, and then Tej Sing send word he had a belly-ache. The fact is that both of these old rogues are in a mutual fright of each other, but if you accompany Tej Sing and I accompany Goolab Sing, they cannot poison each other without witnesses, at all events.

I send this by the Motbir,[7] whom the *Maharajah* despatches to persuade the refractory C. in C.

Is not this like the embassy of Ulysses to the sulky Achilles, when he would keep his tent, and would not come out and wop the Trojans?

Believe me, yours ever,

Herbert B. Edwardes.

Henry Lawrence, in his despatch of the 12th November, reporting to the Government the result of the expedition and installation of the *Maharaja*, adds:

Under any circumstances one officer will go to Huzara, and one remain here until affairs are brought into some order.

Lumsden was deputed to Huzara, whilst John Nicholson remained in charge of affairs at Cashmere.

---

7. Trusted agent.

CHAPTER 4

Lumsden Nominated
to Raise the Guides

The following letter from Harry Lumsden to his father describes his return from Cashmere to the Punjab, and ends with the news of his appointment to raise the Guide Corps:—

Camp Rawul Pinder,
6th February, 1847.

As I have now returned within reach of a *dak*[1] to the provinces, after a three months' exile, I may as well spend my first hours of liberty in writing to give all my dear friends at home an account of my movements, and account for my long compulsory silence.

Passing over all the long time of plots and political shifts on the part of the ex-*wazir* of Lahore (Lai Sing) and the Cashmere rebellion, with its events and consequences, which I have no doubt you must have long ere this seen chronicled in the *Delhi Gazette* much more ably than I can hope to do, I shall at once plunge *in mediae res*, and commence my eventful story from the date of my last communication, which I believe was one I wrote at the foot of a note from Lawrence to your address.

On our arrival at Baramulla,[2] on the withdrawal of the Seikh troops from Cashmere, Lawrence thought it would be well to send a division through the Huzara country, and told me to accompany it and pick up all the information I could regarding the state of the country, the feelings of the people, and, in short,

---

1. Post.
2. Near Srinagar, Cashmere.

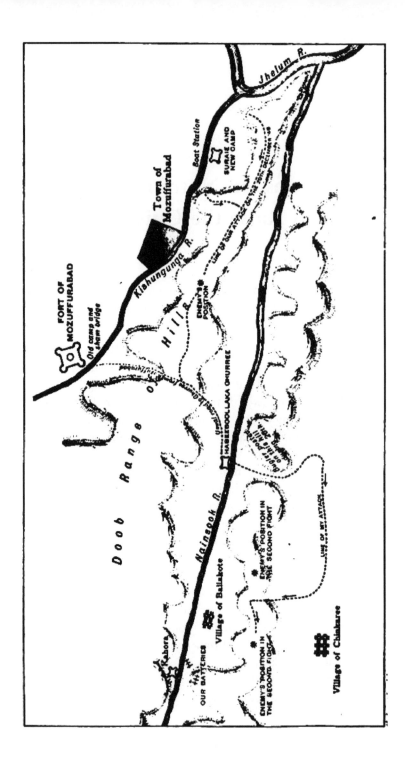

whatever I could find worth knowing.

After a week's delay in collecting carriages, I started with 3000 Seikhs and six guns carried on elephants under my command, and after a week's march arrived at a place called Mozufferabad, on the banks of the Kishungunga stream. I learnt here, to my surprise, that instead of a quiet march through the country, I should have to fight every inch of the way. I had lots of gun ammunition, but the men had not more than twenty-five rounds per man, owing to the carelessness of their officers.

We had before us the operation of crossing a river in the face of some 7000 hillmen, in their own mountains, well armed, but without guns. You may fancy my feelings on finding myself—a griff of a lieutenant—suddenly placed in the position of a general officer, with its accompanying responsibilities, without any officer to consult, and with troops in whose company I had never been before, except as an enemy. However, I determined to do my best for the Government, and, if possible, show that I was not unworthy of Lawrence's patronage and trust, which he has so freely bestowed on me. I sent back orders for all of the ammunition that could be spared from Cashmere to be sent up. At the same time I directed, on my own responsibility, Sirdar Gulab Sing Atáriwala, then at Hirkishun Gurhi, to join me without delay with such force as he had at disposal

I reported the whole state of things to Lawrence, and communicated my intention to cross the river and attack the enemy, so soon as the ammunition and food should have been brought up.

In the meantime, another difficulty had presented itself. "The opium had all run out." The Seikhs, who never touch tobacco, require some stimulant; they are in the habit of swallowing concoctions of opium, made into pills, daily. It seems that these grand old veterans of Runjeet Sing's army can do nothing without opium, and really become so dejected that you might have wapped them with a big stick. It took several weeks to rectify all this before we were prepared to start.

Having made up my mind as to the best plan of crossing the river with the limited means at my disposal (one boat), I determined to threaten to cross about a mile higher up the river, to attract the attention of the hillmen, whilst I should really cross at a convenient spot down the river, opposite a building (a

37

caravanserai) on the other bank of the river, of which I desired to get possession.

On the night of the 21st I moved down the boat to opposite the old *caravanserai*, and 700 picked men with two guns were ferried across, and took possession of the building, which was immediately loopholed, and provided first-rate cover for a small bridge which was shortly constructed, and by the 24th the whole division was crossed without firing a shot, much to their delight as well as to my own.

On Christmas Day we were all ready, and packing our ammunition on mules, and making the necessary arrangements for forcing the pass between us and the Gurhi[3] Hubiboola, which was occupied by the enemies' headquarters with their whole force in strength, holding the pass, ready to oppose us.

It was desirable to prevent the troops in the *gurhi* from joining their friends in the pass; I accordingly detached a brother of the Mozufferabad rajah with about 500 men of his own, armed with matchlocks, to take a detour and secure shelter without observation in broken ground near Hubiboola Gurhi, and occupy the attention of the enemy's garrison.

Having received information that Sirdar Gulab Sing Atáriwala had not moved, in spite of my requisition for his assistance, I consulted with the Seikh generals in the force, and they all agreed that whatever work was to be done we must do for ourselves, and fixed next morning for our advance.

At daylight on the 26th December General Kan Sing's division was divided into two columns, covered by skirmishers, and, supported by three guns, advanced up the hill, driving in the enemy's pickets, and, gaining the crest, were in little less than three hours masters of the first ridge. We hoped our work would now be comparatively easy, as we had been assured that from this point the road continued along the crest. After about three miles, however, we found a stiff ascent of some 800 yards facing us, with the enemy awaiting our assault on its summit.

After reconnoitring the position I determined to attack, but the ground proved very difficult, as we had to take a detour of a mile or so before we could find a path. Here the column divided into two; one half remained where they were, whilst the remainder went further round the hill. I went with the latter, after

---

3. Fort

arranging for a simultaneous attack, and that on no account was the other column to move until we were in position.

We had not proceeded far, however, when the Seikhs lost their temper, could no longer brook delay, and with their war-cry of "*Wah Gooroo*," rushed the position *tulwár* [4] in hand. Seeing this, I sent up my party to support them, and went to see about my guns, which were some way off, but within shot of the crest As the storming party reached within 200 yards of the summit the enemy jumped up and gave the Seikhs a volley. The guns immediately opened, and every shot seemed to tell on the hillmen, who sought shelter among the rocks, and remained without exposing themselves.

The storming party were out of wind and could not take advantage of the moment, and were too glad to remain under shelter. In this way the whole day was spent, the Seikhs holding their ground, but not able to make a rush under the heavy fire of musketry playing on them. What would not I have given for fifty shells for the benefit of the enemy. I never saw such rifle shooting as the Seikh artillery made with their six-pounders. I think it would have astonished some of our bluejackets. They literally prevented the enemy from raising their heads.

The Seikhs would not retire an inch, though unable to advance. As soon, however, as darkness began to come on the enemy decamped, leaving us in possession of the position, but with a loss of 33 killed and 180 wounded.

Next morning we again advanced, but the enemy would not come to close quarters, and evacuated the *gurhi* on our approach.

On our arrival the *Maharajah's* agent, without consulting me, thought fit to make some stupid terms with the Kághán chiefs, by which they were bound to retire to their own country, and give security for their future good conduct, as well as for the punctual payment of their revenues. This arrangement was all made unknown to me, and caused me much trouble, as it tied my hands at a time when the enemy were disheartened and much reduced in numbers, and gave him opportunity to refit Up to this time not a word had I heard from Lahore to assure me that Lawrence would approve of what I was doing, but on the 10th January I received three lines, which put my mind at

---

4. Sword or scimitar.

ease, and gave me fresh spirits.

The enemy, as I was informed by the chief of the district, Hussein Khan, had been instigated by the Sitána Hindustani fanatics, who had succeeded in stirring up men of the Puckli valley to oppose our progress. Many of the Huzara chiefs were with them, as well as the Kághán Saiuds, and their followers.

We halted for some days on the banks of the Nainsukh River. The enemy in the meantime had concentrated on the top of a steep mountain, where it was next to impossible to follow them, except with great loss, as they had only to roll down stones to clear the only paths of everything living that attempted to approach.

At last a villager came in and told me that although the enemy occupied the top of the mountain all day, they were in the habit of coming to springs half-way down to cook and rest at night. Acting on this information, I sent for some herds-men of the district, and showing them a handful of gold coins, promised them to give them if the men would take up a bugler and some odds and ends that they must carry with them to the top of the hill after the enemy had retired from the heights for the night. A bargain was made, and next evening my little party was ready for starting. The bugler was disguised as a shepherd, and the villagers (three in number) carried each half a dozen pots filled with powder, with fuses attached.

These they were to take to the top of the hill and lay out in a row, and at nine at night, on a signal rocket being fired from camp, they were to light all the fuses, the bugler would blow all the calls he knew, and then the whole party were to make the best of their way back to camp.

When the time came a star rocket shot up into the cloudless sky. *Bang, bang, bang* went the powder pots, the sound of their bursting reverberating through the hills, in the still night air, like salvos of artillery, while the shepherds, who had that day lost some sheep—carried off, it was supposed, by the enemy—sent some large stones bounding down the side of the hill

The enemy, who had just retired for the night, rushed to their matchlocks, and concluding that the whole of our force had by some mysterious agency been conveyed up the hill above them, instantly took to flight, those in front firing back on later starters, and each little party thinking his neighbour a pursuing

Seikh. We in camp were too much convulsed with merriment at the complete success of our stratagem to attempt to follow them, if we had had any intention of doing so.[5]

This settled the whole business, and brought the Kághán Saiuds to their senses. They sent in their *vakils*[6] to me to ask for pardon for the past and with every security for their future good conduct What think you, as an artillery officer, of my light artillery? If not very deadly, it is at least portable.

I must here record the fact that when I asked the Seikh officer commanding the force to call for a volunteer bugler he replied, "No, you would then get a really good man; let me pick you out a *haramzada*,[7] and it will not matter if he is killed." Thus ended my first attempt at an independent command, for which I have received the thanks of the Government[8] and, what I prize more, Lawrence's approbation; and I flatter myself it is not every lieutenant of nine years' standing that can say he has commanded 3500 men in two different actions.

Don't put yourself in a fuss when you do not hear from me, or see nonsense about me in the *Delhi Gazette*, as you may depend upon it, if any mishap was to come over me, Lawrence would be the first to hear about it, and would send you a line. I am now so likely to be sent into the jungles at a moment's warning, and kept there for months, that you may be frequently a long time without a letter, but you may depend upon my writing as often as I can.

I have just been nominated to raise the corps of Guides, on 700 *rupees* a month. It will be the finest appointment in the country, being the right hand of the army and the left of the political I

---

5. The story of the whole force of the enemy having stampeded before one bugler and three herdsmen becoming known throughout the country completely broke up the gathering, and is told to this day in those wild regions as a sample of the tricks Lumsden could play at a pinch.

6. Agents or representatives.

7. Bad lot, or base-born.

8. Extract from Agent Governor-General (N.W. Frontier) to Lieutenant Lumsden: "Camp Mungla, November 27th, 1846.—I am much gratified at this acknowledgment of your good services during the recent operations."

Extract Mr. Secretary Currie's letter 455 of 9th November, 1846: "You will convey to Lieutenant Lumsden, attached to Sirdar Tej Sing's headquarters, the Governor-General's approbation. The conciliatory and energetic manner in which Lieutenant Lumsden has performed his duty is most creditable to that officer."

am to have the making of this new regiment all to myself. The arming and dressing is to be according to my own fancy. They are for general service. I consider it as good as a majority and C.B.-ship to any man in the first campaign he may get into. I am, in addition, still to carry on the duties of an assistant in the agency of Lahore, and to have a roving commission to make myself acquainted with the people, the roads, fords, ferries, and forts within and beyond the frontier.

As soon as I have to some extent settled the Huzara country, I am to go for a few months to Peshawur, and assist Lawrence's brother George, who is in charge of the valley. I am to commence to recruit my new corps there, which, in the first place, is to consist of 1 *resaldar*, 1 *resaidar*, 2 *jemadars*, 2 *kote duffadars*, 12 *duffadars*,[9] a trumpeter, and 80 sabres in the Cavalry, with 2 *subadárs*, 2 *jemadars*, 18 *havildars*, 18 *naicks*[10] 4 buglers, and 146 Infantry *Sepoys*.

I have found the Seikhs who accompanied me first-rate men, ready for any work, always in the best of humours, fond of their officers, and just as obedient to orders as our own troops, and not giving one-quarter the trouble that the latter do, though they had no commissariat, nor half the quantity of carriage usually allowed to our men.

Each man carries seven days' supply on his back instead of his knapsack, and fills this store up whenever he can, never expending a *seer* but when driven to it In this way they have come through the wild Huzara hills for three months without a complaint, as happy as possible, and taking the greatest care of me.

Is it not strange that two of these very regiments, only just a year ago, were fighting against us, and repulsed two assaults of Gilbert's division at Sobraon? The men and officers often talked over the whole business with me in the most friendly way. These regiments were commanded by Colonel Bhoop Sing, and are the very corps which I mentioned as retiring in a mass through the River Sutlej, after Sobraon, without breaking their ranks. The little colonel had two horses shot under him, and is as proud as a peacock of the whole affair. He is a great pet of mine, and always accompanies me shooting, whilst General Kan Sing has given me an invitation to his house to see his son's

9. The various native officers of an irregular cavalry regiment
10. Native officers of an infantry regiment.

marriage. Only think of my being "best young man" on such an occasion.

I want you to secure for me the very best telescope you can set your hands upon. I do not mind it being a trifle heavy, provided it is a first-rate one, nor paying the price for it, so long as it is good enough for the officer commanding "the Guides."

My other want is a brace of first-rate pistols, to carry in a belt, as I find the pair you gave me are no longer safe, and I must have something of the sort, just to keep up with the fashions of the place, and make myself on equal terms with my neighbours in my wanderings. A poor man who was holding my horse the other day had a narrow escape from those old pistols, and I dare not attempt to use them longer. Nicholson and I had just got to the end of a long march, on our way up to Cashmere, when he dismounted, and I, following his example, gave my horse to a villager to hold. The man had scarcely taken hold of the bridle when the horse shook himself, and bang went the brace of pistols, blowing out the end of the holsters, and the ball from one taking the point of the poor man's nose off, for which I had to recompense him to the best of my power.

This appears a queer sort of tale, but truth is stranger than fiction, and the accident actually took place before Nicholson, otherwise I should have been afraid to repeat the story.

Never believe a word you see in the *Delhi* or other Indian papers, as they get hold of all sorts of cock-and-bull stories from native newspapers and correspondents, and it would be as much as a man's appointment was worth for one in the agency to write a single line to any newspaper, or for a line of his to get into print by any accident, so that no one can contradict statements put forth by these people. What need any of us care so long as the Government and the G.G.'s agent are satisfied. The only thing is that you dear people at home are apt to get into a fuss if you see that young hopeful is on the top of a hill, with strange folk with strange arms eyeing him.

After this yarn you can never tell me I do not write.

CHAPTER 5

Raising the Guides

In a letter written only a few years ago to Lieutenant G. J. Younghusband, of the Guides, Lumsden thus described the manner of the first raising of the corps.

It is impossible for anyone nowadays to take in the true history of "the Guides" without remembering the state of the Punjab and the border population at the time the regiment was first put together. The following anecdotes will in some measure illustrate the sort of men who first entered the Guides, and the sort of work they were trained to.

I must explain that in 1846 I was an assistant political agent, under Sir Henry Lawrence, and posted to assist Colonel George Lawrence at Peshawur, when the order arrived for me to raise the Guides in addition to my political duties.

The object of the corps was to have trustworthy men who could at a moment's notice act as guides to troops in the field, and collect intelligence beyond as well as within the border. There were no British troops in those days—European or native—anywhere in the Punjab except at Lahore. All the military duties were performed by the old Seikh army, one division of which was at Peshawur under its own general and staff officers, but at the disposal of Colonel George Lawrence.

While the Seikh *sirdars* carried on the administration of the country, a brigade used to be sent out to the Yusafzai district to collect the Government revenue, and according to the custom of the country, collected not only what was the fixed revenue but quite as much more for the benefit of the influential officers of the expedition. These exactions were, as a matter of course, strenuously resisted by most of the tribes, and seldom collected without a fight and destruction of villages.

To obviate this most unsatisfactory state of things, Lawrence sent me on a cold weather trip to see the country, and, if possible, to make some sort of an arrangement with the heads of tribes. During this tour I made the acquaintance of all the most influential men in the country, and soon found there would be but little trouble in settling everything almost as I liked, were the detested Seikh troops only kept out of the way. As I had by this time collected some fifty horsemen and twenty infantry, chiefly down-countrymen and Persians, I got orders to set to work at once on a rough revenue settlement, which naturally brought me in contact with the heads of villages, from among whose younger sons and relations I soon selected a score of first-class Pathan recruits for the Guides. All went on well for a time until a village called Babuzai on the Buneyr frontier, which had once gained a high reputation on the border by repulsing an attack of a whole brigade of Seikhs, refused to pay its share of revenue, and obliged Lawrence to come out with a force of Seikhs to my assistance.

The Seikhs attacked the village in front, while the Guides stole up to the crest of the ridge and dropped down in rear of the enemy, turning all their breastworks and rendering them untenable. Away went the defenders, with my men in pursuit, so close on their heels that Futteh Khan (Khuttuk), then a trooper in the cavalry, got blown up in cutting down a man who happened to be carrying a bag of powder in one hand, and a lighted matchlock in the other. This was the Guides' first taste of powder, and a most trying ordeal for raw troops, as they had to scramble up the hill in the dark, over stones and rocks, but not a man lagged behind or lost his way.

Sometime after this, Arsula Khan, chief of Zeda district, ran off to the Buneyr hills with Government revenue, and made two or three raids on Hindu traders passing along the border, subjecting them to severe torture, in order to extort a ransom.

Entering the hills as soon as it was dark, escorted by a troop of Seikh Regular Cavalry and twenty-five Guide *sowars*, and advancing as rapidly as I could, undiscovered, to the village, I was not a little taken aback to find that my Guides alone had followed me, the Seikhs having remained outside at the foot of the hills. Fortunately the discovery was made while it was yet dark, so that the villagers could not see the strength of our party, and we put them in a horrid fright by keeping our horses clattering round the place, and calling on the men to come out and give up their arms, before we opened great guns on them.

As the women and children were all in the place, and unable to escape, the men lost heart, and eventually coming out, one by one, were tied up and secured, and marched off with all their cattle to the open plains without a shot being fired; but unfortunately the object of the expedition, Arsula Khan, had left the village the afternoon before we visited the place. "Swagger did the trick." Half an hour's warning would have brought two or three hundred matchlockmen on us in a narrow defile.

In the days I am writing about every man ploughed with his sword by his side and matchlock handy, with a piece of dried cow-dung burning near, ready to light the match, while the cattle of the village were escorted out to graze by an armed party from each village. On one occasion, when out hawking, I had, as usual, some half-dozen mounted Guides with me, and finding a flock of little bustard, "*obdra,*" let a hawk after one of them—a very strong old bird, which took us a very long gallop, and eventually was knocked down close under the foot of the hills.

Having a good Arab under me, I had outstripped the escort in the chase, and the ground being covered thickly with thorn bushes, could not find the exact spot where the birds were. Looking all round, I saw a villager frantically waving his *pugree,* and concluding he had seen the end of the chase I at once rode towards him as fast as my horse would carry me; and lucky it was that I had plenty of pace on, for on nearing my man I was saluted with a volley from twenty matchlocks. To turn and bolt to my escort was the work of a moment.

As soon as we were all assembled, and had given our horses time to recover breath, Fakera, a well-known Afridi horseman in the Guides, slipped off his horse, creeping through the bushes like a cat, contrived to stalk one of the enemy, and discovered the party were out with their cattle from one of our own villages, and had taken us for Pullie horsemen. They were more frightened at the discovery of the mistake they had made than I was by their volley, and expected that half of them at least must be hanged for shooting at me, the only white man they knew.

The narrative is continued by a letter written at the time:—

Camp Punja-Sahib, 28th June, 1847.

You must excuse this thick paper, my dear father, as people in the jungles are apt to run short of all sorts of things, and have not Messrs. Blotting Paper and Co. next door, as you more luxurious people have at home. I have sent in an emergent indent (as a quartermaster would say) into Peshawur.

Since my last I have been wandering about in camp with my men. I have secured most excellent drill instructors from the 59th, and nothing could be more satisfactory than the willingness of my recruits and their progress in training and discipline. They are all hard fellows, full of natural military instincts, and will make excellent soldiers.

I like what I have seen of the chiefs and people in Yusafzai, who are beginning to understand me, as I am them. I have just despatched a report as to the present state of the district, which has been forwarded to Government.

Returning from Yusafzai, I was allowed breathing-time for ten days at Peshawur, when suddenly up comes an urgent order from Lawrence to say he was most anxious to have an officer here to look after a set of robbers living in a mountain fastness called Gundgurh, who have been plundering in the absence of any troops to control them, but that he did not like ordering anyone out in so fearfully hot a season. Of course there was no resisting such an appeal, and down I came here as quick as I could on the fourth day from Peshawur.

On leaving Peshawur I took it into my wise head that the Cabul River might float me down some forty miles without much trouble, and that I should be cooler on the water than riding, so I sent on two Guides to get a raft ready. When I arrived at dusk, and to my surprise found no Guides, I stormed for half an hour, and then set to work constructing a raft for myself with the assistance of the *zamindars*[1] from the neighbouring village.

In half an hour we contrived to get two good bullock hides blown out and fastened under a *charpoy*.[2] A Guide, who came with me, and I embarked on the Cabul River and floated down

1. Land holders.
2. Rough native bed.

the stream merrily enough, smoking cigars and blowing a cloud like the fumes from the funnel of the *Great Western* until nearly midnight, when suddenly, without a moment's warning, bang went one of the inflated hides in a thousand shivers with a report like that of an eighteen-pounder, and away flies young Hopeful, headfirst, half-way to the bottom of the Cabul River, from which position he had considerable difficulty in extricating himself, as, owing to his being half asleep, slightly astonished, and having all his clothes on, it took a few seconds to realize the situation. However, he did find his way to the surface, and by kicking and splashing about for a little managed to get rid of his inexpressibles, which, however elegant in a drawing-room, are a great nuisance when one has to kick for life.

As soon as this was accomplished, the getting rid of the remainder of my clothes and the subsequent swim to the remnant of the raft were comparatively easy.

When I got to the raft, however, I found my unfortunate Guide in the last extremities, unable to swim from fear, and too tired to hold on by the remaining skin. Luckily for him, riding on a *mussuck*[3] was an old achievement of mine, so climbing up, without more ado I cut the *charpoy* adrift by undoing the string, and, taking the Guide's *pugree* off his head, passed it round his chest under his arms with the two ends round my own waist, and thus after nearly two hours in the water, with God's assistance made my way to the bank. So far all was well, but now came the rub. We were at least two miles from any village, and as I had thrown away my boots and all my clothes I was much in the state that Dame Nature made me, a precious figure to be seen among chaste Hindoos.

After much laughing and consultation it was agreed that I should take the Guide's *pugree* around me and sit like Patience on a monument, smiling at Grief, while the Guide went out and told our story, and borrowed a suit of clothes and a pair of shoes. He succeeded in his mission, and shortly afterwards out came your eldest son, in a blue *loongee*,[4] for a *pugree*, round his head, a pair of pyjamas wide enough to make the mainsail of a seventy-four, and a flash blue *chupkin*.[5] In this garb I marched

---

3. Inflated hide.
4. Large waist-scarf.
5. Coat.

down the river till we came to a ferryboat, in which we again took ship and were at last landed at my tent at the village of Akora.

Heaven only knows what made the skin under us blow up, for the people in this part of the world come down all the way from Jellalabad on these skins, bringing *maunds*[6] of merchandise with them, and say such rafts are safer than boats. One thing is sure, the whole skin was torn to shreds.

The depredators had decamped before we could reach Gundgurh.

In the meantime you will be gratified by the perusal of the accompanying copy of paragraph 3 of a despatch of the 25th May, 1847, from the Foreign Secretary with the Governor-General to Major Lawrence:

> The Governor-General requests that Major Lawrence may be directed to express to Lieutenant Lumsden His Lordship's gratification at the zealous co-operation he affords his superior officer, who is on his part so anxious to acknowledge it. The Governor-General has been pleased to raise the salary of Major Edwardes to 1000 *rupees per mensem*, and that of Lieutenant Lumsden to 800 *rupees* as a testimony of his approbation of their services since they have been in the Punjab.

If therefore the furlough memorial is granted, I may yet have a chance of seeing *"home sweet home."*

One of Lumsden's chief duties at this period, as a political officer and also as commander of the Guides, was to deal with heads of clans and villages, who were backward and recusant in the payment of their land revenue. Under the Sikhs and Duránis much oppression had been carried on—heavy fines were imposed on the people in addition to the ordinary taxation, and collected sometimes at the point of the sword. The officer in charge of the party would also make exactions for his own private benefit, while an escort under him would maintain their horses and themselves at the cost of the village for weeks together. The result was that when British officers assumed charge of the civil administration it was often found that the impoverished landholders neglected to pay even just demands, till a show of force had been made. Lumsden and his Guides were therefore often employed

---

6. A *maund* = 80 lbs.

in the collection of revenue from malcontent villagers, who, not realizing the change that had taken place in the spirit of their rulers, had attempted to defy the orders of the British agent at Peshawur.

In the spring of 1848 Sir Henry Lawrence was obliged, on account of his health, to return to England. He was succeeded as Governor-General's agent and ruler of the Punjab by a Bengal civilian, Sir Frederick Currie.

The Guide Corps had been fully completed up to its complement in March of that year, when Lumsden and his men were suddenly ordered to Lahore.

It may be well before entering on the causes of this sudden demand for their services to sketch the events which had happened at the capital since Lumsden had left that city for Cashmere. As soon as Henry Lawrence had returned from installing the Maharaja Gulab Singh, a commission of five British officers, civil and military, sat in judgment on the treacherous *wazir* Lai Singh, whose secret orders to Sheikh Imam-ud-din had provoked the rebellion against Gulab Singh. Lai Singh's guilt was proved beyond question before a large audience of Sikh *sirdars*. By Lord Hardinge's order the Queen Regent's paramour was deposed from his office, and sent off a state prisoner to the fort of Agra. His crafty mistress likewise ceased to have any voice in public affairs. By the Treaty of Bhairowál a Council of Regency, composed of eight *sirdars*, guided and controlled by Henry Lawrence, was now appointed to govern the Punjab in the name of its child-sovereign Dulip Singh. The Resident's powers were to extend over every department and to any extent.

In plain fact, from those last days of 1846, Henry Lawrence, still a captain of Bengal Artillery, became, by consent of all his Sikh colleagues, sole Regent of the Punjab. The continued intrigues of the *Maharani* rendered it, in Lawrence's view, necessary that she should be separated from her son, the young king. To give effect to this decision, a proclamation was issued to the Sikh chiefs and nation, announcing that in the opinion of the Governor-General it had become absolutely necessary to separate the *Maharaja* from his mother, an opinion in which the durbar perfectly coincided, and that, accordingly, on the 19th day of August, 1847, her Highness had left the palace of Lahore, and had been taken to Sheikhopoorah.

When Lumsden arrived at Lahore with his Guides, Sir Frederick Currie had already assumed the office of Resident on the departure of Sir Henry Lawrence for England. Intrigue and disaffection were rife amongst the people and soldiery, the *Maharani* secretly doing her utmost to stir up bad feeling against the British. The first task assigned to the Guides was a difficult one. They were called upon to unravel a conspiracy, believed to have been organized by the Sikhs, to seduce from their allegiance certain of the British Native Infantry and Irregular Cavalry who formed the garrison of Lahore. Lumsden chose a Guide, by name Pir Bukhs, who had originally belonged to the 59th N.I., to make a secret inquiry.

Pir Bukhs, with whom were also associated Resáldár Futteh Khan, Khuttuk and Akbar Shah, a non-commissioned officer, both of the Guides, discovered that a Sikh general, Kan Singh, urged on by the *Maharani*, was the leader of the plot, and that some fifty or sixty of our soldiers had already been tampered with, and a day fixed for a general rising of the conspirators. Eventually Lumsden, acting on this information, proceeded with the Guide infantry to the city, surrounded the house of General Kan Singh, arrested his *munshi* and a confidential agent, and took possession of a box of papers, which, in the end, was found to contain sufficient evidence to hang Kan Singh and his *munshi*, and to banish the *Maharani* from the Punjab. The next step, however, was to secure the person of the *Maharani*, and Lumsden was ordered to proceed to Sheikhopoorah and convey her to Ferozepore.

The manner in which this task was carried out is described as follows in the Resident's official despatch[7] to the Secretary to the Government of India, dated Lahore, 16th May, 1848:—

> I have the honour to state that Maharani Junda Khore, the mother of Maharajah Duleep Sing, was removed from the fort of Sheikhopoorah by my orders yesterday afternoon, and is now on her way, under charge of an escort, to Ferozepore. By the arrangements I have made it is expected the *Maharani* will reach Ferozepore tomorrow morning. I have been induced to take this step at the present moment for several reasons. In the letter of the Governor-General, dated the 27th of August last, his lordship directed that in the event of the *Maharani* being found to be engaged in intrigues detrimental to the interests of the Lahore State, she should be removed from the Punjab.
> The Governor-General in council may perhaps like to know the mode in which the removal of the *Maharani* was effected. I had reason to believe it possible that she had gained over the

---

7. Parliamentary Blue Book.

guard and the *sirdars* in charge of Sheikhopoorah to her interest, and that they might refuse to give her up. About a week ago I changed nearly the whole guard at the fort, and relieved the company of regulars by a company from another regiment of Poorbeahs, and added to the Rohillas appointed by Colonel Lawrence thirty new men, the *jemadar* of Rohillas, through whom they were appointed, remaining at Lahore.

I appointed Lieutenants Lumsden and Hodson with the mounted portion of the Guide Corps to be the escort of the *Maharani* from Sheikhopoorah, and I sent with them as bearers of my *moorasilla*[8] to the *Maharani* and the *Durbar purwannas*,[9] Kai Mool Sing (the confidential *vakeel*[10] of Rajah Tej Sing), Dewan Kedar Náth (as representative of Rajah Deena Náth), Sirdar Nar Sing (as representative of the Attaree interests), and Fakeer Noorooddeen. Sheikhopoorah is twenty miles from Lahore. I was prepared if opposition was offered to enforce the execution of my orders. Lieutenant Lumsden's party arrived at Sheikhopoorah before daylight yesterday morning, the emissaries of the *Durbar* having preceded them.

If any opposition was shown in opening the gates I should have known it. Soon after sunrise, and at my request, two squadrons of the 14th Dragoons were saddled at daylight, and two nine-pounders of the Horse Battery ready harnessed to go down at a moment's notice. This force, accompanied by Major Napier of the Engineers,[11] who had made a plan of the fort, might have been at the spot in three hours, and Major Napier was satisfied that they would get into the fort in ten minutes afterwards. Happily there was not the slightest opposition; all was acquiescence and civility from the *Maharani* downwards, very probably induced by the execution which took place a few days ago.

Lahore, 20th May, 1848.

Lieutenant Lumsden returned yesterday from Ferozepore, where he left the *Maharani* under Captain Browne's charge. I have now made all arrangements for her march towards Benares, and she will, I hope, leave Ferozepore in the course of the next three days.

---

8. Letter.
9. Written orders.
10. Agent
11. Afterwards Field Marshal Lord Napier of Magdala, G.C.B., G.C.S.I., etc.

I feel assured that the Governor-General in council will be pleased with the admirable manner in which Lieutenant Lumsden carried out all the arrangements I made for the safe removal of the *Rani* from Sheikhopoorah to Ferozepore.

Lumsden in after days used to recall the excitement of that adventurous ride with Hodson to Sheikhopoorah, and the prospect of what might be before them when they got there. He accompanied the *Maharani* in her carriage along with two of the Sikh *sirdars*, and never lost sight of her until he joyfully handed her over to Captain Browne, the political officer deputed to receive her. The captive lady did not seem to realize her position or destiny until she had traversed a considerable portion of her journey. She then commenced to heap all the abuse she could command on the British Government and on her captor, while the foulest of Billingsgate slang would be thrown into the shade if compared with the language and curses with which she favoured the two Sikh *sirdars* who were also in the carriage.

CHAPTER 6

Lumsden's Account of the Winter Campaign, 1848-49

In the meantime the disbanded soldiers of the Khálsa army scattered throughout the villages of the Punjab were like smouldering fragments of igneous matter ready to burst into flame. Indeed the fire had been kindled on the 20th April by the murder of Agnew and Anderson at Mooltan, and was quickly followed by a widespread rising—the final attempt of the Sikh nation to regain their lost ascendancy by force of arms. Herbert Edwardes has told the tale, how on receipt of Agnew's appeal for help, written the day before he was murdered, he (Edwardes) at once summoned the chiefs and fighting men of the Deraját and Bannu, and pushed down by forced marches to Mooltan. This able and gallant soldier, though too late to save the lives of his brother officers, fully realized the immediate necessity for quelling such an outbreak. On being joined by the loyal *Nawab* of Bhawulpore and General Van Cortlandt,[1] with such troops as they could command, Edwardes immediately attacked the enemy, and after three successive engagements drove Mulraj into Mooltan, and kept him besieged in the fort like a terrier, as Edwardes wrote, "barking at a tiger."

And so things remained until the month of August, when the besieging force was relieved by the arrival of the columns from Ferozepore and Lahore under the command of General Whish.

Harry Lumsden wrote to his father from Lahore on the 3rd May as follows:—

I have so much to think of just now that I consider myself fortunate if I get off half a dozen lines by each mail to say

---

1. An officer who had formerly been employed under the Sikh Government.

that all is well. Since I have come down here I find myself appointed C.-in-C, Adjutant-General, Quartermaster-general, and Commissary-general of the Seikh army, and expected to be as well up to the working of each department as if I had been in them all my life, whereas everything is new to me. However, the work is interesting, the authority unbounded, and the credit to be gained just what I can make it

I am happy to say I have found Sir Frederick Currie quite a different character from what we all expected, for, though his manner at first was not prepossessing, he has turned out well on further acquaintance, and appears to be willing to work agreeably with all under him. With me he has always been remarkably civil, and has given me permission to do just what I like with my Guides, dress and drill them as I think desirable, which is mighty agreeable to young Hopeful.

We are not to do anything against Mooltan till after the rains, which I consider is a great mistake, but the Resident knows best. I don't like the idea of letting any native be "*yaghi*"[2] for a single day, especially one who has murdered two British officers in the cold-blooded way described in my last letter.[3] The example of one successful attempt is likely to lead to a dozen others, and unsettles men's minds, making them doubt the power of our Government, which should always be felt to be irresistible, as well as available at all seasons of the year; should people once take it into their heads that we cannot act in the hot weather, we shall soon have lots of summer campaigns. Had Lawrence been at our head now, we should have been in Mooltan by this time, and most likely Mulraj swinging over the gateway, whereas the latter is looked on as a saint who can laugh at a *Faringhi*. One blow in time saves many.

Lumsden was sent with the Guide Cavalry to join Edwardes at Mooltan in the month of June. When the camp occupied the position on the right of the *nullah* at "Suruj Kund" the cavalry, under Lumsden, charged, and took, though they could not bring away, twelve wall pieces mounted round the Bibi Pákdáman Mosque. Hodson had been appointed adjutant to the corps, but in addition to his military duties he was also an assistant political officer in the Baree Doáb, and had

---

2. Rebellious.
3. This letter has unfortunately been lost.

with him 120 men of the Guide infantry.

On the 28th July, 1848, the rest of the Guide infantry at Lahore, under the command of Subadár Rasúl Khan, a brother of Futteh Khan, Khuttuk, was ordered to attempt to get possession of the important fort of Govindgurh, Umritsur, then held, with doubtful loyalty, by a regiment of Sikh infantry and some Sikh artillery. The detachment of Guides consisted of the commanding officer, 4 native officers, 28 N.C. officers, and 118 men. They left Lahore at noon, and reached Govindgurh next morning, having with them three prisoners, to afford pretext for entering the fort

The Sikhs admitted the Guides unsuspectingly, and the *subadár* forthwith contrived to get possession of the main gateway and cavalier in the centre of the fort, which completely commanded the whole of the works. Next morning the 1st Native Infantry and a regiment of Irregular cavalry arrived, and were added to the garrison. For this service Subadár Rasúl Khan was handsomely rewarded by a present of a sword and one thousand *rupees*, while each Guide in the detachment received two gold *budkis*[4] as a mark of approbation from our Government.

We find a letter from Lumsden to his father, dated Camp Suruj Kund, Mooltan, 14th October, 1848, which sets forth his own position at that time:—

Here we are, well in for a second Punjab war, the result of which must be the annexation of Runjeet Sing's rich province to our Indian empire, and which must lead to a considerable increase of our army. I told you in my last that we had pushed our parallels to within 600 yards of the walls of Mooltan, and a battery of 24-pounders was under construction, the fire from which, on a common brick wall, would in all probability have made a practical breach, and half an hour's rushing about the town with the bayonet would, I have little doubt, have established us pretty comfortably in the city. There is an old proverb about a *cup and a lip* which we were destined to verify. At the last moment Rajah Sher Sing, with the whole of his force—who had hitherto been our ally, or, at any rate, neutral—marched over and joined the enemy, a move which obliged General Whish to suspend operations, and take up a secure position, till such reinforcements should arrive as to make us at least numerically

---

4. An Indian coin.

stronger than Mulraj. Here we are, twisting our thumbs until more troops arrive. I may as well remind you that Edwardes and Lake have a wild and irregular army, which has been bullying Mulraj before the British troops came down here, and that my Guides are attached to this force, while General Whish commands the whole.

In our camp we have only Edwardes, Lake, Cortlandt, James, and myself, to take duty, and of which number Edwardes and Lake are obliged to remain in camp and carry on the office business, leaving only four of us to take duty in the trenches; and as we, during the whole time we were before the place, had three officers always on duty at a time, day and night—two on picket and one with the working parties from our camp—you may fancy the duty was hard enough. It was impossible to give in, with such men working with you, but I several times thought that I should have been obliged to do so, as I have been out of sorts for some time, and my doctor insisted on my going away. Thank God I did not go, for a few days after the force came back I got time to get doctored, and am all right again. I can now go grinding about the country with my Guides again, and the cold mornings and nights do me as much good as a trip to the hills.

My Guides have gained for themselves and for me a good name in the British camp. All the Engineers send for Guides as an escort, when reconnoitring, in preference to regular cavalry. Only think, when I was on duty elsewhere one day sixty-six of my men rode slap through and through ten times their number in the hope of recovering some camels which the Seikhs had driven off from General Whish's camp. They did not get the camels, but covered themselves with glory in the presence of the whole army.[5]

---

5. This feat was no ordinary one, and the following graphic account of it, taken from *Blackwood's Magazine* for May, 1897, may be quoted:—

In the siege of Mooltan, which followed, the Guides again and again distinguished themselves, either individually or as a corps; but one instance must suffice of the fearlessness and dash which thus early made them remarkable, and for which they have ever been famous.

One August day news was brought hurriedly to the British camp that a party of Mulraj's cavalry had driven off a herd of Government camels which were grazing in the open country some miles away. Lieutenant Lumsden was absent at the moment, but those of the Guides who were in camp (continued next page),

Resaldar Futteh Khan, Khan Bahadur, Corps of Guides

Now that Sher Sing has bolted out of Mooltan (leaving Mulraj to make the best fight of it he can here), and is wending his way northward in the direction of Goojerat, and his father, Chuttur Sing, with the whole of the Huzara Brigade, is moving on the same point, while the Bunnoo Seikh force is also closing to the same point, there can be but little doubt, when one knows the ground and looks at a map, that the whole Seikh army will most probably occupy a line on the right bank. There are but three passes—one at Rotás, which will be covered by Jhelum, another at Pind Dadun Khan by the same place, and a third nearly midway between these two, but which is not marked on any of our maps, and would be held by the enemy's centre. This would be the strongest position they could find, with the Jhelum River in their front and endless ravines behind them, through which they could easily escape, in case we should succeed in forcing the passage of the river and drive them from their position. Some people think they will entrench themselves in the open country between the Jhelum and the Chenáb, because Goojerat has been named in intercepted letters from Chuttur Sing to his son; but anyone who knows the Seikhs can easily fancy their being sharp enough to name one point and occupy another only half-way to the named spot, should it answer their purpose.

You cannot think with what anxiety all the old assistants in the

---

(less than seventy horsemen in all) turned out under a gallant chief, Futteh Khan by name, and within a few minutes of the first alarm they were racing across country in the direction taken by the marauders. A gallop of three miles brought the troop suddenly within sight of the enemy, when instead of a small party, as they had expected, they found themselves confronted with the whole of Mulraj's cavalry. The apparition of so superior a force might well have checked the ardour of the pursuers, but no odds were so great as to appal the Guides. Without check or hesitation the gallant little band charged straight at the opposing mass of horsemen, and before the latter had time to face them they had cut their way right through the midst. Rapidly rallying and wheeling about they charged back, as they had come, through the ranks of the confused and astonished enemy, dealing destruction as they passed. Stupefied by the impetuosity of the attack, the Seikhs still stood irresolute, when, before they could decide whether to retreat or retaliate, once again their dauntless foes bore down on them. This settled the issue of the combat Before the whirling line of Guide horsemen could close with them a third time, the enemy broke and fled, closely pursued by Futteh Khan and his victorious band. Nor did either side draw rein till the walls of Mooltan gave shelter to the vanquished and checked the career of the pursuers.

Residency are looking out for the arrival of our old chief, Sir Henry Lawrence. One would think to hear the conversations of an evening at our little mess that he alone of all the Indian community could carry on a war with spirit or rule a district energetically. You hear on every side, "Only let Lawrence get out here, and we shall soon see the end of all this trouble."

We have now in camp some of your old Topkhanah[6] friends who desire to be particularly remembered to you—John Anderson, Day, and Garbett—who are all well, and very proud of their horse artillery, and tell me that I should have been an artilleryman, as young Graham, Swinhoe, etc., etc., to which I reply that "had it been so I should never have been a Guide."

On the departure of Sher Sing with the Sikh army from Mooltan, Lumsden with his cavalry was summoned back to Lahore for further service, inasmuch as simultaneously with the movement of Sher Sing up the Jhech Doáb, between the Jhelum and the Chenáb, the districts about Lahore, and especially under the Jamu Hills, had broken out into revolt.

A characteristic letter of Henry Lawrence to Lumsden's father, one of the last he wrote in England, dated Southampton, 28th November, 1848, 8 p.m., may be quoted here as showing that Harry Lumsden's services at this period were fully appreciated by his chief.

Here we are, safely landed, my dear Lumsden, and ready to embark early on Monday. I cannot tell you how much I regret that we were not able to visit you in your own nest.

Harry's letter was not needed to prove that he is a noble young fellow; there is a quiet soldier-like something in all his despatches that is much more pleasant to me than the flourishes of many others.

His compliments to myself are the more acceptable, as addressed to you. and as he does not usually disperse soft

H. M. Lawrence.

Lumsden's share in the great events which took place in the Punjab in the early months of 1849 are described by himself:—

Camp Peshawur,
15th April, 1849.

No doubt all you good people at home will think you have

---

6. Artillery.

very good reason to be angry with me for not having sent you notes of events in the late campaign, as they have taken place; but if you will only for a moment consider that I have had to play the part of the head of intelligence department and guide to the army, and been responsible for keeping the Commander-in-Chief and General Gilbert informed of every move the enemy have made, in the shortest possible time, I think you will be convinced that a commandant of the Guides has not many hours he can call his own.

My last letter to you was, I think, from Lahore, on my return from Sultankee, where I dismantled some forts and played other little pranks to amuse the Seikhs.

Shortly afterwards I went to Jubba Fort, about thirty miles from Lahore, and after the place had been pounded by some horse artillery guns for several hours the garrison gave in, and I had to march them all in to Lahore, with their hands tied behind their backs. I then received orders to move post haste and join army headquarters' camp at Ramnuggar, but when I reached Eminabad, on my way up, I heard of a party of Seikhs, horse and foot, who had just crossed from the north side of the Chenáb River, and were on their way to Noorpore to create disturbance in our new Jullundur province. I instantly ordered Hodson to join me with my riflemen and gave chase, hoping by long marches to cut this detachment of the enemy off, and, as good lack would have it, heavy rain greatly assisted me, making the Seikhs unwilling to step out, and giving them the idea that we would not move in such weather.

On the fourth day, 3rd January, 1849, about three in the afternoon, we came on the enemy, cooking their dinners, and though there were more than seven to one against us, the surprise was a great point gained, and my riflemen rushed into the thick jungle, where the enemy were encamped, clearing it in no time.

The moment the Singhs came out of this village of Kutova into the open country, on the other side, I led my troop at them, and killed every man, including their famous leader, Gunda Sing [7]

---

7. "So bad," says Hodson, "was the nature of the country over which Lumsden followed them, that at one time more than half of the horses of the troop were down, pursuers and pursued rolling together in desperate strife in the middle of the deep marshes."

The Secretary with the Governor-General wrote to the Resident at Lahore, on the 12th January, 1849:—

> You will convey to Lieutenant Lumsden the approval of the Governor-General of the gallantry and activity of himself and men in his attack against the insurgents, and his lordship's sense of the service he has been rendering.

Which is not so bad for a fifth lieutenant of native infantry! Having finished this little matter, I hunted Ram Sing, another great scamp, into the hills about Deenanuggur, and on the 12th, 13th, and 14th of January was with General Wheeler's column in the operations at the foot of the hills, and on the heights of Dullah, and was mentioned in the General's despatch as one "who had aided me most cordially." After this I moved with my Guides towards the Commander-in-Chief's army, and arrived at Wuzeerabad just in time to catch the Seikhs crossing the Chenab River to turn the right flank of our army. We had just arrived on the banks of the river, when we suddenly came on a large detachment of *Goorchurries* (irregular Seikh horse) who had forded the stream close to Wuzeerabad, and were quite as much taken aback at seeing us as we were at finding them on our side of the stream.

Without hesitation we went straight at them, and drove the lot helter-skelter through a deep ford, and dismounting set to work to make a breastwork, commanding the passage to be occupied by our infantry as soon as they came up. They arrived about 4 p.m., and I instantly posted Hodson off to report what I had done to headquarters. So important was this discovery considered by the authorities there that Colonel Mackeson, now the Governor-General's agent in camp, rode down the other side of the river as fast as his horse could carry him, and was ferried across on a "*shurnai*"[8] by a friendly boatman to my tent

During the night a general officer with a whole brigade turned up to occupy the position. We burnt the only two boats the enemy had in possession here, and remained watching these fords until the 19th January, when the Guides were ordered to join army headquarters. I have always felt the poor Guides got scant credit for their share in this business.

On the 21st we took part in the general battle of Goojerat,

---

8. Inflated skin.

which was an artillery action throughout, and much more like a grand review than a day which was to settle the destiny of the Punjab. A more beautiful sight could not have been on earth than the steady advance of upwards of one hundred guns—horse artillery going to the front at a gallop, and then "Left about!" "Action front!" supported by our cavalry, the heavy guns all the while smashing away at the Seikh artillery, and breaking up their masses of infantry and cavalry. Three times did the Seikh infantry form line to advance and charge at our horse artillery, who coolly watched for them until they came within the range of grape, and gave them a shower of such rain as had never come within the range of their conception.

Their lines at first halted, shook backwards and forwards like a field of wheat in a heavy wind, and at last broke and bolted like a flock of wild sheep, the horse artillery following at a gallop, and keeping up a murderous fire on them for miles. Our cavalry took up the pursuit when the horse artillery left off, and finished as pretty a day's work as any army in India ever got through. Thank God, the loss on our side this time was comparatively nothing, though you will be sorry to hear that poor Anderson[9] was killed at the head of his troop in the thick of the action.

The moment the scrimmage was over the Guides were started off after the broken enemy, following them up to Aurungabad Serai, on the Jhelum, where we were in time to cut up many stragglers, and prevent their crossing over to join the division of Sirdar Uttur Sing, encamped on the right bank. Here we had to remain until General Gilbert came up with his division and forced the passage of the river. No sooner were we across the water than the Guides were again off, and met, after three marches, Colonel George and Mrs. Lawrence, with other prisoners, at Pucka Serai, and escorted them back to the Jhelum, and again rejoined the pursuing division at Rawul Pindi, and was joined by John Nicholson.

When we arrived at Attok the General found himself on the bank of the Indus, with an escort of thirty Guide *sowars* and a company of Guide rifles, which I had managed to keep up with me by picking up each man alongside of my cavalry. The latter immediately lined the rocks on the edge of the stream, and

---

9. A brother officer of Lumsden's father.

63

opened such a nasty fire on the Afghan infantry that they were glad to cut away the bridge of boats, which swung over to our side of the stream, and was secured to us. Next morning, before daylight, two boat-loads of Guides crossed the Indus, and took possession of the fort at Khyrabad, which enabled a bridge to be reconstructed and a brigade of infantry to be crossed over. Three days afterwards the Guides entered the city of Peshawur, and here is the commandant, doing the duties of the political agent on the north-west frontier of India. However, George Lawrence will be back tomorrow, when I hope to get a little rest.

Don't show this letter to anyone, for people will say that H. B. L. is an egotist, whereas I know that you good people want to learn what your own hopeful son has been at. Thank God that in spite of the past year's hard work, in the shape of exposure, anxiety, and long marches, I am still as well as ever I was in my life.

By a most unfortunate mistake my name was left out of the Commander-in-Chief's despatch. However, the old general wrote and told Nicholson that he was so very sorry for it, and had written to the Governor-General on the subject It is a pity, but cannot now be helped. I have now gained three medals, and, please Providence, hope soon to come home and show them off. I have made up my mind to come home in two years, and to stick to my Guides till I do come, should Government not like to retain me in the double capacity as half-political, half-Guide.

I have come to this conclusion from seeing a list of the new district officers to be appointed in the Punjab, from which it is evident that all we unfortunate military officers, assistants to Sir Henry Lawrence, who have borne the brunt of the late outbreak, and stood to our posts till the ship split, are to be kept as we are, without gaining a single step in the political ladder, while dozens of civilians are put in over our heads, many of them junior to us in the service, and men who have never been out of a drawing-room in their lives.

Sir Henry, who, fortunately, is back again in the Punjab, is ill-pleased, but can do nothing more, having already done everything he could for us. He has again given me the choice, which I most readily avail myself of, to avoid what I consider a disgrace. I would rather command the Guides for love all my life than serve on 5000 *rupees* a month under some of these civilians, junior to me in the service.

CHAPTER 7

Drilling of the Guides by the 60th Rifles

H. B. LUMSDEN TO HIS FATHER.

Peshawur, 23rd April, 1849.

I sent a sort of abstract account of my share of the late campaign, and hope that, though addressed to my dear mother, it will have proved amusing to you all; I can conscientiously assure you that I could not have sent you monthly letters if a *lakh* of *rupees* depended on the arrival of each. No man on earth knows better than you do the sort of work expected from a deputy quartermaster-general of an army in the field, and when his duties are combined with those of assistant political agent and the head of a young Guide corps, you must admit they are enough for any man's power. Thank God, I have got through with credit to myself and the fine set of men I have the good fortune to command; though the unfortunate mistake of the C.-in-C. in leaving me out of his despatch is a great pity, as it might have given me a lift towards a brevet hereafter.[1] However, everything is for the best, though we poor blind mortals cannot always see how it may tend to our own good; and I have every

---

1. The omission, however, had meanwhile been repaired.
Extract from the Commander-in-Chief's despatch to the Governor-General, dated Camp Kullala, 15th March, 1849:—"On perusal of my despatch relative to the operations of the 21st February at Goojerat, I regret to find that I omitted mentioning the names of Lieutenants Lumsden and Hodson, of the Guides, and Lieutenant Lake of the Engineers, attached to the political department. These officers were most active in conveying orders throughout the action, and I now beg to bring their names to the favourable notice of your lordship."

reason to be most thankful to Providence for the many advantages I now enjoy above thousands of older and better soldiers than myself. Last month I was indignant in the extreme at the influx of a lot of civilians into the new Lahore Government, and had made up my mind to throw up the political line altogether rather than serve under them, and to stick to my military appointment as commandant of the Guide corps alone, should it be determined that I could not hold both.

My old friend, Henry Lawrence, however, has again stood out for me, and recommended that I should remain as an assistant, as heretofore, holding command of the Guides; and that, in consideration of the augmentation of my corps to four hundred cavalry and six hundred infantry, my own pay should be increased to 1000 *Rs.* monthly. I have not yet been nominated in the Government orders, but George Lawrence tells me there is no doubt of my getting this, which, with the certainty of remaining in the Peshawur district under him, is all I could have wished for under the sun.

I have made up my mind to come home after two years, and, if I can save cash enough to keep me from starvation, for one year at all events; and if I can stay longer all the better. You will scarcely credit it, but the last six months have made me quite homesick, and I can now think of nothing else but rambling about the hills and rivers of Aberdeenshire, in the green fields, and quietly fishing about Ballater, as I now remember what my boyish ideas of the place were. All of you good people know as well as I do that were I to live a single man in India a thousand years, in the best appointment in the country, I should never save cash enough to retire from the service. . . . . My only desire now is to be quiet for two years, save enough to take me home for my furlough, and allow me to see all my friends once more; I shall try to pick up a good sort of young wife, who will look after the cash while I make it, and enable me to cut John Company altogether by the time I am entitled to a pension. I would not give a rap to go home after all my old friends have gone the way of all flesh, and find myself a stranger in my own country, and when I am too old to enjoy myself and see what home really is.

I am to be stationed here, as I have just told you, and go over in a day or two, through the Afridi Pass, into the Kohat district, formerly held by the Sirdar, Sultan Mahomed, for the purpose of arranging for the occupation of the defile and collecting the Kohat revenue. This, I expect, will take me some six weeks to carry through, after which I return here, leaving young Pollock to carry out the work. There must, for the next two or three years, be constant little fights with the different hill tribes in our neighbourhood, which will give ample practice to our troops and keep our hands in. I only wish the order for my additional men would come out at once, to enable me to get them polished up and made good shots by the cold season.

Old Brigadier Wheeler, in his report to the Commander-in-Chief of the Sam Sing business, speaking of my two companies with him under Hodson, says, "they are the finest light infantry companies I have ever set my eyes on, in every way—cool under fire, first-rate shots, good judges of ground, and drilled to a perfection seldom equalled in our regiments of the line. The only fault to be found with them is their small numbers." Not so bad for a corps that has only been in existence two years.

Pray send me a package of fresh vegetable seeds for the garden here. We require a lot, as the garden is very large, and you might add some flower seeds also. Peshawur gardening has never yet been tried, but as clover grows here a perfect weed, I have great hopes that by getting lots of English seed we shall be able to cut out the gardens in the provinces; if they are sent out at once they will be out overland before the rains set in. Don't be frightened of sending too much.

About this time, by the kindness of that excellent soldier, Colonel Bradshaw, of the 60th Royal Rifles, a number of chosen men from the Guides were thoroughly drilled by the 60th on their own parade ground; and it was to the advantages gained from these exercises that Lumsden ever afterwards attributed the special steadiness of the Guide Infantry on parade. During Colonel Bradshaw's expedition into the Lundkhor valley, which will be described later on, the Guides brought down two or three wounded men of the Rifles from the hillside; and one Guide, after having been returned "missing" for two days, was found in the 60th hospital, having made his way there while severely wounded, and having been cared for during the absence of his own regiment from camp.

By Government order of the 19th June, 1849, the Guides were

increased from one to three troops, and from two to six companies. A second in command (Lieutenant A. Hardinge) and an adjutant (Lieutenant H. N. Miller) were posted to the regiment.

The Punjab Frontier Force was now raised. The object of the creation of this body, which did such good service in 1857, and to which the Guides were eventually attached, cannot be better told than in the words of the late Sir Henry Daly, who himself, in Lumsden's absence at Candahar in 1857, commanded the Guides at the siege of Delhi In a lecture to the Royal United Service Institution in 1884, Sir Henry Daly said:—

> My own reminiscences have this merit, they carry us back to the earliest stages of the Punjab Force; for I believe Sir John Coke, that rare leader of Pathans, and myself are the only survivors of the original commandants.
>
> Captain Coke and Lieutenant Daly raised the 1st Punjab Infantry and the 1st Punjab Cavalry, and within seven months of their embodiment both corps were reviewed by Sir Charles Napier, and served in the field under his command.
>
> > "As to Coke's," wrote that heroic soldier to George Lawrence, "I have seen nothing superior to it in drill; it is admirable. And both you and I saw how this brave corps fought under its excellent leader in our five days' campaign."
>
> And in the general order detailing the fighting he writes:
>
> > As Captain Coke and the 1st Punjab Regiment of Infantry sustained the brunt of this skirmishing, the Commander-in-Chief thinks it due to this admirable young corps and its excellent leader to say that their conduct called forth the applause of the whole column.

The stately proclamation of Lord Dalhousie, dated 29th March, 1849, recounts how the Punjab became part of the British Empire. The treacherous murder of two British officers—Vans-Agnew and Anderson—at Mooltan in April, 1848, was followed within twelve months by the destruction of the Sikh army, the capture of Mooltan, the battle of Goojerat, and the expulsion of the Afghans across the Indus to the mouth of the Khyber Pass. Sir Henry Lawrence was placed at the head of the new Government, with unlimited power of selecting the civil and military officers under him, Lord Dalhousie stipulating only for his agent in the war, Colonel Mackeson.

The defence of the frontier from Huzara to Mithunkote, at the junction of the five rivers, was a heavy task to face. It meant the control of lawless tribes, whose trade was warfare and plunder, numbering in all not less than 100,000 fighting men, levying blackmail on travellers and merchants, never combining save against the powers at Lahore or Cabul.

For a thousand years and more the valley of the Indus under the Suleyman range had been studded with a line of forts and towers—ruins of which still remain—as positions and outposts against the ceaseless raids of mountain marauders.

In times not long past, in a country so difficult for military operations—with narrow defiles, mere fissures in the rocks—marauders assembled from long distances, well armed and well mounted, and carrying their food on their backs. They sacked towns, exacted ransoms, murdered Sikh governors and people, getting back to their fastnesses with impunity.

The first duty which fell on Sir Henry Lawrence was the defence of his Trans-Indus frontier, and ten regiments, five of Cavalry and five of Infantry, were organized for employment.

Before proceeding further, it will be well to turn to the small body of Guides which owed its origin to Sir Henry Lawrence in December, 1846. Their organization must have been in his mind when he conceived the idea of a frontier force.

Sir Henry, during the first Afghan war, had seen the difficulties our army, British and native, encountered in the passes, amongst the hill tribes and northern nations, in the absence of guides and interpreters; and he resolved that in the future, within our own ranks, there should be hardy men accustomed to every region and accident of service, and familiar with every village dialect.

The Guides, originally one troop of cavalry and two companies of infantry, were raised by Major-General Sir Harry Burnett Lumsden, then a lieutenant. Lumsden possessed characteristics for the task in a rare degree. A daring sportsman, full of endurance, hardy and strong of frame, with an instinctive knowledge of men which gave him a power which none under him ever questioned. life in the Punjab in those times was full of incidents, and few were the days which did not test self-dependence and soldierly intelligence. Henry Lawrence quickly gauged Lumsden's genius. In addition to the strength begat by the stirring scenes in which he moved, Lumsden breathed among giants. The Lawrences, Edwardes, the Nicholsons were his associates.

It is hardly enough to say that on the enrolment of the Guides each man's personal history was known to Lumsden. Men from every wild and warlike tribe were represented in its ranks— men habituated to war and sport, the dangers and vicissitudes of border life: Afridis and Goorkhas, Sikhs and Huzaras, Wuziris, Pathans of every class, and even *Kafirs*, speaking all the tongues of the border, Persian, Púshtú, etc., dialects unknown to the men of the plains. In many cases the Guides had a camp-language or patois of their own. Lumsden sought out the men notorious for desperate deeds, leaders in forays, who kept the passes into the hills, and lived amid inaccessible rocks. He made Guides of them. Tempted by regular pay and enterprise, many joined the corps, and became conspicuous for daring and fidelity. On the border, and in the ranks of the Guides, tales, abundant in humour, were told of Lumsden's interviews with men who had defied all authority, and had never been seen in the plains but for murder and plunder.

A sketch of Diláwur Khan, who died on the path of duty, a *subadár* of the Guides, whose name is familiar in every village between the Khyber and Cashmere, will illustrate this:—

When Lumsden first visited Yusafzai in search of recruits—in his own words—"of men accustomed to look after themselves, and not easily taken aback by any sudden emergency"—Diláwur Khan was notorious. He had been brought up by Muhammadan priests, and was intended for the priesthood, but kidnapping bankers and rich traders, carrying them across the Indus into Yusafzai, was too attractive in adventure and remuneration, and he forsook the sacred calling.

Diláwur's capital consisted of his sword, a piece of rope, and a huge bullock's skin, which he could inflate at pleasure, and so carry himself and his guests across the "sacred river." Once there, a messenger was sent to settle the sum the firm or family would give as a ransom for his guest This was Diláwur's occupation. Lumsden, thinking that Diláwur must have rare local knowledge and pluck to carry on such a trade successfully, sent him an invitation to his camp, promising him a safe return to the hills. The very novelty of the invitation took Diláwur's fancy, and to the astonishment of the chiefs of the district he appeared in camp. Lumsden received him with all courtesy, pointed out that in a short time posts would be so established throughout the country that his calling would be impossible, and the risk of hanging great, and ended his moral by proposing to make him a Guide. Diláwur fairly burst into a fit of laughter at the proposal, and took his departure across the border. Six weeks afterwards he voluntarily turned up at Lumsden's tent, saying he had come to join the Guides, but pleaded hard to be excused the degradation of the "goose step"; but Lumsden held out stoutly for the absolute necessity of his being taught the complete art of war, and finally had the satisfaction of seeing the most dreaded man on the frontier patiently balancing on one leg at his bidding.

Such is Lumsden's own account, and he adds: "about half my first recruits were of this stamp, while the other half were sons and nephews of the chiefs of the district," who, as representatives of their family, sought the Englishmen, and eventually rose to the higher ranks. So popular became enlistment under Lumsden, that thirty or forty young Afridis, or Pathans, fed and clothed by their relatives in the ranks, passing through their first drill, awaited vacancies. Great was the excitement at the rifle-butts when a vacancy, as a prize, was shot for by these aspirants.

The headquarters of the corps were fixed at Murdán, in the midst of Yusafzai. A rude fort was constructed, and there, in a rich valley, bounded on the north and east by the Swât mountains, with the Indus and the Cabul River south and west, Lumsden held civil and military sway over a people the Sikhs had failed to subdue, and who had withstood an army with guns led by Ranjit Singh in person.

It seems fitting to quote here some part of a record of further incidents in the life of one whom Lumsden described as the "sharp, observant, and faithful Diláwur Khan, who soon rose to be a native officer, and one of the most trusted men in the regiment, finally falling at his post of duty as a Guide, basely betrayed on a mission on which he of all men should never have been sent."

The Rev, T. P. Hughes, a member of the Afghan Mission at Peshawur, in a pamphlet printed in 1876, writes as follows:—

Diláwur (the brave) was a native of Jahangira, a village on the banks of the Cabul River. He belonged to the tribe of Khatak, and could trace his descent from the great poet chief, Khushhál Khan. When a youth he was sent to the village mosque, and received instruction in the rudiments of Arabic and of Muhammadan theology. Being then of a studious turn of mind, he soon left his native place for a more advanced teacher, and for some time sat at the feet of a learned *moulvie* in the village of Zeydah. But the sedentary life of a theological student was not suited to the physical energy of Diláwur Khan, and in due time he exchanged the life of the sanctuary for that of the highway, and commenced to earn his living by plunder and robbery. The Sikhs were then the unwelcome rulers of the district, and it was thought consistent with the principles of religion and piety to despoil and pillage the *infidel* conqueror.

The occupation of a highway robber amongst the Afghans in those days was an honourable profession; and the danger and risk attending it were great attractions to Diláwur. Moreover, the *modus operandi* of Diláwur's maraudings was both curious and novel There is nothing like it even in the histories of Turpin and Macheath. For example, hearing that a wealthy Hindu shopkeeper was about to be married, he would, in company with others of his tribe, lie in ambush on the east bank of the Indus and await the arrival of the expectant bridegroom. Armed to the teeth with pistols, sword, and dagger, the Afghan brigands, led by Diláwur Khan, would attack the bridal party and seize the rich shopkeeper, bedizened with wristlets and chains. The unfortunate man was dragged to the river bank and placed inside an inflated cowhide, upon which one of the party mounted himself and paddled it across the river.

The shopkeeper was then carried to the Khatak hills, and a letter sent to his sorrowing friends, informing them that the ransom demanded for their relative was the moderate sum of two hundred *rupees* (£20). The Hindus, true to the instinct of their nature, would commence haggling as to the sum to be paid, when Diláwur Khan would cut short their negotiations by informing them that if the sum demanded was not sent within a week the head of their captive would be struck off and sent to them as an offering of peace (*nazr*), and that in consequence of the expense incurred in feeding their unwelcome guest, the ransom would be increased to three hundred.

In all cases the demand was acceded to, and the frightened trader restored to his home. Amongst his own people Diláwur Khan had found great inconsistency of conduct, especially among the Muhammadan priests, and he had not served in the Guides long before he learned that the English were actuated by principles of truth and justice. Already his heart was drawn towards the religion of the conqueror. He delighted to argue with and to listen to the precepts set forth by Dr. Pfander and the missionaries of the Afghan mission in Peshawur. He was presented with a copy of Dr. Pfander's *Mizan-ul-Haqq*, and thought and studied assiduously.

In the end of 1856, when the Háfiz Ji—the high priest of Cabul—accompanied the Amir Dost Muhammad Khan to Peshawur, he invited the mullahs of the city and surrounding country to discuss subjects of Moslem theology with him. Diláwur was one if those who responded to the invitation, and, hungry for argument as he always was, he introduced a point of doctrine for debate which created such discord in the assembly, that, although they did not actually kick him out, they accused him of being a *kafir* (an *infidel*) and forced him to retire. This treatment had a great effect on his mind. He thought there must be something wrong in a religion the teachers of which were afraid to face discussion.

Eventually, after the siege of Delhi, in which he displayed unwavering loyalty and devotion to the British, he was baptized at Peshawur, in 1858.

Mr. Hughes writes:—

The superstitions of the Muhammadans came in for his most severe condemnation, and he would ridicule their saints and shrines in the most unmeasured terms. It is related that some time before his baptism he was crossing the Indus in a boat which, being overladen, showed symptoms of collapse. The boatman and the other passengers at once set up a cry of distress, and sought the protection of their saints, "*O Ali! O Hosein! O Káka Sahib!*" when Diláwur Khan commenced crying out at the top of his voice, "*Lumsden Sahib! O Lumsden Sahib!*"

"What are you doing, you *infidel?*" exclaimed the passengers, "why do you supplicate *Lumsden Sahib?*"

"Why," exclaimed Diláwur, "your saints have been dead ages

ago, but *Lumsden Sahib* is living within thirty miles of us, and I think it wiser to pray to a living man than to a dead saint."

Many years later—in 1869—the Government had occasion to employ a trustworthy Afghan on a secret mission to Central Asia. Diláwur Khan was selected for the duty, and no doubt in respect to general ability and spirit of enterprise he was well qualified. But at that time age had begun to tell upon him, and had the political officer who made the selection been fully aware of Diláwur's religious history, he assuredly would not have chosen him. There was not a tribe on the frontier which did not know Diláwur Khan of the Guides, and did not look upon him as an irreconcilable enemy of the Moslem faith.

Mr. Hughes thus describes the last service of this remarkable man:—

It was not until January, 1871, that I became informed of his fate. The story was related to me by Shahzadah Akbar Khan. It was as follows:—

"I and my uncle, Shahzadah Yahayah Khan, started on a journey on special service for Government. After sixteen days' march we arrived at the village of Shishi, in the country of Chitral, where we fell in with three Afghans, who were sitting on the roadside under a tree, eating their breakfast. Upon inquiry we found their names were Diláwur Khan, Ahmad Jan, and Lall Jan. Lall Jan was a native of Hazarah, in Afghanistan, and did not appear to be connected in any way with the other two.

"We engaged in conversation, and we soon understood that we were each employed in the British service on some secret mission, although we did not allude to the subject, but conversed on general topics. We then proceeded on our journey, but we were soon overtaken by one of the servants of the ruler of Chitral, who said that strangers were not allowed to travel through the country without the permission of the king. When we heard this we decided to return to the city, but as we found a 'caravan' was about to start, we determined to renew our journey. We stayed the night at the village of Shugat. In the middle of the night six of the ruler's soldiers seized the whole five of us, and bound us hand and foot In the morning our bonds were loosed, and we were ordered to return to the city of Chitral in company with the soldiers.

"On our way, as we passed the river, Diláwur Khan threw a

small bundle of papers into the water. My uncle, observing this, took the hint and did the same. (They must have been letters of introduction which they had received from the British Government.) We were then brought into the presence of the king. His Majesty asked us our names. Diláwur Khan said he was 'Mullah Diláwur,' to which the king replied, 'It is untrue; you are a Subadár Diláwur; you are a heretic (*wahhábi*), a Christian (*Christán*). A letter has come from the *Kazis* of Peshawur, and therefore I know you are a Christian, and a spy from the British Government.'

"Diláwur Khan replied, 'It is quite true that I was a *subadár*, but I am now a *mullah*, and I am going to study in Bokhara. If you think I am an *infidel* (*kafir*), bring the *mullahs* and let them discuss religious questions with me.' We were then searched. Diláwur had ten Bokhara sovereigns (*tilas*), and a book on science (*Ilm-i-hikmat*). We were imprisoned fourteen days. On the fourteenth day one of the king's servants told Diláwur that the *mullahs* (priests) had held a council, and had decided to stone him. He replied, 'It must be God's will'

"In the middle of the night Diláwur Khan said to us that, as the *mullahs* had decided to stone him, he may just as well jump into the river and drown himself. Being an excellent swimmer he no doubt hoped thus to escape, but my uncle seized him and would not let him attempt it.

"To our great surprise, the next morning the king came himself to us, and said we had nothing to fear, and that he would help us on our journey. We were, however, kept in prison two months longer, although kindly treated. By this time there had been very heavy falls of snow in the surrounding hills. We were at last released. The king gave each of us a blanket and some bread, and supplied us with two mules. Three of his servants also accompanied us. After four days' journey we came to the entrance to the pass over the mountain known as Kotri Nuqsan. Here we found the snow nearly two feet deep. One of the servants then took the mules back, and the other two remained with us. As we ascended the mountain the depth of snow increased. Night came on, and we slept under a rock; the cold was intense.

"In the morning the two servants of the king said they would try and collect wood for a fire. They went away, and we never saw them again; they must have returned to Chitral. Having travelled a few miles more, night again came on, and we slept in a cave on the hillside. In the morning the snow was quite three feet deep. We decided to press on, but the snow increased, and we did not proceed more than two miles. Another night was spent under the shelter of a rock, and in the morning Ahmad Jan, Diláwur Khan's comrade, was found dead. We left his body in the snow, and journeyed on for about four miles more. We took refuge for the night in a cave, but Diláwur Khan soon complained of the cold, and said his body was benumbed. We soon found that he was frostbitten and dangerously ill. We rubbed his limbs and did all we could to promote circulation of the blood, but with no avail.

"While we were rubbing his body, Diláwur Khan said, 'I feel I am dying. It is quite true that I am Subadár Diláwur Khan of the Guides at Murdán. I am a Khatak, and a native of the village of Jahangira. I am on a secret mission for the English Government If either of you live to return to Peshawur, go to the Commissioner and tell him Diláwur is dead. I have served the English faithfully, and I am happy to die in the service of the British Government.' He soon fell asleep—it was the sleep of death."

CHAPTER 8

Causes Leading to the Affair of Sangao

Lumsden's personal narrative is continued in the following letters:—

H. B. LUMSDEN TO HIS FATHER.

Peshawur, 10th August, 1849.

I came in here yesterday, and find that it is overland day, so must send you a few lines. I am disgusted at finding my name left out of the brevet just published I had more hard work and marching in the hot weather, and received more letters of thanks, both to myself and my regiment, from Government, during the Punjab campaign, than most men. My name also was mentioned by the C.-in-C. as "having done my duty at Goojerat," whilst in General Whish's letter of the 23rd January last to the Adjutant-General, "Lieutenant Lumsden, Assistant Resident and of the Guides, performed useful service for the two months he and his men were in the allied camp"; and yet I am left out of the *Gazette*. . . .

Sir Henry Lawrence has been again very ill, and must, I fear, go away to the Cape shortly if he does not soon mend.

George Lawrence is also on his back with fever, and looking very ill I wish he would take my advice and go away to Simla while he has strength to move. The Peshawur fever never leaves a man until he has change of air, and Lawrence has now had three sharp attacks within the year. He will not leave his post, he tells me, at a time when it would be inconvenient for Government to lose his services; but I say it would be much more inconvenient, both to himself and Government, if he should stay just one day too long here.

From what I can see of the new way of carrying on business in the Punjab, I have every reason to be satisfied with the choice I made in giving up the civil for the Guide line of business. We military men, who have not been ground at points of law practice, do not enter the ring on fair terms with even younger civilians, who have these things at their finger ends; and though it is bad enough to be superseded by a military man, it is nothing to receiving a wigging daily, and to be told "that the youngest civilian in the country would not have done so-and-so," or to having a young gentleman of the black cloth put over one in a province.

H. B. LUMSDEN TO HIS MOTHER.

Peshawur, 29th October, 1849.

You want to know my reasons for having made up my mind to quit the political line, and keep to my original field as a soldier. They are as follows:—

In the first place the Lahore agency is not now as heretofore a political agency for the affairs of the north-western frontier, but has resolved itself into a new civil government of the Punjab, where all of our civil regulations are to be introduced. This being the case, I thought that I should have no chance with young civilians, who have all their lives been learning the regulations, and must know something about them, while I should have everything to learn before I could possibly teach others. It would not be very agreeable to have the Board writing letters and telling me that Mr. So-and-So, who had only been out two years in the Civil Service, would not have made the mistake which you have fallen into. When Major Edwardes, who is one of the cleverest men in India with his pen, finds this, what hope should I have of getting out of such scrapes? Major Lawrence even is thinking of leaving the Punjab as soon as he can conveniently do so, and he has two brothers on the Board.

On the other hand, at the head of the Guides, I have three fine young officers under me, with three hundred sabres, and six hundred rifles. I rather flatter myself there are not many men in the Army who can cut me out, and I have work to do which I like and understand, such as must, sooner or later, lead to distinction, and which has already got for me the promise of a majority as soon as I get my company regimentally; and, to crown all, through Sir Henry Lawrence's exertions in my favour, I have, together with all the officers under me, got all the powers of an assistant commissioner in the Punjab, which will enable me to hold political power, in the event of a war, in any quarter, and my being a Guide secures for me the certainty of seeing every service that may be going.

Will Father, under these circumstances, think that I was a griff to give up, or rather decline to enter, a line in which I could have little hope of even holding my own, instead of holding on to the appointment I feel myself a master in, and which opens out to me a wide field for distinction as well as remuneration.

Sir Henry has been very ill, and must go to the Cape or home next hot weather. He is to be here in a day or two, on his way from Cashmere to Lahore, and I need not tell you how delighted I shall be to see him.

No news here. We are to have a little *tumasha* (excitement) here in a month or two, bringing some of these hill gentlemen in this neighbourhood to order for plundering; but it will be a very slight business after what we have been accustomed to for the last year or two; and what will please you more is that, from having H.M. 60th Rifles to do the light infantry skirmishing, there will be no work for the Guides beyond pointing out the best roads into the fight.

Before giving an account of the operations anticipated by Lumsden in writing to his mother, it may be well to quote a description of their causes, and of the field in which they were to be carried out, from a report of Mr. K. Temple,[1] Secretary to the Punjab Government.[2]

From the time of the annexation of the Punjab the Swâtis uniformly proved themselves bad neighbours to the British. The sub-divisions of the Peshawur district adjoining the Swâtis, Ranizais, and Utman Khels, are Lundkhor, on the north-west corner of Yusafzai, and then Hashtnagar; and these tribes seem to have regarded the plains of Peshawur, especially Hashtnagar, as a hunter does his hunting-grounds. Plunderers and marauders—sometimes in bands, sometimes in twos and threes, some-

---

1. Afterwards the Right Hon. Sir Richard Temple, Bart, G.C.S.I., C.I.E.
2. Paget's *Record of Frontier Expedition*, 1st Ed.

times on foot and sometimes mounted—issued from Swât, passed through Ranizai, and proceeded to the plains of Hashtnagar and Yusafzai. They would not usually make regular raids, and they would refrain from molesting Pathans, their fellow-clansmen; but they would attack persons of all other classes—cultivators, petty traders, cattle graziers, wayfarers, and the like. They would carry off Hindus in particular, for the purpose of putting them to ransom.

Again, the Swâtis harboured renegades, refugee criminals, internal malcontents, and external enemies, the names of whom are too numerous to mention. For years the valley was a rendezvous for any and every person hostile to the British Government, and among them were several persons who had been dismissed from British service; and one man named Mokaram Khan, who had been dismissed from the Peshawur Police, in particular was received with great favour, and enjoyed a large landed grant in Swât. Not only did Swât receive and support enemies of the British, but it encouraged them to commit depredations in British territory. Further, the Swâtis took every opportunity of inciting British villages to set authority at nought. They invited their fellow-Pathans to throw off British yoke and acknowledge a nominal allegiance to Swât For this purpose they would not only assemble troops in Ranizai; or Utman Khel, but they would even send horsemen into British villages, partly as emissaries and partly as representatives of authority.

In October, 1849, it was reported by Lieutenant H. B. Lumsden, Assistant-Commissioner in Yusafzai, that the whole of the Utman Khel villages of the Lundkhor division of Yusafzai had positively refused to pay revenue, that they had warned the native revenue collector against sending any Government servants into the country, that the people were all busy preparing for war. In reporting this matter to Government, and urging the despatch of a military force, lieutenant-Colonel George Lawrence, the Deputy-Commissioner of Peshawur, said the Sikhs were in the habit of sending yearly from 1200 to 1500 men, with two or four guns, to make the Yusafzai collection, which, though it harassed the country, had a salutary effect; and as no troops of ours had, up to that time, been seen beyond the cantonment of Peshawur, an impression had got abroad among the ignorant hill tribes throughout the frontier that we had either no force, or were afraid to approach their fastnesses.

In sanctioning the employment of such a force, the Governor-General recorded that in "all ordinary cases the employment of British troops for the mere collection of revenue is a measure to be avoided. But the refusal of the villagers in Lundkhor to pay the little revenue demanded of them is not merely a denial of the revenue which they owe, but is, in fact, a test and trial of the British power, and of the authority which was to be exercised over them. It was therefore quite indispensable that the demands of the Government should be fully enforced, and a conspicuous example made of these men, the first in this newly-conquered province who had dared to resist the orders of the British officers."

It was further ordered that if resistance should be attempted it was to be put down severely, but without any unnecessary harshness; and, under any circumstances, the headmen of the villages were to be brought prisoners to Peshawur, there to await the pleasure of the Government. . . .

Immediately after Colonel Lawrence had sent in his report, two forays on British territory were made by horsemen from the village of Pali.

On the 3rd December a force moved from Peshawur, under the command of Lieutenant-Colonel Bradshaw, C.B., Her Majesty's 60th Rifles, and accompanied by Lieutenant-Colonel Lawrence, the Deputy-Commissioner.

After much difficulty in crossing the Cabul River at Nowshera, there being no ford and but few boats, the force reached Kátlung on the 10th, a village at which Lumsden, with his Guide corps, had been encamped, protecting the country, for the past month. On the morning of the 11th the force advanced, to carry out the successful and well-managed affair at Sangao. Great natural difficulties of ground had to be faced and overcome before it was possible to engage the enemy. The village of Sangao is situated in a nook formed by the range of hills (3000 feet high) which borders the Janikhor valley on the north, and a spur (500 feet high) projecting therefrom at an angle of fifteen or twenty degrees. Across the angle was constructed a wall, behind which and on the spur the enemy took up a position, showing numerous flags or standards.

On the force approaching within 1200 yards, two of our guns

opened fire on the spur, whilst the 60th Rifles covered the right attack, the Guides and 1st Punjab Infantry (Coke's) advancing along
the main spur to the left, so as to obtain possession of the only line
of retreat that appeared possible. The main body, with the remaining
four guns of Fordyce's troop, moved to attack the village in front. So
quickly did the Guides accomplish their task, that an artillery officer
deliberately laid a gun on them, and was on the point of ordering it
to be fired when a keen-eyed gunner called out, "Lord! sir; them is
our mudlarks!" referring to their mud-colour[3] uniform, then for the
first time seen in action by British troops, though now so generally
adopted by the whole army when in the field.

With some twenty casualties the possession of the place was secured and the village destroyed, whilst the Utmanzais, deserting everything, fled over the hills to Swât.

On the 14th December a like punishment was inflicted on the
villages of Pali, Zormandai, and Sherkhán in the Bázdara valley, after
which the force returned to Peshawur. This example had the happiest
effect. In a short time the headmen all came in to Lumsden, acknowledged their sins, and paid their revenue.

As this was the first punishment of the kind inflicted by us on
the Peshawur border, it may be well to set forth the general policy
by which the Punjab Government was guided for many years in its
treatment of the neighbouring hill tribes of the north-west frontier. In
1864, the Secretary to the Government of the Punjab wrote as follows
in regard to such expeditions[4]—

Whilst any hasty exertion of physical pressure to the exclusion
of other methods of adjustment is confessedly impolitic, there
is a point beyond which the practice of forbearance may not
be carried. As without physical force in reserve there can be no
governing power, so under extreme and repeated provocation
its non-employment is not distinguishable from weakness. In
each case separately, therefore, it must be judged whether or not
offensive measures have been justified It must be noted that the
despatch of an expedition into the hills is always in the nature
of a judicial act. It is the delivery of a sentence and the infliction
of a punishment for international offences. It is, as a rule, not in
assertion of any disputed right or in ultimate arbitration of any

---

3. Khaki.
4. Paget's *Record of North-West Frontier Expeditions.*

contested claim of its own that the British Government resolves on such measures, but simply as the only means by which retribution can be obtained for acknowledged crimes committed by its neighbours, and by which justice can be satisfied or future outrages prevented.

In the extreme cases, in which expeditions are unavoidable, they are analogous to legal penalties for civil crime—evils in themselves inevitable from deficiencies of preventive police, but redeemed by their deterrent effects. Considerations of expense, of military risk, of possible losses, of increasing antagonism and combination against us on the part of the tribes, all weigh heavy against expeditions; and, to set them aside, there must be an irresistible obligation to protect and to vindicate the outraged rights of subjects whom we debar from the revenge and retaliation they formerly practised.

To permit a *moulvi*, openly preaching war against us as infidels, to occupy our villages with his armed retainers or murderously to attack the encampment of our officials; to suffer a British officer to be murdered in our territory whilst travelling on the public road; to allow a populous town to be plundered by an invading force; to sanction passively the returns of fanatical conspirators, robbers, and murderers to a post from which we had expelled them by military action—this is the degree of inaction—this is the ignominious attitude to which the British Government would be reduced were it admitted that the expeditions recorded have not been fully justified, have not been fully necessary.

The question is, indeed, much less one of moral right than of political expediency and of military practicability.

Morally we have the fullest right. As a Government it is our bounden duty, in proportion to our ability, and after exhausting all milder measures, to chastise, in their corporate capacity, tribes or sections of tribes who openly and habitually rob and murder our subjects, or violate our territory. This is also a condition of our political existence—the extension of protection in return for submission. And if by refusing the surrender of the actors in the crimes committed the tribes leave no alternative but hostilities available, the responsibility is theirs.

But, politically, the advantages to be obtained will always much depend on the concomitant circumstances. The military success which, in varying degrees, has always attended expeditions, and the demonstration that their roughest hills can be penetrated by our troops, have done much to subjugate the minds and compel the respect of the hill populations, and to reconcile them to peaceful pursuits. Success less distinguished might, on the contrary, excite them to continued rapine and resistance.

CHAPTER 9

Peshawur and the Neighbourhood, 1850–51

Brigadier-General Sir Colin Campbell was appointed to command the Peshawur district about the end of November, 1849, and in January, 1850, the commander-in-chief, Sir Charles Napier, arrived at Peshawur. In the meantime the Punjab Frontier Force had recruited, trained, and numbered 11,000 men of all ranks, with 64 guns, including those in position on the walls and forts of Bannu and Kohat. Of this force, the 1st Punjab Cavalry and the 1st Punjab Rifles had, from the beginning, been raised at Peshawur on the type of the Guides, whilst the rest of the force was organized and detailed to stations along the frontier from Huzara to Sind. The 1st Punjab Rifles, under Captain Coke, had already shown their efficiency in action at Sangao, and the time had come for these two corps to go over and take up their allotted posts at Kohat.

That station is separated from the Peshawur valley by a defile known as the Kohat Pass, the *kotul*, or summit, of which is within three miles of Kohat. The road lies through mountainous and independent country occupied by Afridi tribes. Early in February, 1850, a detachment of sappers was sent, under escort of irregular levies, by Lieutenant F. R. Pollock,[1] the Assistant-Commissioner of Kohat, to improve the road over the *kotul*; the detachment, however, was surprised and many of the men killed by the Afridis, who thereupon closed the pass. It became necessary, therefore, to reopen our communication and to punish the offenders.

The commander-in-chief, being himself at Peshawur, immediately

---

1. Afterwards Major-General Sir Richard Pollock, K.C.S.I.

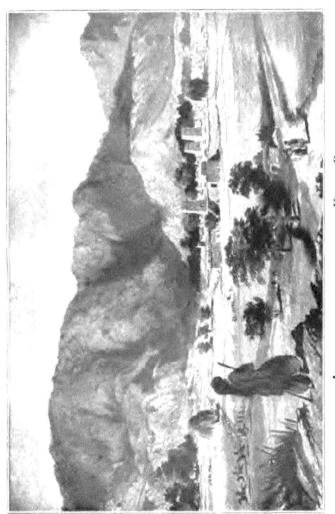

AKORA VILLAGE, ENTRANCE TO KOHAT PASS

directed Brigadier Sir Colin Campbell to detail a force adequate to the undertaking, and personally to proceed in command. Sir Charles Napier also accompanied the force which moved from Peshawur on the 8th February, and by the 13th had successfully carried out the operation.

The Guides under Lumsden, and the 1st Punjab Rifles under Coke, covered the flanks of the column in its advance, and the latter corps held the pass until the withdrawal of the troops. The details of this operation were published in a despatch, and the thanks of Government conveyed to all concerned.

John Coke and Harry Lumsden were the greatest of friends, and had much in common. They both commanded regiments, and were rulers of their respective districts of Kohat and Yusafzai. Coke, like Lumsden, was first a military and then a political officer. He was the picture of a soldier—tall, broad-shouldered, and of commanding appearance, with dark hair and beard. He was a Herefordshire man, and in after days, when he had left the service and settled in that county, he was as much respected by his neighbours at home as he had been by the chiefs and people of the border when he was Deputy-Commissioner at Kohat.

A journey on horseback through the Kohat Pass was often not altogether without excitement. If an Afridi matchlock had remained too long loaded, it might as likely as not be discharged in the direction of a passer-by. This used to happen sometimes in the neighbourhood of Shirukki, a straggling group of huts situated in a narrow portion of the defile. When Lumsden was acting as Commissioner he had occasion to go from Peshawur to consult Coke at Kohat. The latter went out a abort distance to meet his friend, and naturally asked if he had come through the pass all right. "Oh, yes," said Lumsden, "but no thanks to you, John."

"Why?" asked Coke.

"Well, at Shirukki, as I passed, out came one of your Afridi friends, blowing at the match of his matchlock, and vociferously inquiring whether I was. Coke! Nothing but my being able to assure him that I was Lumsden, not Coke, saved my skin." The name of "Coke" rather handicapped its possessor amongst Muhammadan races. "*Khok*" in Púshtú signifies a pig, and the temptation, on occasion, to emphasize a guttural was too much for excitable Pathans.

There used to be a good deal of rivalry between the Guides and the 1st Punjab Rifles in border expeditions. While the former were styled *"Khákis"* from their dust-coloured clothing, the latter went by the name of the *"Siah posh"*[2] owing to their being clothed in invisible green, like British Rifle Corps.

HARRY LUMSDEN TO HIS MOTHER.

Peshawur, 11th May, 1850.

Many thanks for your letters of the 14th March, from which I am delighted to find that the good people at Aberdeen approve of the conduct of the Guides at Sangao; but as I have got hold of a fine set of young lads in the corps, who don't care a pin's head for being shot at, I consider that a Belhelvie man who could not (as John would say) go ahead with them, deserves to be kicked out of the parish as disgracing the porridge of *"Bon-Accord."* There is little credit due to a white-skin for going on so long as he has good men to back him; and the Guides are Al.

George Lawrence has, I am sorry to say, been obliged to go to Simla for this hot season, as the doctor told him the consequences of another fever, like what he had last year, would be fatal, and when the hot winds once set in there's no getting away from Peshawur.

The Board of Administration have put me in charge of the district, so your first-born is now *"Burra Sahib"*[3] at Peshawur, as well as Commandant of Guides. I told Government distinctly that I did not wish to have the charge if by taking it I should lose my regiment, and the Governor-General, Lord Dalhousie, has given in. I must get home next year. I look upon it that I have had quite enough of India now, and the sooner I get out of it the better. I am half killed with work of all sorts, and often when I am bothered wish myself back with the 59th N.I.

I have sent to old Nain Sookh to Futtehgurh to have a tent sent to Billy[4] at Meerut. His corps is, I believe, a good one, the 68th, and at Meerut, if he only keeps quiet, and works for a short time at Hindustani, I have no doubt he will do well.

Peter is a pet of Sir Charles Napier, and will remain in the Quartermaster-General's department all his life. If he has the luck of an old cow, he should be Quartermaster-General of the Army as soon as he is a major, and what better could he wish for?

---

2. Black-coated.
3. The "big man" or district officer.
4. William, his youngest brother.

Lumsden being now, as he tells his mother in the preceding letter, not only Commandant of the Guides, but principal civil officer of the Peshawur district, it may be well to recall to memory some of the main features of the city of Peshawur and the immediate neighbourhood before the present cantonment had been built and occupied.

In those early days the British troops were chiefly quartered in an old caravanserai called the Ghor Khatri, in the heart of the native town, and in the large fort which commanded the city on the north-west. The Zakha-Khel and other marauding Afridi tribes of the Khyber regarded the temporary barracks, guardhouses, and stables of the British as happy hunting founds, from which they often succeeded in stealing with impunity horses and arms. Lumsden himself lived in an old *burj* or tower, the Guides being in tents or huts hard by, while the officers' mess occupied the house subsequently known as Mackeson's.

The trunk road to Lahore was at this time being laid out by that most energetic of engineers, Lieutenant Alexander Taylor.[5] The journey from Peshawur to Rawul Pindi, a distance of about one hundred miles, could only be made on horseback or on foot. The town and fort of Attock, on the left bank of the Indus, about forty miles from Peshawur, was more picturesque than at present—to those who beheld it from the right bank. It was still unspoilt by Public Works' barracks, the eye falling only on the crenulated walls, gateways, and half-ruined towers, piled one above the other, on which so many hungry Central Asian hordes had gazed as they pressed forward to secure wealth by the plunder of India.[6]

Lumsden's "*burj*" was situated just outside the so-called cantonment of Peshawur, and was surrounded by a garden. The *burj* was built on a truncated cone or mound of rough masonry, to which ascent was made by a flight of steps. No record remained of its builder or original purpose; it might have been the halting-place or "*derah*" of a wandering saint. The masonry was strong and well cemented. A wide verandah, used as a general sleeping apartment, surrounded, at a somewhat lower level, the central octagonal hall. Lumsden's companion in the tower was Lieutenant Pollock, who had recently been transferred from Kohat[7] to Peshawur as Assistant Commissioner. He was one of

5. Afterwards General Sir Alexander Taylor, G.C.B., R.E., late Governor of Cooper's Hill College.
6. See illustration p. 19.
7. Sir Richard Pollock has given the following interesting description of his position at Kohat, previous to Sir Charles Napier's expedition:—
"In the spring of 1849 I found myself at Kohat, the (continued next page),

Sir Henry Lawrence's picked men, the youngest of them, being only twenty-two years of age when he left his regiment, the 49th N.I., and went with a small force, after the siege of Mooltan, to assist Major Reynell Taylor in besieging the fort of Lukki in the Bannu district. His arrival at a critical moment secured not only the surrender of the fort, but also the immediate withdrawal of Sirdar Muhammad Azim Khan, the second eldest son of the Amir Dost Muhammad Khan of Cabul, from the Bannu territory to Kurram.

In those days officers always had their arms within reach. One night Lumsden and Pollock found themselves respectively stalking each other in and around the *burj*, each having heard the sound of someone moving on the premises. At the door of the hall hung a short stick with a loaded knob, which Lumsden in his wanderings in Yusafzai had wielded with much effect as a weapon to be hurled at the many fierce dogs which rushed upon his horse. The men of the Guides gave this stick the name of "Cease firing," because Lumsden on parade, when some of his excited young soldiers would heed no bugle-call, found that "Cease firing" lodged between their shoulders commanded instant obedience. So great was the respect in which this apparently harmless weapon was held that not a few of the Guides would salute it as they passed.

There was a standing order at Peshawur that no officer should

---

only white man in the place, and the first officer to assume charge of the district I was military commandant, district officer (under George Lawrence at Peshawur), with no telegraph, and the Kohat Pass independent between me and my chief, no police, and for garrison I had Lahorah Sing's troop of Sikh horse artillery, and some Multani Pathan horse and foot levies. Except for the loneliness it was a very pleasant, interesting, and responsible life. I lived and worked in Sirdar Sultan Muhammad Khan's house. There was only a rough footpath between this and the lines and parades, so I started road-making, for which I employed the artillerymen. There was an old mound of very hard earth on our line of road, and this we determined to blow up.

"One evening, when the mine was nearly ready, my dinner was announced, and Lahorah Sing said, (If you will go down to your meal I will send word when the charge is ready, and we will fire the train when you come back.' I turned out again when the work was completed, and it was by this time quite dark. I took up what seemed to me a fairly safe position, gave the signal, and up went the mine, and simultaneously some large substance whizzed past my ear. Sending back men to see if they could find anything, they returned with a human thigh-bone; and then we realized what, I am afraid, the Sikhs must have guessed, that we had disturbed a disused Muhammadan graveyard. If I had been killed, or even injured, it would have made a glorious story for the faithful—how a young English officer had insulted a saint, and how this had been promptly resented."

THE GUIDE BURJ, PESHAWUR

go about the district unarmed. This rule was obviously necessary in a country where every native carried arms, and where any unarmed officer was liable to be taken at a disadvantage, while the very possession of a weapon would ensure respect. It was, at the same time, very irksome to some officers, unaccustomed to such a habit, to carry sword or pistol. On one occasion a young officer was brought up to Sir Colin Campbell for disobedience of this order, upon which the old veteran, characteristically shaking his fist at him, remarked, "I'll tell you what it is, young man—you may go without your breeches, but d—— it, sir, you *shall* carry your sword."

Besides office routine, Lumsden had to spend no small portion of his time in receiving and interviewing chiefs and representatives of border clans, as well as landowners of the district. These personal interviews generally took place in the *burj*, and were useful as a means of securing information and gaining knowledge of character. The Zakha-Khel Afridis were then, as they are now, amongst the most determined marauders of all the Afridi clans; their deeds were as notorious in Cabul as in Peshawur. Sirdar Ghulam Haidar Khan, the heir-apparent of the Amir Dost Muhammad, used to relate how a noted Zakha-Khel thief in Cabul, on being disturbed in the operation of cutting out a horse, attempted to escape through a hole in the wall. When his head and shoulders had emerged on the outside, his legs were seized by someone from within. Screaming out to an accomplice who stood near, he begged him to cut off his head rather than to leave him to be recognized by those who would gloat over his capture.

One afternoon the chief of these Zakha-Khels awaited Lumsden's return to the *burj*. The old man looked ill. Lumsden observing the fact, and remembering that he had not seen him for two months, asked whether all was going well with him. The chief looked up for a moment with his keen eyes, and said, "No, *sahib*, it is not all well with me."

"What is the matter?"

"I cannot tell you, as I might get into a scrape."

"Don't fear," said Lumsden, "for if it is anything short of murder you may speak on; you shall go home safely."

Placing his turban on the ground, and pulling his skull-cap tightly on his head, he said, "Well, *sahib*, the last time I was here, after visiting you, I returned to sleep for the night in the town of Peshawur. There I met a number of young lads of my clan, who were bent on stealing officers' horses in the cantonment. Of course, *sahib*, I am too old and too respectable nowadays to join in such sport as that, but I could not resist the temptation to see how these youngsters did their work. So I went down with them, and the first stable they commenced to cut the wall of was that of the Topkhana[8] adjutant. Well, the boys were not quiet enough, and made a noise which disturbed the adjutant *sahib*; but, will you believe it, the fool of a fellow instead of firing at them fired at me."

Then throwing open his *chogah*,[9] the old man displayed a breast well peppered with shot marks, and, shaking his head significantly, added, "By the blessing of the Prophet, I may get my change out of him yet." It may as well be added that, as the adjutant's period of appointment was just up, the desire of the Zakha-Khel chief was never accomplished.

Another frequent visitor was Rahmut Khan, the chief of the Orakzais, who had great influence amongst the Aka-Khel, Basi-Khel, and other tribes bordering on the Kohat Pass. At one time he was the agent on the part of the Government for controlling the affairs of that pass. Rahmut Khan was physically a fine specimen of a man, with strongly marked Jewish features, and full of energy and impulse. In argument he was always impatient, and could scarcely keep himself from interrupting friends or foes with the exclamation, "*Zara puigi.*" So frequently did he use these words that he was known by the name of "*Zara puigi*," which signifies in Púshtú, "Just understand a little." Lumsden wrote of this man:

> I cannot help telling the way that an Afridi chief of the Orakzais settled a disputed succession to the leadership of his clan, as an apt illustration of the state of the north-west frontier at the time I have been writing about Rahmut Khan, a younger son of the redoubted chief of the Orakzais, but son of a lady of good family, had for some time disputed the succession with his elder brother, who was the offspring of a woman of no family. Part of the tribe followed each claimant, and many lives had been sacrificed on either side without bringing the dispute any nearer a close. A bright idea struck the younger son. He called a council of the elders of the clan, put them down to adjudicate the case, and promised to abide by their award, which was in due time given against him.

---

8. Artillery.
9. Loose flowing robe.

He at once resigned all claims, and at the suggestion of his relations, gave a feast on the happy occasion of the reconciliation of the family, to which he in due time escorted them all, including his elder brother. The supper was given in his own residence, under which he had carefully lodged a heavy charge of gunpowder. When all had feasted and were in great spirits, Rahmut Khan duly presented the pipe of peace. It was passed round, and whilst the curling smoke ascended, he quietly slipped out of the door, lighted a match, and ran for his life, whilst an explosion blew his brother, home, and relatives into eternity. He told me this little tale himself, remarking, "I had but little trouble after that."

While quartered at Peshawur frequent patrols of the Guides used to be detached to traverse the roads in the vicinity of the city, in search of professional marauders from the neighbouring hills. These gentlemen, in quest of horses or arms, did not hesitate to take the life of anyone who stood in their way. They used to dig through the sun-dried brick or mud stable-walls in order to carry off horses. They were armed to the teeth, and unhesitatingly risked life and limb in their desperate undertakings. On one memorable night, a Guide belonging to a patrol, passing an old gateway some little distance out of the city, suddenly observed an unusual protuberance on the sky-line of the building. Thinking it not unlike a human head, he stopped to look further. The object suddenly disappeared, on which the soldier, without hesitation, scaled up a winding staircase.

No sooner did he show himself above than a pistol was snapped in his face. Providentially it missed fire, and the Guide, sword in hand, rushed on his assailant, who then sprang over the parapet of the gateway into the road, where another Guide instantly put a rifle-bullet through his heel, and secured "*Razza*," one of the most noted robbers in the mountains, who for years had been the terror of the whole country, and had been "wanted" for over a dozen murders. He had evidently been hiding until the early hours of the morning, when he could enter the city in the hope of clearing out some Hindu.

CHAPTER 10

Lord Dalhousie at Peshawur

Sir Colin Campbell, who had been absent on a visit to Cashmere, returned to Peshawur in the autumn of 1850, and immediately entered into the closest relations with Lumsden, both as regards the policy to be adopted towards the tribes, and the measures necessary for the protection of the frontier.

An extract from the *Life of Lord Clyde*, by Lieutenant-General Shadwell, published in 1881, relating to these important subjects, may appropriately be quoted as showing, amongst other things, the arduous nature of Lumsden's duties and responsibilities at the time:—

> Sir Colin's attention was again called to the unsatisfactory relations existing between the Afridis and the British authorities on the subject of the free passage of the Kohat Pass. Lieutenant Lumsden, the deputy commissioner, had recommended to the Lahore Government the propositions made by the tribes to renew their former friendly relations with us. This policy was cordially endorsed by Sir Colin. The information he had collected about the country inhabited by the tribes occupying the district of Teerah, in the vicinity of the Kohat Pass, led him to the conclusion that an attempt to subjugate these people would be an enterprise requiring serious consideration.
>
> The movement of a column of troops, with its encumbrance of baggage and stores, through a pass such as the Khyber or that of Kohat, the extent and difficulties of which are known, is an affair of not very difficult management; but the movement of a body of our troops, with its baggage and ammunition, in the interior of these mountains, which are without roads, is an undertaking of a more responsible character, where every man is

armed and an enemy. . . .

Sir Colin wrote:—

> I scarcely think one could manage in such a country to drive
> them into a corner, even by the employment of two or three
> columns; because it is their practice, I am told, to abandon their
> mud-houses or huts which they occupy during the summer
> months in the Teerah districts, and remove with their cattle and
> families to the lower slopes of the hills on this as well as the Af-
> ghanistan side of the range, and inhabit caves which they dig in
> the sides of the hills. When alarmed they send off their women,
> mounting the aged and sick on their cattle, and hide the little
> grain they possess, the men taking to the hills to oppose those
> by whom they have been disturbed.

Sir Colin was of opinion that to:

> . . . . . . effectually reduce these hill people immediately in our
> front to our rule, or at any rate to afford a fair chance of doing
> this, operations should be undertaken at the same time from
> both sides of the range of hills which they inhabit, when one
> party would be able to drive them upon the bayonets of the
> other party. . . .

The difficulties attending the operation and the probable insig-
nificant result of them led him to believe that Sir Henry Lawrence
would be:

> . . . . . glad to take advantage of the opening the Afridis have of-
> fered by their petition to Lumsden to accept their terms, if the
> security they have offered for their future behaviour is at all to
> be depended on.

H. B. LUMSDEN TO HIS FATHER.

Peshawur, 13th October, 1850.

Very many thanks for your kind letter of the 20th August, in
which you advise me to come home at once and acquire a
knowledge of the value of £ s. d., a subject to which, I regret
much to say, I have as yet paid but little attention. I am also most
sensible, my dear father, of your kindness in offering me every
assistance in your power to enable me to enjoy my furlough;
but at present I do not see how I am to come home under two
more years' service. I have just been called upon to pay some

four thousand *rupees* for regimental steps. I cannot refuse to purchase steps without the risk of repenting it hereafter, besides getting a very bad name in the service; and, after all, the paying for these promotions will only oblige me to remain two years more where I am, which will be just two years less to serve when I come back again.

As for drawing on your savings to help me when I come home, and to enjoy myself, I would just as soon think of shooting myself, or any other mad trick. Considering my good fortune in the service, and the handsome pay I have drawn for the last eight years, I should have saved a very pretty little purse by this time, quite enough to have enabled me to have paid for my steps and enabled me to go home too. As I have chosen to spend my cash in horses and dogs, perhaps foolishly, I must now pay the penalty, and work until I can afford to play. That's "bus."[1]

Both for my health and my purse I shall try and get Sir Henry to let me go up to the hills above Cashmere next hot season on duty as a Guide, which will enable me to get up amongst the snow, at the same time save cash. One cannot expend much money among snow bears and *burrel*.[2] This I have no doubt of being able to manage when Sir Henry and the Governor-General come up here in January.

All the big-wigs are to be at Peshawur this cold season, and I shall have to do the honours, a bit of duty I should most willingly make over to anyone fond of such work.

I cannot help thinking that we shall have a grand row in the hills this cold weather, though I cannot as yet point out the spot. The hill people are all boiling, and ready for a row. Peshawur has been most sickly this year, and at this present moment every hospital in cantonments is as full as it can hold, though, strange to say, we have had a cooler season than has been known for years.

The Marquis of Dalhousie, Governor-General of India, visited Peshawur in the month of March, 1851, and at once entered into consultation with the local authorities on the numerous pending questions regarding the future protection of the valley, and the policy to be

---

1. Enough.
2. A species of wild sheep.

followed towards the hill tribes. Sir Colin Campbell was desired, after taking counsel with Lumsden, to lay before his Excellency a memorandum on the project of defence. The Governor-General took the greatest interest in all that was going on, and he expressed to Lumsden the confidence he had in entrusting to him the political and civil charge of the Peshawur border until the return from furlough of that experienced political officer Colonel Mackeson.

Lord Dalhousie felt confident that Lumsden would work cordially with Sir Colin Campbell, and that between them they would do everything to project and carry out the necessary measures for the safety of the frontier and the protection of our own subjects. It must be remembered that we had only a short time before taken the Peshawur valley from the Sikhs into our own hands. It was therefore eminently desirable to observe the effect of blockading and other defensive measures on marauding tribes, which we had not the slightest wish to annex or to interfere with.

In the meantime our own subjects had to be protected, and to secure this end a system of frontier defence organization was fully considered, which allotted Yusafzai and all of the country east of the Swât and Cabul Rivers to the corps of Guides which was to be located in a defensive central position at Hoti Murdân.[3] The country to the west of the Swât and Cabul Rivers, bordering on the hills inhabited by the Momund and Afridi tribes, was to be protected by the garrison of Peshawur. The rest of the frontier, including Huzara on the left bank of the Indus, and from thence to Sind, was allotted to the care of the Punjab Frontier Force.

One of the difficulties of the problem to be solved by the political and military authorities at Peshawur was the fact that many of the hillmen belonging to independent tribes held lands both inside and outside the border, and systematically, upon every favourable opportunity, attempted further encroachments. There were ruinous walls, towers, and villages, with occasional hamlets, scattered along the line of the border, the inhabitants of which, in continual intercourse with the agricultural population of our own villages, secured information, projected raids, and afforded shelter to marauders going and returning from forays into British territory. Such localities presented shelter for bad characters, for whom their own home in the mountains had been made too hot, owing to blood feuds or other causes, and were in

---

3. So called from two villages, Hoti and Murdân. In later years the station has generally been called Murdân.

themselves the source of constant disturbance.

On his return journey to Attock the Governor-General took the opportunity of inspecting the Guide Corps at Akorah, and in a letter dated "Attock, 24th March, 1851," caused the following communication to be made to Lieutenant Lumsden:—

(1) I am directed to inform you that the Governor-General had much pleasure in casually meeting the Guide Corps in camp at Akorah. His lordship would have been glad, if time had permitted, of his doing more than merely passing down their ranks, but even the passing glance his lordship was able to afford was sufficient to show him the smart, active, and soldier-like appearance of the corps, both in cavalry and infantry.

(2) Their gallant and effective conduct has won for them, on many occasions, the approbation of the Government. The Governor-General is happy to mark the occasion of seeing them in person, and to evince to their commanding officer the sense he entertains of their services under him in the field, by bestowing on one of their native officers a public distinction in honour of the service he has done.

(3) The conduct of Futteh Khan Khuttuk, *Resáldar* of the Guides, has been conspicuous on many occasions. The Governor-General has satisfaction in conferring on him the title of *"Khan Bahádur"* and his lordship requests that the honour which has been conferred on him, and the sentiments herein expressed, may be made known to the corps in regimental orders.

H. B. Lumsden to his Father.

Peshawur, 11th July, 1851.

I am sorry to find that I have raised hopes among you good people at home, which must be deferred for a year. I cannot come home until the cold season of 1852, when, please Providence, I shall be a major in the Army, and take the little I can save with me to expend at home.

The Marquis of Dalhousie gave me a chance the other day to try to get home for a year, keeping the Guides; his reply[4] I send to you at the risk of being scolded for putting you to the expense of postage, as it will please you, and show that the Governor-General is not ill-pleased with my work.

---

4. This letter has apparently been lost.

I have to establish a chain of posts all round the district in the cold season, and the Governor-General is evidently anxious that I should do so rather than anyone else, and, as the proposition originated with myself, I cannot well get out of the business. Next hot weather the Guides are to occupy Yusafzai, so we must build a shed of some sort for ourselves.

Peter is living with me in our old tower, which we find much cooler than the big house. We have been very lucky in getting together at the same station, and, as he is to be permanently at Peshawur, we may have a good spell of it Should any chance bring any of you in the neighbourhood of one Rob Roy Adams,[5] who was lately my second in command in the Guides, I hope you will be kind to him, for he is a great pet of all the Guides, and went home sick. I am very sorry to hear so bad an account of poor ——; it only shows that, although we have a hot climate here, and lots of knives and bullets going now and then, quiet people at home do often not last so long as we poor subs in India; when the time comes a bed is just as bad a place to give up one's last breath as a ploughed field.

H. B. LUMSDEN TO HIS FATHER.

Peshawur, 18th October, 1851.

I have for a long time been thinking over my position, and wishing to come home to Belhelvie for three years. The present would appear to be the best for such a break in my Indian career, for the constant exposure in the hot season year after year has told a little on my constitution, and things on the frontier look as if they would remain quiet for a year or two. I have been in political charge of the frontier for two years, and am now about to be relieved, so that there is nothing on the score of appointments to keep me excepting the command of my pets, the Guides. . . .

The only thing that bothers me is that my doctor tells me I should go home, and that he will give me a certificate if I like; he wants me to go by sea, which is a great nuisance. I have told Lord Dalhousie that I will remain another year, establish my regiment comfortably in their new line of outposts, and then run home in December, 1852.

We are to have a new line of posts all round the Peshawur dis-

---

5. Afterwards Deputy-Commissioner of Peshawur, assassinated in 1864.

trict to keep out our mad neighbours, which will tend much to quiet the temper of our own people, by cutting them off completely from the influence of starving adventurers, and leave them a little time to think of improving their own condition by cultivating their land instead of rushing about the country in armed groups cutting each other's throats. The regular army are to occupy the southern and western border, while I, with my Guides and a squadron of irregular cavalry, protect the Yusafzais, and keep them in order. We have got the best part of the frontier to live in, but the worst and most troublesome to protect Mackeson will be here, I fancy, about the middle of December, when I shall make over all the civil work to him, and retire to the command of the Guides and charge of Yusafzai.

CHAPTER 11

Building of Fort Michni

Throughout the summer of 1851 Saadut Khan, the Momund chief, whose headquarters were at Lalpura, on the Cabul River, in Afghan territory, and who had opposed us in the Afghan operations of 1841-42, continued to instigate the tribes to harass our border. Detachments of the Guide cavalry and infantry, posted for defence at the village of Mutta, were constantly engaged in petty skirmishes. As autumn approached the Momunds increased in boldness. The followers of the Michni and Pindiali chiefs actually came down, set fire to houses, and destroyed some of the crops of our villagers. Lord Dalhousie thought it desirable that a punitive expedition should be sent into Momund country; but on the advice of the authorities at Peshawur consented, in the first instance, to try a system of preventive vigilance rather than one of armed retaliation.

On the 15th October, on the commencement of the cold season, the Supreme Government directed that the Momund fiefs in the *Doába*[1] should be confiscated, that the defensive posts should be strengthened, and that British troops should operate against the offending Momunds and destroy their lodgements in the plains.

On the 25th October, Sir Colin Campbell, at the head of a force of 2500 men, moved from Peshawur into the *Doába*. Lumsden, with 250 Guide infantry and some *sowars*, accompanied the troops, whilst the remainder of the corps went to Hoti-Murdân, in Yusafzai, which was to be their future headquarters. The *Doába* is a richly cultivated tract of country to the north of Peshawur, bordering on the Momund frontier, and confined by the Cabul and Swât Rivers from the points of their entry into the plain to their junction. It presents a front of some

---

1. *Doába* = land lying between two rivers.

twelve miles, in the centre of which, two miles from the border and eighteen miles from Peshawur, is the happily selected military post of Shubkudr, erected by the Sikhs on their first occupation of the valley.

It was and still is connected with Peshawur by a gun road, which crosses the Nágumán branch of the Cabul River by a boat-bridge. The object of Sir Colin Campbell's expedition was to cover the operation of erecting a fort at Michni, on the left flank of this line, six miles from Shubkudr; to destroy the numerous Momund walled enclosures and villages, which offered shelter to marauders; and to allow the civil authorities to remove the few scattered inhabitants to other localities more under control.

The details of the military operations carried out by the troops in the field under Sir Colin Campbell in this and subsequent Utmankhel and Ranizai campaigns, with mention of the services of Lumsden and his Guides, are so fully detailed in the official documents published in the *Records of Expeditions against the North-West Frontier Tribes*, that they need not be repeated at length. Suffice it to say that the troops were engaged for months on the Momund frontier in most trying and harassing duties.

The fort of Michni was constructed by working parties from the force, whilst the remainder of the troops covering the operation were constantly called out, night and day, to meet threatened attacks, or to dislodge the hillmen as they collected in bodies and attempted to secure strategical positions in the vicinity of the camp. The cavalry at the pickets thrown out well in front of the force had always to be on the alert, and had successive sharp skirmishes. In feet, owing to the confined nature of the broken country, bodies of the enemy could collect without being observed. Galloping horsemen came in constantly, calling for supports. Patrolling was incessant day and night; but the numerous ravines draining the mountain ridges rendered it impossible altogether to prevent small parties from breaking through to our villages along such an extended line.

Saadut Khan himself was continually threatening in force, but not until the 8th of December did he really advance. Then, at the head of some four or five thousand men, he came out towards Mutta, a village on the right bank of the Swât; but as soon as his men came under fire of our infantry and artillery, they rapidly broke up and were driven back. By the middle of December the Michni Fort was, for all practical purposes, completed. Thereupon the troops, under Sir Colin's command, leaving a garrison for the post, moved to Miankhel, some three miles nearer to Shubkudr, in order to complete the frontier patrolling road, and to destroy the numerous walled enclosures. Some eleven or twelve towers were blown up before the detachment quitted Miankhel.

Several large fortified enclosures—the latter, built of what was locally known as "*puska*" work (*i.e.*, of chopped straw and mud dried in layers in the sun)—were very difficult to destroy. Some of these were long, two or three feet in thickness, and very high. After the troops had undermined their base, all the available elephants in camp would be marshalled for a feat of strength and skill. The huge beasts, their trunks protected by leather shields, would advance together in line, and in the cleverest manner use their heads as rams. They seemed to know instinctively when a wall was just tottering to its ruin. They would then suddenly recoil and, with a shriek, rush back from the consequences of their own action, as the wall fell in a cloud of dust before them.

On one occasion a Momund *mullah*, who had remained behind his people, was sitting with two of his disciples in one of these huts. A Muhammadan soldier of one of our regiments warned him that, as the order had been given for the destruction of his house, he had better depart in peace. The angry priest, however, not only reviled the soldier as a follower of *infidels*, but dared the British to touch him. While still hurling anathemas at all around, he was suddenly startled by a crash, followed by the appearance of two elephant trunks upheaving the roof. The effect was miraculous. In a moment, with his unwound turban flowing like a pennant behind him, he hurriedly shook the dust from his feet and bolted up the hill like a rabbit from a hole, the two disciples following.

Lord Dalhousie was not given to panegyric, but the following letters show his high appreciation of the manner in which Lumsden had carried out the special duties entrusted to him during the absence of Colonel Mackeson:—

> From P. Melvill, Esq., Secretary to the Board of Administration, to Lieutenant H. B. Lumsden, Officiating Deputy Commissioner, Peshawur, D/Lahore, 5th January, 1852. No. 26. I am ordered to forward to you the annexed extract, paras. 3 and 4, of a letter from the Secretary to the Government of India, written on the occasion of appointing Colonel Mackeson, C.B., to be Commissioner of Peshawur.

(2) It is highly gratifying to the Board to convey to you this cordial expression of the Most Noble the Governor-General's approbation of your services during the time you have been in civil charge of Peshawur.

(3) Colonel Mackeson left Lahore for Peshawur two days ago. The Board request that on his arrival you will hand over charge of your office to him.

> Extract, paras. 3 and 4, of a letter, No. 3926, dated the 20th December, 1851, from the Secretary to the Government of India, with the Governor-General, to the Board of Administration for the affairs of the Punjab.

(3) Lieutenant Lumsden's temporary civil employment as deputy commissioner will now cease. His Lordship has recently taken occasion, on the occurrence of this officer's name in the correspondence with the Commander-in-Chief, to bear the highest testimony to his merits and to the manner in which he has discharged the civil duties entrusted to him. The appointment was neither sought by Lieutenant Lumsden, nor, as his Lordship believes, was agreeable to him. He had no previous experience in civil duties, and was at once placed at the head of them.

Lieutenant Lumsden has fulfilled these duties assiduously, with great discretion, and excellent judgement. His promptitude, energy, and determination, joined with admirable temper, and a tact which is proved by the unbroken harmony of his official intercourse with the civil and military officers with whom he has been brought in contact, have rendered his conduct of civil duties at Peshawur eminently successful, and have entitled him to the approbation and to the cordial thanks of the Government, which the Governor-General has the great satisfaction of now conveying to him.

(4) Your Board are directed to transmit to Lieutenant Lumsden a copy of the foregoing para, of this communication, as also of the accompanying extract, para. 21, of a letter from the Most Noble the Governor-General, addressed to the Adjutant -General of the Army, on the 17th October last

(21) Having thus expressed the Governor-General's views on the several topics which have been brought to his Lord-ship's notice connected with the defence of the valley of Peshawur, his

Lordship directs me now to advert to the testimony which has been borne by the Brigadier-General to the merits of Lieutenant Lumsden, testimony very honourable to that young officer, deriving additional value from the marked notice which has been taken of it by his Excellency the Commander-in-Chief. No task could be more agreeable to the Governor-General than to record his very cordial concurrence in the approbation which his Excellency and Sir Colin Campbell have so warmly bestowed on Lieutenant Lumsden. A braver or a better soldier never drew a sword.

The Governor-General places unbounded confidence in him, and in the gallant body of men he commands; while his conduct in the chief position in which he has been placed, and amidst the difficulties of a duty to which he was unused, has earned his Lordship's high approbation. The harmony and goodwill which have been apparent in the conduct of public affairs upon the frontier of Peshawur, and which are of such infinite value to the public interests, have long attracted the Governor-General's attention, and commanded his applause, and his Excellency seizes this opportunity of offering to Sir Colin Campbell the warm acknowledgments which are due to him, as well as to Lieutenant Lumsden, for the zeal and concord with which they have laboured together in the important position they have held upon the frontier.

In the last days of 1851, or in the beginning of 1852, Sir John Lawrence first inspected Hoti Murdân. An incident which occurred during his visit is thus described by Sir Henry Daly in the lecture which we have already quoted:—

Sir John Lawrence, as ruler of the Punjab, was wont from time to time to make tours through all parts of the country. On one of his early visits to Murdân the chiefs from the hills, with their followers, and every village baron, gathered at Murdân to pay the great man obeisance. Revenue assessments and cases were discussed, and appeals received Lumsden, from early ties, was probably easy in criminal and civil matters with a people whom he found cultivating their fields with sword and matchlock by their side, and who had never paid revenue, except by force of arms, and who had no law but tradition and the will of the Kázis. Sir John, though cordially relying on Lumsden's judgment, spent two or three days in cultivating a personal knowledge, as was his habit, with all that came before him; and thus it seemed to the men of the Guides that their leader was harassed by explanations instead of being with them as usual in the field, or at sports.

The night before Sir John was to march with his retinue from Murdân, Lumsden, after Sir John had gone to bed, went outside and sat on the parapet of the fort. After a while an Afridi orderly, who always attended Lumsden in sport or fight, crept up to him and said, "Since the great Lawrence came you have been worried and distressed; many have observed this, and that he is always looking at papers, asking questions, and overhauling your accounts. Has he said anything to pain you? Is he interfering with you? He starts for Peshawur tomorrow morning; there is no reason why he should reach it"

The incident tells its own tale; but when Lumsden read Daly's account of it, he added the following pencil note:

It may seem strange, nowadays, that any private soldier should make such a proposal to his commanding officer, but the man only characteristically displayed what might have been the natural procedure of a chief of his own clan at his own home, and only meant to show me that he was loyal to me, but cared not a straw for any other man living. It must be remembered that for nearly two years I was absolutely alone with my Guides in the Yusafzai country, and on the most intimate terms with the native officers and men, having no one else but the chiefs and people of the country to converse with.

In a letter written on the 1st April, 1852, Lumsden describes a raid by trans-border marauders, which took place a short time before.

I must send you a few lines to say we are all well, and to prevent your being anxious, should you see in the newspapers the account of a night attack on my first troop at Goojur Gurhi by a superior force of Swât cavalry under one Mokurrum Khan, from that country. The facts of the case are, that I was ordered to furnish an escort for a Mr. James, of the Survey Department, who came into Yusafzai to fix some points for the great trigonometrical survey. I gave the gentleman thirty riflemen to escort his tents, and ordered my first troop, only thirty-four strong, to Goojur Gurhi, to meet Mr. James before he went to the border of the Swât country. Mr. James changed his route, and did not go to Goojur Gurhi, and my troop remained expecting him.

In the middle of the night of the 7th March the troop sentries observed a large body of horse coming towards camp, and, challenging them, received for answer "Friend!" and on inquiry, "What friend?" were answered "*Sahib.*" This put the sentries off their guard, and the Resaldár Futteh Khan ran out of his tent to meet the supposed *Sahib.* He had no sooner got to the end of the camp than he saw that the party coming towards them had lighted matches, and therefore could not belong to any regiment in our service, and, with great presence of mind, called out to his men, "Draw swords; the enemy are on us."

The troopers, surprised but not frightened, rushed to their arms just as 180 of the enemy's cavalry, headed by Mokurrum Khan, charged into camp. My *duffadars* (who carry lances) went like men to the front, and received the brunt of the shock, while the troopers, sword in hand, got into knots, and resisted at every point, and the enemy could not penetrate beyond the skirts of the camp. Eight or ten of my best men then got on their knees, and in the dark, creeping under the horses' legs, cut the poor animals down, sending the riders flying in the air. The business was short and sharp. Scarcely a tent in camp escaped untouched, but in half an hour the enemy were thrashed out of camp and driven back to their hills, leaving two men dead in our camp and five horses, besides carrying off no end of wounded and dead. Thank God, my loss was only two men killed and five *syces*[2] wounded. We did not lose a single horse, whilst we took five from the enemy.

When you consider the surprise, and the odds against my Guides, it is very clear that nothing but God's blessing could have saved them from utter destruction, though as men my troopers behaved themselves like true soldiers, determined not to give an inch of ground until it was lost. I am most thankful for the escape of my brave native officer and men, and proud of them as belonging to my own regiment. If the men could only have got on their horses before the enemy burst into camp, or had my thirty riflemen been there to have kept the enemy off

2. Grooms.

for only a few minutes, what a lesson the Swât cavalry would have received. But *all is well that ends well.*

I hope, if all is well, to start for home round the Cape by some vessel leaving Bombay or Calcutta in January, 1853. I cannot leave Yusafzai this year, for the frontier has been twice attacked, and my corps is ordered to protect it, and the Governor-General has put me in civil and military charge of Yusafzai. My own doctor and others in Peshawur have told me that I must go home soon, and if possible by sea, as they think the sea air will do me more good than anything else. I cannot make out exactly what is the matter with me, and doubt if the doctors can, though they look very grave when the question is put to them, and say it 's all the climate and too much exposure. However, I will take good care of myself for the next eight months, and then come home.

The gallant conduct of Resaldár Futteh Khan, "*Khan Bahádur*," in the affair just described, and of the detachment of Guide cavalry under his command, received the highest approbation from the Commander-in-Chief and the Governor-General.

Chapter 12

Adventure of Sam Fisher and Lumsden on Gunga Mountain

The Guides were not long left in peace to build their fort and settle down at Hoti Murdân. Mokurrum Khan's attack on the Guide detachment, and the assembly of several thousand Swât troops at the foot of the Mora mountain, in the valley of Ranizai, necessitated the immediate despatch of a considerable force from Peshawur, in order to check the further spread of disaffection.

Mokurrum Khan, the leader of the raiders, held a *jághír*[1] from Say-ad Akbar, the ruler or king of Swât, half of which was situated in the valley of Ranizai, on the Yusafzai side of the Malakund Pass. When bent on plunder, Mokurrum Khan used to assemble his people in Ranizai, but was prepared to retire to Swât should danger threaten. It was therefore determined to bring such pressure on the Ranizais as would make them feel that they could not, with impunity, afford to allow refugees from British territory or raiders from Swât to embroil them with our Government.

A force, under the command of Brigadier Sir Colin Campbell, moved from Peshawur on the 11th March, 1852. Lieutenant-Colonel Mackeson accompanied it as Commissioner, whilst the Guides, under Lumsden, joined it on the march to the Ranizai valley, which was reached on the 22nd. The negotiations with the Ranizais were carried on by Lumsden, who, as Assistant-Commissioner, was in charge of the Yusafzai district. The strength of the force forbad any opposition. A reconnaissance of the Ranizai valley up to the Malakund Pass was made by the troops. A fine of 5000 *rupees* was imposed on the inhabit-

---

1. Rent-free grant of land.

ants for their participation in Mokurrum Khan's and other raids into Yusafzai, while ten *maliks*[2] of villages were taken away as hostages for the payment of the fine. The Peshawur force withdrew, and Lumsden, with his Guides, remained on the frontier.

On the 15th April Sir Colin received intimation from the officer commanding the Shubkudr outpost of a threatened invasion of the Doába between the Cabul and Swât Rivers, by Saadut Khan, the chief of the Momunds, at the head of a large body of horse and foot. The Commissioner did not accept the rumour of this invasion as trustworthy, but Sir Colin immediately proceeded to Shubkudr, in time to place himself at the head of three hundred sabres of Native Cavalry, two Horse Artillery guns, and two companies of Infantry, with which, at Punjpao, he frustrated Saadut Khan's intentions, drove the enemy back into the mountains, and broke up the gathering.

On the withdrawal of our troops from Ranizai, however, disaffection, instigated by the powers in Swât, showed itself on the Yusafzai frontier. One Ajun Khan, part-proprietor of the village of Tangi, in Yusafzai, desired to possess himself of the whole. He, moreover, demanded exemption from attendance at our courts and non-interference in his affairs by our revenue and political officers. As these demands could not be complied with, he at once adopted the course, not infrequent under Duráni and Sikh rule, of removing to the hills across the border, placing himself at the head of a band of adventurers, and doing his utmost, by rapine and plunder, to create discontent amongst the villagers in the plains. The matter was the more serious as Ajun Khan possessed influence amongst the Utmankhel population on the border, owned lands in Swât, was a vassal of Sayad Akbar the Ruler, and also a follower of the Akhund.

On the 28th April Sir Colin, accompanied by the Commissioner, Colonel Mackeson, again took the field, and after crossing the Swât River at Abazai, was joined by Lumsden and his Guides. On the 11th and 12th of May the troops attacked Ajun Khan in his strongholds of Nowadan and Prangurh, utterly defeated his Utmankhel and Swât followers, and drove the rebel himself to seek safety by flight.

In the meantime, however, as the Ranizais withheld the payment of the fine which had been imposed on them, repudiated their hostages, expelled the families of the latter from their valley, and proclaimed themselves subjects of Swât, further coercion had become absolutely necessary. Sir Colin accordingly, with a force amounting to some 3270

2. Headmen.

of all ranks, moved on the 18th May on Shahkot, the capital village of Ranizai, where were now assembled, not only the people of Ranizai and adventurous spirits from adjacent valleys, but also some four or five thousand Swât troops. The village was at the foot of commanding heights, and located on the perpendicular banks of a deep ravine, through which our men had to cross to the assault. The troops at once attacked, and, after considerable resistance, carried the position. The enemy retired over the heights in their rear, and along the high road to Swât, and, breaking up, were pursued and cut up by the Guide cavalry for some three miles, as far as Dargai at the foot of the Malakund Pass. Great punishment was inflicted on the enemy, our losses only amounting to eleven killed and twenty-nine wounded. In his despatch Sir Colin Campbell said:—

> This action, though fought against hillmen and amidst the difficulties of a *nullah* of extraordinary steepness and width, with broken and stony ground in its neighbourhood, was essentially one of the plains, and not of the mountains. The Artillery had full scope, as had the Cavalry. This circumstance accounted for the considerable results, and the very heavy chastisement the force was able to inflict on the crowds opposed, who could not have been less than 6000 in number. They had shown great resolution, and had held the *nullah* in a manner which extorted the admiration of the troops. . . .
>
> Nothing could be more satisfactory than the conduct of all, particularly of the Guides and Gurkhas, on whom the brunt fell, when making the great assault on the *nullah*. With the readiness of the Guides under Lieutenant Lumsden, Sir Colin said, the Commander-in-Chief was well acquainted, and he added that he was particularly happy in having been able to employ the 66th Gurkhas, under Lieutenant-Colonel Troup, in an operation requiring all those qualities for which Gurkhas are so famous.

The troops remained in the valley, completing its subjugation, until the 24th May.

In the meantime a difference of opinion had arisen between Sir Colin Campbell and Colonel Mackeson. The Political officer urged upon the Brigadier the advisability of following up his success by an advance over the Malakund Pass into Swât, in order to enforce the responsibility of the rulers of that country for the disturbances created by their instigation within our borders. Sir Colin Campbell was prepared to enter on such an enterprise provided he could be assured that the object of the expedition would be confined to three or four days' operations. Without, however, properly equipped hill-carriage, mules, ponies, and bullocks, and without an addition of 2500 men to his force, Sir Colin was not prepared to commit the troops under his command to an unlimited and indefinite campaign.

The hot season having now set in, the force marched back to Peshawur, leaving Lumsden and his Guides to look after the frontier. Within a month of the withdrawal of the force the Ranizais made overtures for peace, accepted all our terms, and settled down to reconstruct their houses and to till their lands.

In accordance with the scheme for frontier defence of the Peshawur valley, as drawn up by Sir Colin and Lumsden, a fort was now being constructed at Abazai, and the Guides, in addition to completing their own work at Hoti Murdân, had to provide a strong detachment under a British officer to cover the workmen engaged at Abazai as well as cavalry to patrol the frontier.

It was during these days that Lumsden had a narrow escape of being surprised by his friends of Sangao. We quote his own account of it:—

On one memorable occasion, Sam Fisher (Colonel 15th Bengal Cavalry, killed by his own men in 1857) and I determined to have some wild-goat[3] shooting on the Gunga mountain, as Ajub Khan of Chargolie had reported that many of these animals had come down from the upper ranges to feed on the young grass, which sprouts some weeks earlier on Gunga than elsewhere.

Our party consisted of Fisher, Ajub Elian, and myself, with four *shikáris*[4] and four men of the Guide corps. We started before daylight in the morning, and toiled over the hills till four o'clock, without having the luck to come across any game, and then it was put to the vote whether we should start for home or camp out for the night, as it would not be possible to work our way down the precipitous rocks by the dim evening light

As the weather was fine we determined to try our luck for another day, and, having each a blanket with us, we made the best of our way to springs close by a cave which is known as

---

3. *Markhor.*
4. Native huntsmen.

the Cashmere Cave. Here our little store of provisions of cold fowls, etc., was opened, pipes lighted, and preparations made for passing the night comfortably in the cave, when I heard the *khan* and Marfut Shah, my head huntsman, arguing in Púshtú (the language of the country), and my ear caught enough of what they were saying to know that they did not quite like the idea of resting in the cave, so close to the Buneyr frontier, but at the same time considered it by far the most comfortable place for Englishmen at night.

I at once settled the matter by asking the *khan* to show the way to the most eligible spot, and we scrambled up the ledges of rock, some eighty or one hundred feet, on to a flat piece of ground, immediately overhanging the roof of our cave. Here our attendants cut grass for beds, and we turned in under our blankets, with rifles at our hands, and *shikáris* told off to watch, an hour at a time, till daylight

Just before dawn the *shikári* on duty woke the man next him, and said that he heard something moving below us. The other replied, "It's only a wild goat"

"Wild goats don't break sticks," was the *khan's* reply, and next moment we were all up, rifle in hand, ready for any work.

As the day broke and more light was thrown on the scene, we could make out numbers of heads, peeping from every bush round the mouth of the cave, and now and then a fellow would try by various tricks to discover whether it was really occupied, without at the same time exposing himself to any bullet that he felt certain would instantly follow his being seen. They threw stones, coughed, and even pushed up a turban on the end of a matchlock in front of the cave, getting no response, but could not, any of them, make up his mind to risk a peep into the place. All this time we were sitting motionless, watching every movement, and amusing ourselves by covering first one man and then another, as each exposed himself to our aim, but determined not to fire a shot except in self-defence.

At last one man looked up and saw Sam Fisher's deadly rifle pointed full in his face, and, without a moment's hesitation, he gave a scream of terror and bolted down the side of the hill, taking at least two hundred men with him. They appeared to rise from every bush and rock on the hillside, and would doubtless have made the place very hot for us had we been, as they

115

fondly hoped, hopelessly pent up inside that cave.

As it was they jumped to the conclusion that the whole affair was a deep trap, laid by us to draw them to destruction. We, in the meantime, sending a shower of stones and rocks down the hill after them, to keep them moving, were only too glad to make an unmolested return home, with a determination never to sleep in caves for fear of catching colds.

In the month of June of this year Sir Colin Campbell resigned the Peshawur command. The Commissioner, Colonel Mackeson, had, as already stated, proposed that an expedition should be made into Swât, with a force which Sir Colin considered too weak for the task. He had pointed out the difficulty which would be experienced in maintaining communication and operating with a small body of men in a mountainous and thickly inhabited, yet practically unknown, country. The Governor-General, however, was disposed to make light of these objections, and to cast reflections upon Campbell's refusal to undertake the operations. Sir Colin at once requested to be relieved of his command. He had, as we know, expressed his readiness— although he did not approve of the measure—to force the Malakund Pass and conduct an expedition without baggage, to last for two or three days.

But operations of this kind he always regarded as half measures, entailing great loss of life without corresponding results. Campbell's judgment was confirmed by our experience ten or eleven years later, in the Umbeyla campaign, when some five thousand of our troops, armed with weapons superior to those in use in 1852, and with carriage equipment suitable for mountain warfare, encountered the tribes of Swât, Buneyr, and Bajour. The struggle with these hillmen, roused to action by the Akhund and fanatical preachers, was a very severe one, our loss being above nine hundred officers and men killed and wounded.

It is interesting to reflect that, if Sir Colin had not resigned his frontier command in 1852, he would most probably have still been at Peshawur in 1854, when the Crimean war took place, and gave him opportunities of earning much distinction at the head of his Highlanders, and led to his great career as Commander-in-Chief in India, soon after the outbreak of the Mutiny.

Harry Lumsden's relations with Sir Colin Campbell were always of the happiest nature, and the younger soldier delighted to recall the example, sayings, and doings of the veteran who, on his marches, was wont to recount the experiences of his long service. Speaking of a regiment which had been very severely handled in action, and had lost a number of officers and men, Sir Colin said:

> My young friend, take my word for it, that battalion will not get over it for years, and should be well nursed. I have known cases where a corps still showed the effects even after twenty years. If you are ever called upon to use British troops in a real tough business, and you have a choice, don't select veterans, for they know too well what to expect, but a fresh corps, which has just been entered on something easy and carried everything before them, and they themselves believe that nothing can stop them.

Sir Colin always disliked the burning of villages and the distress thereby inflicted upon women and children, and never would expose a man under him, or lose a single soldier unnecessarily. But, however careful he was of others, he never spared himself, and was always in the right place in the hour of action. Most popular with British soldiers, Campbell knew exactly what they could do, and how they should be handled upon every emergency. It was his practice, if possible, always to reconnoitre and to examine for himself the ground to be worked over. In all retirements he stuck doggedly to the rearguard until he saw the last of his column safely out of danger.

CHAPTER 13

Leave to England

Lumsden had now completed some fifteen years of continuous service. His health demanded rest and change. Having obtained a medical certificate, he started for England in November, 1852, taking the long sea route *via* the Cape. The command of the Guides fell to Lieutenant W. S. R. Hodson, who had already done much good military service with the corps during the Punjab campaign of 1848-49.

Lumsden's services in the Peshawur division were thus acknowledged by Brigadier-General A. Roberts, C.B., Sir Colin Campbell's successor, in an order of the 30th October, 1852:—

> Lieutenant H. B. Lumsden having made over command of the Guide Corps and of the troops in Yusafzai and Hashtnagar, preparatory to proceeding to Europe, the Brigadier-General desires to offer him most cordial thanks for the able manner in which he has conducted the duties of his command for so long a period on this frontier. The Brigadier-General has not had the pleasure of service with Lieutenant Lumsden, and the Guide Corps has only been incidentally and occasionally placed under the orders of the senior officer at Peshawur; but the records in this division abundantly show the estimation in which Lieutenant Lumsden and the distinguished body of men under his orders were held by the late commanding officer, Brigadier-General Sir Colin Campbell, who was so able to judge of their merits from frequent service with them in the field.
>
> Lieutenant Lumsden's personal influence in many parts of this valley, and his thorough acquaintance with the frontier, render his departure a great public loss, but he leaves behind him a fame which has been repeatedly acknowledged by the highest

authorities in India, and a corps which, raised and commanded by himself for the last six years, whilst constantly employed in various quarters of the Punjab and Trans-Indus territories, in all situations and under all circumstances has done credit to its gallant leader.

The final parting with his "Guides"—the soldiers he had created, and who had been associated with him so intimately and served him so faithfully—was a severe trial to Harry Lumsden. He had no option, however, for in those days officers of the Indian service gave up their appointments when they went on furlough, and could only trust to their luck for suitable re-employment on their return. The sea voyage restored Lumsden's health almost entirely, but he suffered much distress regarding Lady Dalhousie, a passenger on the same ship. Her ladyship had embarked in a very weak state, and, being a bad sailor, succumbed at last just before reaching home, her death being accelerated by tempestuous weather at the end of the journey.

Harry Lumsden had been so long isolated from his family, and from so many of his best friends and comrades, that the pleasure of meeting them again, with all the associations of home, had the happiest effect in renovating a constitution which had been severely tried by constant exposure and anxiety. Time slipped by so quickly that he had scarcely realized that he had nearly worked out his three years, when the following letter from Lord Dalhousie announced to him the happy intelligence that he was once more, on return to India, to be placed in command of his old corps.

TO MAJOR H. LUMSDEN.

Ootacmund, 31st March, 1855.

My dear Lumsden,—You will probably have heard from Bowie before now that I am keeping the Guides for you. . . . I have just nominated Reynell Taylor to hold command temporarily.

If you will be out here by the end of December, and if I am to the fore, you shall have your old friends again.

There is not a man in the Army who has so good a right to them, or to whom I should be so well pleased to give them, before I leave India, as yourself.

Your father will be pleased to hear that said. Tell him I bade you repeat it to him, with my compliments.

Always, my dear Lumsden,

Yours very truly,   Dalhousie.

Meanwhile Lieutenant Lumsden had been promoted to a captaincy, on the 1st March, 1853, and to a brevet majority for services in the field on the 6th February, 1854. In the spring of 1856, after he had rejoined, and had been with the Guides at Murdán for several months, he wrote to his father on the 27th April as follows:—

We have had a sort of parade round the border for the benefit of some recusant villagers, who, however, thought better of the matter as soon as they saw that we were determined to have our own way, and preferred paying a fine for their past misconduct rather than be made animated targets of for the practice of Guide riflemen. We have now again returned to our quarters here, and settled down to cantonment life. Brigadier Cotton, commanding at Peshawur, did us the honour of a three days' visit, and inspected everything, expressing himself extremely satisfied with all he saw, which is most satisfactory from a man like him, for he has the character of being one of the strictest hands in H.M. service, and we are not under his immediate orders.

Our brigadier is that glorious soldier Neville Chamberlain, of the Punjab Irregular Force, but he has never been near us since he got the command. He sent me a most kind letter, however, saying that he had no wish to interfere with me in any way, but, on the contrary, would be most happy to forward my views if I would only write to him a note on any subject in which he could help me, so I fancy we shall get on well enough. The commandant-ship of the Guides is not now, however, such an independent one as it was before I went home, but I am a most fortunate man to tumble in for it again on any terms, seeing that I had thrown it up on going home, and was succeeded by a younger man.

During the parade along the frontier above described, a party of the Guides, with their commanding officer, were encamped at Abazai. Major Lumsden then made the acquaintance of that enterprising and sturdy soldier Jack Peyton, at that time a subaltern in the 87th Royal Irish Fusiliers, who was acting assistant-engineer in charge of the forts of Michni, Shubkudr, and Abazai. The two men had much in common. Both were greatly interested in animals. Peyton presented Lumsden with two young white leopards, which Lumsden was delighted to receive, especially when he learnt how they had been acquired. The story cannot be better told than in Peyton's own words:—

In the year 1853 or '54 I was appointed an executive engineer officer at the frontier forts of Michni, Shubkudr, and Abazai My duty was to visit each fort at least three times a week. On one occasion I crossed over the Swât River from Abazai in the large ferry-boat for the purpose of inspecting the works that were going on at Michni and Shubkudr. The river was very much swollen. On my return in the afternoon it had turned into a roaring torrent, two hundred yards wide at least. Major James, then military secretary to Sir John Lawrence, had come out from Peshawur on duty connected with the force, and I was under the impression that Peter Lumsden was with him. The former gave orders before the flood came down, that the boat should be taken across to wait for me, but as he considered it dangerous he sent me word to come over or not as I liked.

On my arrival I made up my mind to chance it and cross over. I took my favourite mare Begum, three boatmen, and eight or ten Swâtis with me, who were on their way to their homes in the Ilm range of mountains. When we got in midstream the boat swung round from the force of the torrent, my mare jumped overboard, and with sorrow I saw my beautiful animal disappear under water. She never rose again, as the currents of the Swât are very bad. At the same moment a young and singularly handsome Pathan, of about seventeen, became much excited, and fell overboard.

Maddened by the loss of my mare and the Mussulman cry to *Allah* for help, I jumped, with my sword and revolver on me, straight on to the back of the sinking young Pathan. Luckily I caught him by the *kummerbund*, and floated down the torrent, swimming by degrees towards the bank, which I reached about a quarter of a mile further down. I was very near done, but the young Pathan, fortunately for me, was insensible, for had he struggled he must have drowned us both. I gave my young friend all the brandy in my flask, which made him very sick, and he recovered.

By this time the boatmen had got the boat over, and came down the other bank to see what had become of us, as they thought we were drowned. On reaching the fort Major James, who was looking on at the occurrence from the ramparts, came to meet me, and in his cheery, genial manner congratulated me on our escape, and told me he would report the matter to Sir John Lawrence, from whom I received a most flattering letter, of which I need not say I was very proud.

Some days afterwards an old Pathan chief came to see me. With tears in his eyes he threw his arms round my neck, and, pointing to the Ilm range, said, "I have come down from those snowy peaks with two young leopards, the only property I have worthy of your acceptance. You were the young officer who jumped into the Swât and saved the life of my son, who is the joy of my old age. The two men. carrying the leopards are of my clan, and were in the boat when you jumped into the wild torrent of the Swât I heard all about it from them. We know you are a *shikári*, as my men have often seen you shooting at the bottom of our hills, and longed to kill you, but now by God's will you are our friend. Come and shoot and eat salt with us. You will be as safe as you would be in your father's house, and may no Pathan's sword or bullet injure you, if we ever meet in battle."

The old man spoke good Persian, and, as I spoke and wrote Persian fairly well in those days, I have tried to give as literal a translation of the old man's words as I can. I visited my old friend frequently, who always sent horses to meet me, and had some nice sport, with the satisfaction of knowing that no other European had ever dared to enter his territory as a guest Of course, no one but my dear Pathan servant ever knew of it I should have lost my appointment had it been discovered. I gave the two young leopards to your gallant and distinguished brother, then commanding the glorious corps of Guides.

Lumsden always held that Peyton's noble deed had a very happy effect upon the people of that part of the frontier. The leopards were kept as pets for some time, running about the camp. In the course of a few months, however, instead of stalking fowls, which was their first sport and a very amusing one to witness, they aspired to higher game, and began to stalk children. So, in the absence of zoological gardens in that remote corner of the world, they had to be quieted by a little prussic acid.

In further illustration of the character of this chivalrous friend of Harry Lumsden, it may not be out of place to quote an account of a previous adventure of danger and difficulty from which Peyton, by his activity and presence of mind, managed to rescue himself:—

In the year 1851, or 1852, 1 obtained six months' leave to go to Cashmere, accompanied by Surgeon Wray, of my regiment, an excellent sportsman and the best of good fellows. We went *via* the Peir Punjal, where we were lucky enough to get a couple of very fine *markhor*. We arrived in Cashmere early in March, and lost no time in getting into the Wurdwun Valley, in those days famous for large-horned ibex I knew the place well, as I spent six weeks there before, on my way to the *ovis ammon* ground at the bottom of the Kari Koram in Thibet. We established our headquarters in a village nearest to the ibex cliffs. The country was all under snow.

The headman of the village who accompanied us gave us an empty house to live in; the house was built on piles of wood. The lower part, in which the cattle were kept, was given over to the servants to live in, while we occupied the upper part, which we got up to by a ladder. The snow came down very heavily for some days, which obliged us to remain indoors, and Wray, who was a splendid musician, amused the villagers by playing his violin to them. At last the sun came out, and we heard several avalanches coming down. Our men were very much averse to going out, and I must say I thought they were right. However, poor Wray, in a jocular manner, said we "funked." This settled the matter, and out we went.

We proceeded up the valley about seven miles along the banks of a small river, which divided the mountains on both sides of it We saw a herd of fine male ibex, some of them with large horns. In consequence of the heavy snow, we were unable to creep round by a circuitous route, and stalk the herd from above. So we[1] spread a blanket in a ravine next to where the ibex were, and sat down close together upon it to keep ourselves warm. Suddenly we heard a noise like distant thunder, then spray and stones followed. Our men called out, "an avalanche is falling." Although I had seen several fall, this one seemed to me quite different—more like a landslip. It covered a breadth of at least a hundred yards, three or four hundred yards long, and fifty or sixty feet in depth.

This enormous mass, like a small mountain, tearing with it

1. *Viz.*, Wray, myself, Abel Khan (my old *shikári*), and our guide, the headman of the village.

rocks, earth, etc., moved towards us much too quickly for us to get out of its way by running down before it. The whole thing looked weird and supernatural. Death stared us in the face. On our right side there was a precipice which cut off our escape in that direction. On our left a very wide trench, which separated us from the shoulder of a mountain large enough to protect us from the approaching avalanche, if we could jump the chasm and get shelter under it. I pointed out to my companions our only chance of escape; by this time the avalanche had approached within fifty or sixty paces of us.

I led the way, made a spring for my life, and landed safely on the side of the chasm and crouched under the shelter of the hill, which was only three or four paces from the side I jumped on. Looking round, to my horror I saw my poor friend Wray and the other two men dashed forward by the avalanche, and buried under a mountain of snow. My dear old *shikári*, Abel Khan, who had all the nerve and activity of an ibex, could have jumped the chasm, but the others were in his way, and he had my heavy Lancaster rifle on his back. The thought haunts me to the present day. Had he a fair run, he would have saved his life by clearing the chasm as I had done, although it was a big jump.

By this time Puttoo Khan (brother of Abel Khan), who was placed to watch the ibex about a quarter of a mile to our left, came to the cave in which I had taken shelter; the former had witnessed the whole occurrence, and saw his brother killed. He cried most piteously, lamenting over the loss of his brother and myself also, who he thought was killed. I cried out, "Puttoo, fate has been hard upon us. I am safe." He seemed bewildered and cried out, "No, you are only the spirit come back to tell me. My beloved brother and our young *Sahib* are gone."

The avalanche still continued its course across the river at the bottom of the valley, and jammed itself about a hundred yards up the side of the opposite mountain, completely stopping up the flow of the river. In this way the snow bridges of the Himalayas are formed—an extraordinary sight it is. With difficulty I persuaded the grief-stricken man that I was alive. He became a little composed, and told me, "We shall not escape long; the headman of the village has been killed, and we shall be killed in turn by the villagers."

We went quickly home, and arranged on the way to get out fresh ammunition and rifles, as all the rifles out with us were buried under the avalanche. I had two Pathans from Peshawur, who remained at home to cook for us. We informed them of what had occurred. We all of us got into the loft, and drew the ladder up after us, and prepared our spare rifles and ammunition for an attack. By this time the villagers had armed themselves, and swore they would burn us out. I told them they could do so, but we would sell our lives dearly.

At last they allowed us to take our departure without carrying out their threat, and we crossed over the pass leading into Cashmere. On arriving there the *Maharajah*, Gulab Singh, sent for me. He was very kind and sympathetic in his manner. I remained there for some weeks, waiting for the snow to melt, which took place soon after. The *Maharajah* sent a company of soldiers with me to dig out the bodies, which we found; Abel Khan and the headman of the village were buried there. I took Wray's body down with me to Cashmere. On the way the young *Maharajah*, Rumbheir Singh, met us and placed with his own hands a valuable Cashmere shawl over the corpse. Poor Wray was buried in it, and the officers of the Royal Irish Fusiliers put up a monument to his memory in Cashmere, as he was much respected and beloved in the regiment.

Some time afterwards I brought up to Cashmere a large quantity of glass, a thing never seen there before, and I had the mosque in which my dear old *shikári* worshipped glazed in with it in honour of his memory. A finer man or a better *shikári* I have never seen. I forgot to mention, in digging for our lost comrades, we found several bodies of the ibex we were stalking, no doubt killed by the avalanche, and smashed to pieces. Only one large head, with grand horns, escaped being broken, which I had put on to an artificial skull and gave it to Mr. Eardley-Wilmot Holt, a friend and good companion of mine in many a pleasant day's snipe and cock shooting and salmon fishing in Ireland, and he has it in his hall amongst several handsome trophies of moose and other game, killed by himself and his friends.

Here ends the avalanche story of the "*Kehl Ke Bucheh*," or "Son of the Ibex," a name which my kind Muhammadan friends in Cashmere always called me in chaff.

I have a faint recollection that the first European I met on my way to Cashmere was Lieutenant Probyn, now the distinguished Sir Dighton Probyn, V.C, but of that I am not quite certain.

In continuation of the above, the following little story is worth relating. One evening my friend Wray and myself returned from a successful stalk on the Peir Punjal after *markhor*. He seemed rather depressed. I asked, "What is the matter with you?"

He replied, "I have an idea that only one of us will return from this trip alive. I know you like my 'Sam Smith' rifle; if I am killed you are to have it."

I said, "Nonsense. However, you like my Lancaster two-groove; if I am killed you shall have it."

A memorandum to that effect was found in his note-book. Both the rifles were buried under the avalanche, and I recovered them from the bodies of our own men who were killed. I valued the rifles very much. Unfortunately they were taken away by the mutineers in 1857, when they looted Sealkote and burnt my bungalow with all my papers.

CHAPTER 14

Afghan Affairs from 1842 to 1854

The next well-marked period of Harry Lumsden's life is that which comprises his important mission to Candahar in 1857-58. In order that the object and scope of that mission may be fully understood, it is necessary to give a brief account of the chain of events which led to it. It will be remembered that after the first Cabul war the British withdrew from Afghanistan, and Dost Muhammad returned to that country as *amir*. Thereafter, for a period of twelve years or more, communications between the Governments of India and Cabul were few, and generally unimportant. In 1848 Sirdar Muhammad Akbar Khan, the Afghan heir-apparent, died, his younger brother, Sirdar Ghulam Haidar Khan, being nominated in his stead to be the successor of Dost Muhammad. In 1850 the *amir* annexed the province of Balkh to his kingdom, and appointed his eldest son,[1] Afzal Khan, to be governor of the newly-acquired district.

In 1854 a serious insurrection, stirred up by the *Amir* of Bokhara, took place in Balkh, while difficulties arose both at Herat and Candahar through the intrigues of Persia, and the rulers of the Candahar territory, the half-brothers of Dost Muhammad. A correspondence arose about this time between the Commissioner of Peshawur, Major Edwardes,[2] and the Governor of Kurram, Azim Khan, also a son of the *amir*. Azim Khan professed himself most anxious for a British alliance. Major Edwardes replied that he had little doubt that a letter addressed by the *amir* to the Governor-General would receive a favourable answer. The *amir*, from the first, seems to have been inclined to make friendship with the British. His position was a critical one. Menaced by the threats of Persia on the one hand, and alarmed by the rumours

---

1. By a lady of inferior family to that of the mother Ghulam Haidar.
2. Colonel Mackeson, the former Commissioner, had been assassinated in 1853.

of the advance of the Russians, and of the disturbances in Balkh, on the other, he felt alone in the midst of his enemies.

On the 23rd October, 1854, Major Edwardes reported the arrival of an envoy from Cabul, bearing letters of goodwill. Sir John Lawrence received the envoy at Abbottabad, when the latter, with much earnestness, declared his assurance that the sole object of the Amir in his overture was the establishment of friendly relations with the British Government. The *amir's* letter to the Governor-General was forwarded to Calcutta, and a most courteous answer was returned. Lord Dalhousie expressed his pleasure at hearing from the *amir*, informed him of the successes of the English and the French in the Crimea, and proposed that the friendship of the British and the Afghans should be recorded in a valid treaty. The *amir* was invited to depute a *sirdar* of high rank and wisdom to Peshawur to meet a British officer, who would be appointed to act as agent of the Governor-General, and who would have full power and liberty to enter into and execute a treaty.

In response to this invitation the *amir* deputed the heir-apparent, Sirdar Ghulam Haidar Khan, to Peshawur to act as his plenipotentiary. The Governor-General had at first resolved to entrust to Major Edwardes the duty of negotiating with the expected envoy from Cabul, but when it became known that the *amir* had appointed the heir-apparent to represent him, and had specially expressed a wish that the Chief Commissioner of the Punjab should receive his son, the Governor-General considered that such an act should be met in an equally friendly spirit. Sir John Lawrence was accordingly directed to proceed to Peshawur, and was invested with full powers to negotiate with Sirdar Ghulam Haidar Khan.

The meeting took place in due course, and the treaty was concluded at Peshawur on the 30th March, 1855. It was guaranteed that we should respect the *amir's* possessions in Afghanistan, and never interfere with them, while the Amir engaged, similarly, to respect British territory, and also to be the friend of our friends, and the enemy of our enemies.

In the beginning of August, 1855, Kohandil Khan, the chief of the Candahar *sirdars*, died. His death was followed by disputes between his heirs, and by a rebellion in the frontier province of Herat. The Amir Dost Muhammad determined to proceed to Candahar in person in order to assert his suzerainty. This he was able to do without opposition. He easily made himself master of Candahar, but his position there, in the beginning of 1856, was a very critical one. He failed either to conciliate or to restrain his brothers and nephews, whose territory he had annexed, and whose property he had confiscated. Their indignation was extreme. One by one they fled from Candahar, and took up arms against the *amir* in various parts of the province.

Nor was Dost Muhammad more popular with the common people of the newly-acquired territory. Instigated by the *mullahs*, the Candaháris were taught to believe that to fight against the *amir* would be to engage in a holy war. The *amir* had allied himself with the British, and promised to be the friend of their friends and the enemy of their enemies, and whereas Christ was their friend, and Muhammad their enemy, the *amir* must be held to have renounced his religion, and all Muhammadans were bound to oppose him.

There can be no doubt that, although the *amir* met the difficulties of his position with apparent equanimity, he was, nevertheless, full of anxiety as to the final result of the expedition to Candahar, and he did not conceal his desire to receive the advice and assistance of the British Government. This desire became more intense when, some months later, the Persians laid siege to Herat. The *amir* returned from Candahar to Cabul, and soon after he entrusted an Afghan native officer of the British Army, who was about to return to Peshawur from leave, with the delivery of a verbal message to Colonel[3] Edwardes. The *subadár* was authorized to say that the *amir* was ready to raise troops if the British Government would muster and pay them whilst employed against Herat, but he desired to have a consultation with the British authorities before taking any farther steps.

Colonel Edwardes was much in favour of the proposed interview. Sir John Lawrence, in referring the matter for orders, said he did not think much good would result from a meeting, because it could hardly be anticipated that the views of the *amir* and the British Government should coincide. If the *amir* should fail in obtaining what he wanted, his dissatisfaction would be a positive evil. The Governor-General admitted the force of Sir John Lawrence's objections, but considered they should be set aside if the *amir* was in earnest in desiring a consultation. Dost Muhammad was accordingly invited to an interview at Peshawur, the Chief Commissioner being authorized to arrange for the payment of a subsidy, if the *amir* would enter into an engagement to undertake operations for the purpose of driving the Persians from Herat.

---

3. Major Edwardes had now become a colonel.

The *amir* left Cabul on the 7th December, 1856, and was met by Sir John Lawrence at the mouth of the Khyber on the 1st January, 1857.

Colonel Edwardes accompanied the Chief Commissioner, while Harry Lumsden and a party of his Guides formed their escort. Bands of Afridis crowned the heights on either side of the pass. The greatest excitement prevailed amongst them and amongst the *amir's* Afghan retainers. Dost Muhammad pitched his tents in British territory on a convenient spot, south of Jamrud, selected for its proximity to Sir John Lawrence's encampment at Burj Huri Singh, on the high-road between Jamrud and Peshawur.

Many interviews took place between the *amir* and our representatives, with the result that, on the 26th January, 1857, a formal treaty was duly agreed upon and signed by both sides. Among other conditions the *amir* bound himself, in consideration of a monthly subsidy of one *lakh* of *rupees*, during the continuance of hostilities with Persia, to keep up a certain number of regular troops for the defence of Afghanistan. Previous to the articles being signed, they were read out in the presence of the whole *durbar*, after which Sir John Lawrence recapitulated those points of the arrangement which appeared most important. One of these was that three British officers should start as soon as possible for Candahar by the Kurram, Paiwar, and Loghar route, in order to satisfy themselves that the subsidy was duly applied to the purpose for which it was granted, and to assist the Afghans in every way in military matters when called upon to do so.

Accordingly a mission, composed of Major Harry Lumsden of the Guides, Lieutenant Peter Lumsden of the Quartermaster-generals department, and Dr. Bellew,[4] assisted by Ghulam Sarwan Khan Khágwáni, was appointed to proceed to Candahar. It was arranged that the members of the mission should retain a lien on their permanent appointments, Captain Henry Daly of the 1st Punjab Cavalry and Lieutenant Frederick Roberts, R.A.,[5] being nominated to be temporarily commandant of the Guides and deputy-assistant quartermaster-general respectively.

The *amir* returned towards Cabul a few days after the close of the conferences, but before he did so he received frequent visits from Harry Lumsden and his brother, who were deputed to gather as much information as they could regarding the Amir's views and the gen-

---

4. Dr. Bellew was at this time attached to the Guides.
5. Afterwards Field Marshal Lord Roberts, V.C., G.C.B., etc.

SKETCH OF AMIR DOST MUHAMMAD KHAN, 1857

eral state of Afghanistan. The *amir* received his guests most graciously, caused them to sit by him on carpets spread on the ground, invited them to drink tea served from Russian *samovârs*, and to smoke at will, while he talked freely on many subjects of great interest.

Dost Muhammad Khan was now getting on in years. He was a patriarch among his people. He had passed through many vicissitudes of life. He was tall, of fine physical development, and he truly looked a king. An artist would have rejoiced to secure his prominent Jewish features as a typical model for an Abraham, Isaac, or Jacob. His manner was courteous, whilst his keen eyes and vigorous conversation conveyed the idea of great determination, combined with astuteness and appreciation of humour. He delighted to dwell on the experiences of his adventurous life; at the same time, he did so merely as a prelude to matters in which he had immediately much greater interest. He called a spade a spade, and never hesitated to confess that, although personally he had the happiest remembrances of his association with the British, yet as a Muhammadan ruler imbued with the tenets of his faith, he would, if he had the power, sweep unbelievers from the face of the earth.

But, *Sahib*, (he would say), as this cannot be, I must cling to the British to save me from the cursed *Kujjur* (Persian), and having made an alliance with the British Government, happen what may, I will keep it faithfully till death.

The natural character of this great Asiatic ruler burst out on one occasion, when pleading for pecuniary assistance from Sir John.

See these coarse garments, (said Dost Muhammad, opening his vest), how old and patched they are. Are these the proper robes for a ruling prince? This shawl around my head is the sole piece of finery I possess. I have no money whatever. My sons and my chiefs take everything I have. They leave me nothing, and they tear me into pieces with their dissensions. I live from hand to mouth among them, a life of expedients. I wish to heaven I could turn *faquir* and escape from this heavy lot.

Occasionally, however, the *amir* would be quite carried away by hope and enthusiasm. Referring to the intended advance on Herat, he exclaimed one day to the chief commissioner:

If you say take more troops, I will take more; if you say less will suffice, I will take less, but with your money and your guns I will mine the walls of Herat, blow up its towers, and take the place at the point of the sword. Indeed I will kindle such a flame in the country round Herat up to the gates of Mashhad that Persia will be glad to withdraw.

During the Lumsden interviews the *amir* was wont to dwell on his sayings to "Jan Larrens" (as he used to style Sir John Lawrence), and on the chief commissioner's remarks to him: thus, for instance—

Jan Larrens wants you to go to Cabul, and impressed upon me the necessity of your doing so; but I pointed out to him the impossibility of it, for you see, Lumsden Sahib, that although I might delight to have you there, yet I have under surveillance in Cabul all the bad characters in the country with their followers; and you know how my elder brothers, Sultan Muhammad, or Pir Muhammad, and others would rejoice to bring me to trouble by getting someone to put a bullet into you or any of the *sahibs*. There is no reason why you should not be with me in Cabul, or in any other place in Afghanistan, except my want of power to protect you there; and it must not be.

On another occasion he remarked:

Jan Larrens asked me how I was able to carry on the administration of Afghanistan if, as I had pointed out to him, the country was so poor that ends could never meet; also how I managed with regard to the accumulating annual deficits. Well, I told him that I took in the English paper, the *Delhi Gazette*, and if he would look back to that he would see how lately I, the *amir*, had been at the point of death. On that occasion, by the blessing of Providence, I got over my ailments by summoning all the respectable Hindu merchants in Cabul to my bedside, and by explaining to them the nature of my complaint; that I was dying from anxiety of mind regarding the debt due to them who had invariably supplied the needful to replenish my exchequer; that they knew the justness of my rule and the safety insured by my power, but that now I was actually dying from the thought of what would occur to them in case of my death, as anarchy would inevitably ensue, and that they would be the first victims. These Hindus are shrewd men; they realized the position, and restored me to health by striking the debt off their books!

With quite a twinkle in his eye, the *amir* on another occasion described the anxiety he and his family always had for the welfare of his people. He pointed out how, in a country producing little but men and stones, it was clear that either the chiefs or the people must perish, and "Do you know," he said, "after the fullest consideration by my sons and myself, we have arrived at the conclusion that *we* must live for the sake of the country, whatever may be *their* (the people's) fate." The *Dost* more than once described the advantage gained to his constitution by the introduction of a tax, styled "*Juz*," levied on Hindus, and especially set apart for the expenses of his, the *amir's* cuisine, "Muhammadan digestion improves," said he, "when pampered on Hindu property."

On the 28th January, Dost Muhammad Khan broke up his camp at Jamrud, bade farewell to Sir John Lawrence, and departed for Cabul.

CHAPTER 15

Lumsden's Diary

Perfect quiet seemed, at this time, to prevail over all India. The Governor-General and the subordinate governors in that vast empire were congratulating each other on the peaceful prospects before them, little dreaming that the quiet current along which they were gliding would, in a comparatively few days, cast them into a boiling abyss in which, for months, they would have to struggle with fire and sword for the very existence of the empire.

The following letter from Lord Canning, dated Calcutta, 19th January, 1857, communicated to Major Lumsden the Governor-General's views on the charge entrusted to him:—

My dear Sir,—It is hardly probable that this letter will reach Peshawur before you leave it. Nevertheless, I write it for the purpose of assuring you of the confidence with which I have agreed in the proposal of Sir John Lawrence, that the mission to Candahar should be entrusted to you, not only from my trust in his judgment on such a matter, but from everything that I have been able to hear in regard to yourself from those who know you.

Your task is a delicate, and may become a difficult, one. We have evidence of this already in the impediments raised to your passage by way of Cabul in company with the *amir*, and although you may abstain, as I am sure you will, most scrupulously from even an interference in the internal affairs of the government and people of Afghanistan, it is certain that you will be met by suspicions and jealousy at every turn. The only precaution to be taken, and I fear it will not be an effectual one, is to confine yourself to your avowed duty of seeing or ascertaining that the treaty is fulfilled on the part of the *amir* by the equipment and maintenance of the force prescribed in it, asking for explanation, if any be needed, to show that this is done, but not hastily, and even forbearing to do so if you should see an honest desire on the part of the *amir* and his officers to discharge their obligations on this head. You should not tender advice, even on military matters, unless invited; but if invited, the more you can help them upon any subject the better.

You cannot impress too strongly upon every man you meet that the British Government does not desire to send into Afghanistan a single man, armed or unarmed, except with the full consent of the Afghans themselves; that you are there for a temporary purpose only, that of assuring your Government that the aid which it has bound itself to give is turned to good account, and that if the war were to cease tomorrow your mission would be at an end. Endeavour to convince them of the truth, that what we most desire is that they would govern themselves and defend themselves, after their own fashion, without any thought from us; and that, in return for contributing to their defence, we ask for nothing but confidence in ourselves and their resistance to the common enemy.

I look forward with interest to your reports,, for with time and patience you will, I have no doubt, be able to collect much useful information, political as well as military. The extent of Persian influence, and whether it is increasing, the extent of disunion amongst the Afghans, and the chances in the event of the *amir's* death, the degree of interest felt about Herat out of the *amir's* camp, and the hands in which it might be placed when recovered from Persia after the *amir* has passed away, are points upon which I shall be glad to hear your opinions when you have had time to form them.

Pray write to me very unreservedly, and do not scruple to put into your letters impressions and suggestions which you might hesitate to record in a formal despatch.

Believe me, my dear sir,

Yours very truly,

Canning.

It was not until the 13th March, after having received intimation from the *amir* that all necessary arrangements had been made for provision and escort through his country, that the mission left Peshawur. Nawáb Foujdar Khan, who was to be the *vakíl*[1] of the British Government at Cabul, started at the same time. For escort Lumsden had a native officer, two non-commissioned officers, and sixteen troopers of the Guide cavalry, with two *havildars*,[2] two *naiks*,[3] and twenty-four Guide infantry. The mission proceeded via Kohat At Thul-biland-khel, on the border of Afghanistan, they were met by Naib Ghulam Ján, the deputy of Muhammad Azim Khan, the Governor of Kurram, with an escort of two companies of infantry and two or three hundred horsemen. Lumsden learnt from the *Naib* that from the time the mission set foot on Afghan soil its members were to be the guests of the *amir*.

On the 23rd March the mission reached Kurram, and was hospitably received by the young Sirdar Muhammad Surwar Khan in the absence of his father, Muhammad Azim Khan. Muhammad Azim Khan was unavoidably absent at Cabul, having been hastily summoned to concert measures with his elder brother,[4] Muhammad Afzal Khan, the Governor of Balkh, regarding the force which might be sent from there to co-operate with an Afghan army from Candahar against Herat. Muhammad Surwar Khan acquitted himself marvellously well, and by his quiet self-possession and *savoir faire* excited surprise.

Although the limit of this sketch will not allow of the setting forth of minute details of the route traversed, it may be interesting to enter here, in Lumsden's own words, his record of the journey across the Paiwar and Shutar Gurdan passes, which were fought over and traversed by the force under General Sir Frederick Roberts, on his march to Cabul in 1879.

Kurram Fort, 24th March.—Naib Ghulam Jan, with two mountain train guns, two companies of regular troops, a clump of *sowars*, with a number of Juzailchees, started for the Paiwar Kotul, which is said to be held by Jajis, who refuse to allow us a passage, and the *Naib*, before starting, warned us that in case of matters coming to a crisis he might require reinforcements, in which case we had better get inside the fort.

Kurram Fort, 27th.—The Naib Ghulam Jan returned about noon from the Paiwar, with the pleasing intelligence that the Jajis have giv-

---

1. Agent.
2. Sergeants.
3. Corporals.
4. By the same mother.

en up all idea of resistance, and promised to pay 3000 *R.s.* as a fine for their misconduct, and that the gathering of Munguls which had joined them had broken up.

The whole movement is said to have been got up by an Akhund-zada, who, residing in the village of Legrai, on the borders of Khost, possesses priestly influence among these Jajis. It is further reported that the obstructions thrown up on the pass by these people are too formidable to be removed in one day, and that we shall have to take another route for a few miles and then drop into the pass road

March 29th. Alt Khel, about 18 miles.—For reasons already given in. my diary of 27th, we took the Speen Gowie route in preference to the Paiwar, sending on two companies of infantry and two mountain train guns at 2 a.m. to secure the crest of the *kotul*. Instead of going through the village of Paiwar we turned sharp to our right up the bed of the deep ravine (east of the village) which comes down from the Siki Ram peak. At three miles from Hubeeb Killa, passed the Goondie Khel offshoot of the Paiwar village, consisting of about thirty houses, in a strong position on one of the Siki Ram spurs.

In the ravine we noticed large piles of stones collected, and were told that they were cairns marking spots where Hindus had been burnt, and that the village of Paiwar contains almost as many *khut-trees*[5] as Mahomedans. These carry on a thriving trade by importing wholesale from Cabul and retailing their goods through Kurram and adjacent districts.

From Goondie Khel[6] there is a regular ascent to the top of the *kotul*, in many respects preferable as a military road to the Paiwar *kotul*, as it has no regular zigzags to obstruct the passage of artillery and baggage. It passes the range a little higher up the spur than the Paiwar, and joins that road at Zuburdust Killa.

As far as Goondie Khel the road is commanded by steep heights on each side, covered with oak jungle; here the ascent commences and, rising out of the *nullah*, passes through a forest of pines, deodars, oaks, and yews, to the summit of the ridge. The ascent towards Hurriab is very gradual, through a succession of beautiful glades, now sprinkled with about a foot of snow and presenting beautiful alpine views. The descent is about two miles longer than that from the Paiwar. By that route, after leaving the village of Paiwar, the road crosses several deep

---

5. Hindu traders.
6. A Tooree village.

ravines, passing through broken country covered with oak jungle, but gradually ascending towards the bottom of the *kotul,* the ascent of which, though by a zigzag pass, is rather less than that of the Peshawur side of the Kohat *kotul.*

At the summit, covered with pines and *deodars,* there is a tower, occupied by a Jáji guard for the protection of the road. From Zuburdust Killa the road runs along the bed of a small rivulet the whole way to Ali Khel.

About half a mile from that village we were met by a body of about a hundred armed Jajis, dancing with drawn knives, and at a short distance beyond the village a larger party saluted us in a similar style, passing us within a few paces, scowling and howling out a peculiar call, which we did not at first detect as a war-cry, never having heard it before. It was like the word "*A-wook,*" pronounced first in a deep bass and several notes higher the second time, but nothing shrill about it like an Afridi or Momund yell. These parties passed on from time to time until we reached camp.

A few hours later at Ali Khel some thousand men, armed to the teeth, with dishevelled hair, drums and drawn knives, came round camp, evidently in a most excited state, and showed such unmistakable signs of ill-will, that Nawab Foujdar Khan (a man not to be easily moved by demonstration) sent down to my guard of "Guides "to know if they were accoutred. The party, however, moved on after hanging about camp for some time, and we had a quiet night. The *Naib* came over in the evening to assure us that there was not the slightest cause for apprehension, as the Ali Khel section of the Jájis were with him. I could not, however, help thinking differently, but kept my counsel to myself.

We were roused at 4 a.m. by bugle call, but just as our cattle were being laden the *Naib* came with a very long face and the pleasing intelligence that Heaven knows how many Khels had occupied the strong ground two miles ahead, and that the country behind us was anything but safe, our old friend the *Akhundzada's* son being at the head of the first-named party, so that we had better delay our march till something was settled.

Nawab Foujdar's men also told us that they had heard parties of men passing the camp all night.

The *Naib* sent on some of the Ali Khel *mullicks* to arrange matters, while he himself went more devotedly to his prayers than we have yet seen him. Time wore on, and the Ali Khel mission produced no beneficial results, but bodies of Jájis continued to cluster round camp, while distant *"nigaras"*[7] warned us that more men were gathering.

On this a council of war was held, to which we were invited, and at which it was finally arranged that horsemen should be sent in haste to Kurram and towards Cabul for succour, while we took up a defensible position, commanding water, and made the best fight we could for our existence. At first no horseman could be found to risk the experiment of such a trip, but at length one started for Kurram.

The cloud around camp still thickening, and the Ali Khel turning out armed and joining in the Jáji war-cry, the *Naib* determined to proceed himself, and make one more diplomatic effort as a last resource.

Two mortal hours did we sit in momentary expectation of a rush into camp by the mad mob around us, who were getting more and more excited every instant, and screaming out yells of derision at the *sirdar's* regular troops.

In the midst of strangers it was refreshing in the extreme to see the Mooltanee *sowars* calmly clustering round their chief, and the small bunch of Guides, rifle in hand, looking as confident as if they had a brigade at their backs. Such moments bring out men's characters, and the coolness of the *Nawab* Foujdar Khan and Ghulam Surwar Khan was an earnest of their mettle.

Suddenly, as if by magic, the yells of the Jajis ceased, and in half an hour the *Naib* returned and told us that all would be well if we moved off at once, as he had made arrangements, sworn to on the *Koran*, with the *Akhundzada*, the Ali Khel and Shamoo Khel *mullicks*, for our safe passage; but from his evident hurry to get us out of the place, anyone could see that he placed no great confidence in Jáji oaths, while their unwillingness to retire made it equally plain that they reciprocated the compliment.

We moved at once in fighting order, cavalry in front, a company with guns immediately behind them, then the baggage, followed by a rearguard of infantry. At every turn we met an ugly bunch of armed Jájis, and were not at all sorry to meet on the road a fine, strapping young Ghilzai chief with only a few followers, who met us on the border of Ghilzai land (to which he had been sent by the *amir*) to escort us safely, on the part of his father, Doulat Khan, through his country. He spoke of the Jájis as dirt, and said he could summon any number of his own clan in twenty-four hours.

---

7. War drums.

Naib Ghulam Jan subsequently informed us in camp that at his interview with the Jáji *mullicks*, the cry was not against us, but their district officer, one Atta Mahomed, and that he, the *Naib*, had sworn on the *Koran* to give them justice on his way back to Kurram, and from the bearing of the men we saw on the march it was evident that their dislike was more to our escort than to us. . . .

On the 8th April, the mission moved down the Sher Dahan Pass on Ghuzni The Sher Dahan Pass is one of the traditional gates of old Ghuzni, which in the time of Mahomed is said to have occupied all the space between the pass and those of Gurdan-i-Musjid and Shutur Gurdan (the latter towards Khilat), which would give a fabulous area of some twenty miles square, and make a city with a population far beyond what the surrounding country could support, nor do the ruins, now visible, in any way bear out this supposition. Beyond the Sher Dahan is an extensive basin enclosed by an amphitheatre of low hills, the drainage of which has but one exit, to the south. Two *karezees*[8] tap the springs in this basin, and carry the water to the gardens of Rozeh, or old Ghuzni This tract is about six miles long by some four miles broad, and is known as "*Talkgar*," and the village of the same name in the centre of it is said to have been the birthplace of Mahomed of Ghuzni, whose tomb is just beyond the old town, to the right of the road.

On viewing this dilapidated old ruin, it is melancholy to think that any Englishman should have ever dreamt of trailing its gates down to the Agra magazine, or of supporting Hindu superstition by the desecration of so time-honoured a tomb. On the broken ground between the old and new cities rise two lofty minarets, said to have marked the entrance to the reception halls of Mahomed of Ghuzni; their structure affords a splendid specimen of the perfection to which brickwork had been carried in his day. The one to the east is superior in dimensions and finish to its fellow, and said to be the handiwork of a master-mason, while the other is that of his pupil. The first mentioned has a large hole through its centre, about half-way up, said to have been created by a round shot during the wars of the Chagattai Government. The tombs beyond are said to be those of the Sultans, Ibrahim and Mahmood.

Ghuzni is a position to this day of remarkable strategical value, holding the highest point of the road between Cabul and Candahar, at the junction of routes from Bamian, Cabul, Dera Ishmail Khan,

8. Subterranean water-canals.

Quetta, and Candahar. If not the most important, it is at least one of the most important strategical positions in the whole country. Ghuzni and Logur are considered the principal granaries of Cabul, while rice is imported from Jellalabad. . . .

Most police cases are settled by the *Naib* (or Deputy) at Ghuzni, whose chief punishments are imprisonments or fines, even in cases of affray or aggravated homicide. Noted highwaymen and thieves are forwarded to Cabul, and generally hanged, even without plans of the spot where the depredations were carried on being required, for here a man's headless body is accepted as dead without a doctor's certificate. To the judicious adoption of this vigorous system may be attributed the general safety of the high road between Cabul and Candahar. The few robberies now heard of are committed by strong parties of Munguls coming over from the adjacent district of Zoormut, who watch their opportunity for spoliation and hurry back to their own country.

Altogether, the *amir's* arrangements for the government of the country, as far as we have seen, are much better than he generally gets credit for, and his people appear to be fairly clothed and fed. There is a marked difference, however, perceptible between the administration of the districts under Sirdar Mahomed Azim Khan in Kurram and those of Sirdar Shere Ali Khan[9] in Ghuzni In the former there is evidently scarcity of means, and all Government functionaries, as well as troops, are in arrears, while in the latter everything required is easily procured, and no grumbling or complaints are heard. Perhaps that is not so much attributable to the difference in character of the individuals administering the districts as to the *amir's* policy in placing the richer provinces in the hands of the family of the heir-apparent, thereby strengthening them for the day of trial

The mission left Ghuzni on the 12th April, and reached Kelát-i-Ghilzai on the 18th. To our right we felt ourselves in touch with the Hazarah tribes, whose confines here border with those of Turrukis and Ghilzais, and whose lofty peaks at intervals presented themselves to the north, whilst the drainage of the district generally flowed southwards towards the great lake of Abistuda.

To the northwards of the Goolkoh is an extensive elevated *plateau*, called Nawar, on which, on the melting of the winter snows, appears a luxuriant vegetation, attracting a considerable number of the adjacent

---

9. Afterwards the Amir Sher Ali Khan. He became heir-apparent on the death of his own brother Ghulam Haidar Khan.

Ghilzai and Hazarah nomadic tribes. Here also is the greater portion of the *amir's* stud of brood mares. A curious custom prevails in this part of the country of working three-year-old colts at this season of the year till they lose a greater portion of their flesh and become quite thin, by way of preparing them for a full allowance of green clover and lucerne, with which they are plenteously regaled for the next three months, and are said thereby to gain in bone and muscle.

From Gholjan, about half-way, the Shinkai Pass leads into the Hazarah country. This village is on the border between the Ghilzais and the Turrukis, and on a low hill in the centre of the valley are two large stones, called Khakein, marking the spot where, about the beginning of the last century, Nadir Shah erected a pile of Ghilzai heads, after the battle in which he crushed the power of that clan. Sirdar Sher Ali Khan, only four years ago, also erected a similar pile of the same material a few miles lower down the Turnuk stream, near the village of Shamilzai, to commemorate a victory in which he completely subjugated the tribes, after six conflicts, seizing the chief, Abdool Rehman Khan, with two of his sons, and obliging the clan to pay revenue into the *amir's* treasury. These Ghilzais are now as quiet and well-behaved a tribe as is to be found in the *amir's* dominions. The black tents of wandering Ghilzais, with their flocks, are to be seen scattered over the plains, while their guardian is lazily watching them from some adjacent peak.

This valley of the Turnuk is but one of six (belonging to the Wurduk Ghilzais) running parallel to each other, and separating the country of the Kakurs on the south from the Hazarahs northward. Each valley has its stream flowing down and fertilizing it. They are all tributaries of the Urghundáb, which joins the Helmund below Ghirisk. These valleys are called respectively Urghundáb, Turnuk, Nowa, Murgha, Afghasun, and Goondour or Learurgi (the last having both names).

We heard at Sir-i-asp on the 17th from Mirza Khuidad Khan, a confidential *moonshee* of Sirdar Futteh Mahomed Khan, that his master had just received the intelligence of the fort of Lurwan having been made over to a party sent from Furrah. It is the capital of the district of Ghor, a dependency of Herat. The *khan* of the place made it over to the *amir's* party to prevent it falling into the hands of a rival put forward by the Herat authorities.

Before reaching our camp at Kelát-i-Ghilzai, we were met by Schagassie Mir Akbar Khan and Nazir Bahadur Khan, confidential agent and comptroller to the household, sent forward by the heir-apparent, Sirdar Ghulam Hydur Khan, to escort us to Candahar, and under the walls of the fort were welcomed by Sirdar Futteh Mahomed Khan (son of the late Sirdar Mahomed Akbar Khan), and received by a guard of honour and a royal salute from the guns of the place. We accompanied the *sirdar* to his comfortable quarters in the fort, and spent a good half-hour in conversation tod tea. On our arrival at our tents we found a profuse Afghan repast prepared for us, by the care of the ladies of the household, the cooking of which would have done credit to Soyer.

Since the occupation of Herat by the Persians the *amir* has thoroughly remodelled and renovated the fort of Kelát-i-Ghilzai, where, without going back to the days of Sultan Babur, Major Halkett Craigie, in 1841, with a small garrison of Bengal *sepoys*, held the temporarily patched-up and dilapidated works against the combined Ghilzai tribes, and repulsed their final assault with a loss to the enemy of a hundred and forty slain, and left on the glacis of the fort.

On the 21st April, at Jaldak, one march out of Kelát-i-Ghilzai, we received our first post from Peshawur, with the news of the conclusion of the Persian war, consent of Persians to give up Herat and withdraw their troops, the abandonment of Bushire by the British, and the willingness of the Persian Government to Mr. Murray's return and honourable reception at Teheran, which, of course, presented to us the probability of a rapid termination to the mission and to its sojourn in Afghanistan.

On the receipt of this intelligence Lumsden addressed the following letter to the Governor-General:—

> Camp Deh Akhoon (two marches from Candahar),
> 23rd April, 1857.
>
> My diaries will have shown your lordship that, up to this date, everything has gone smoothly with our party, and that the Afghans have everywhere evinced the strongest inclinations to show us respect and win our good opinions. This is the effect of direct orders from the *amir*, who appears to have a much firmer hold of his people than we have hitherto given him credit for, and certainly the general safety of the roads has completely taken me by surprise.
>
> People go about their ordinary avocations unarmed, while travellers pass up or down, by day or night, in the most perfect confidence. His system appears to be to divide the country among

his sons, allowing each to govern his district in his own fashion, but holding him responsible for its tranquillity, the *amir* himself being accessible to the meanest of his subjects, whose complaints are frequently listened to.

In the division of the country, he appears to have purposely given the richer provinces to the heir-apparent and his brothers by the same royal mother, leaving the other sons to pick up what they can from the wilder and less productive corners.

From what I can gather in conversation with different classes, it is evident we are strongly suspected of having secret views of our own in connexion with the *amir*. All appear exceedingly anxious to know what is to become of Herat in the event of the Persians giving it up, and cannot believe we do not wish to hold it ourselves; and, though ready enough to try and worm out our views, all are extremely cautious in communicating their own opinion. One thing, however, appears very clear, and that is that no independent chief will be found to hold Herat on his own account Whoever gets it will in a few months be, if he is not already, pledged either to Persia or Cabul.

As for the relations of the late Yar Mahomed Khan,[10] all parties agree that they are either totally wanting in character, or mere children. The grandson, Nadir Khan, is said to be but eight years old. I shall be better able to speak more positively on the subject after being a short time at Candahar, but as your lordship has asked me to write freely, I send ideas as they strike me.

The main difficulty in disposing of Herat seems to be the uncertainty of who may succeed the *amir* in Cabul, for there is little doubt that Herat would be better in the hands of Afghanistan; for the great portion of the population of the Herat district belong either to the Duráni or Char Aimak tribes, and are aliens in blood and creed to the Persians, and should therefore (if properly treated) prefer an Afghan government. But when the *amir* dies, if Herat chances to be in the hands of the stronger party among the sons, it will remain Afghan; but if in the keeping of the weaker, it will go with them over to the Persian interests. It must be remembered that Herat is now in a very different position to that which it occupied while the *amir's* "Candahari brothers" held their country independent of Cabul. The annexation of Candahar brings the *amir* in direct contact

---

10. Ruler of Herat.

with tribes of Herat territory, all of his own kith and kin—a circumstance which would make it difficult for any chief to remain independent of Cabul.

Under these circumstances, it appears to me better to make over Herat to the *amir*, and let him appoint his own governor, for he will be sure, in doing so, to study the interests of the heir-apparent and his family, and thus afford the best prospect of Herat remaining an Afghan dependency instead of becoming a Persian province, and ultimately a Russian *depôt*.

I see, from papers just received, that there is every prospect of Herat being shortly given up, and the war terminated Should this be the case, our mission here will be at an end, unless your lordship should wish us to move on as far as Herat to see that the terms of the treaty are complied with, and at the same time avail ourselves of the opportunity of ascertaining the feelings and position of parties in Central Asia from a nearer point of view.

CHAPTER 16

Arrival at Candahar

On approaching Candahar the mission was met outside the city by one of the *sirdars* and an escort of cavalry, and forthwith conducted through the Cabul gate and the principal *bazaar* to the heir-apparent's residence in the citadel. In the square in front three remarkably fine-looking regiments of infantry and twelve guns were drawn up. They received the mission with a formal salute. Sirdar Ghulam Haidar Khan's residence was a most unpretending building, approached by a small entrance through a corner of an extensive courtyard. A masonry basin of water lay in the centre. Footpaths and *parterres* of flowers in full bloom had been laid out with considerable taste; luxuriant vines covered the walls.

At the end of one of the paths the heir-apparent received his visitors and escorted them to his *durbar*, which was assembled in a large vestibule opening on the Afghan garden just described. The heir-apparent made the usual kind inquiries regarding the health of the Queen, Governor-General, Chief Commissioner, and half the commissioners in the Punjab. Harry Lumsden replied to the best of his ability, and had also to give a full, true, and particular account of the state of his own health! and of that of his companions. The mission then took leave, and were forthwith conducted by the *sirdars chighási*[1] to the residence prepared for them hard by. Their quarters were much the same as those of their royal host, with a similar courtyard and garden.

According to Eastern custom the *sirdar* sent a lordly feast to all the officers and men of the mission, and later in the afternoon a *ziáfat* of 3329 Candahar *rupees*.[2]

1. Master of the ceremonies.
2. Value about a shilling each.

Ghulam Haidar visited the British officers towards evening, and Major Lumsden was especially struck by the improvement in the *sird-ar's* figure, which had become considerably reduced since his visit to Peshawur, and also by his happy manner and extreme intelligence.

In conversing on the subject of his army, Ghulam Haidar used an expressive simile. He said:

Soldiers to be of any real value must be well cared for at all times, as it is useless to give a large amount of grain to a starved horse when he arrives at the foot of a steep ascent Money expended on a standing army is put out at good interest, and must prove a good investment in twenty years.

In a letter to his father, of the 30th April, Lumsden writes:—

Heaven only knows when you may get this letter, but here are a few lines just to say that we cure both flourishing, and would not change our present position for any in India. We arrived here on the 25th—strange to say, the very date on which nineteen years ago the advance of Sir John Keane's army, with Shah Sujah at their head, arrived to upset the *amir's* government, while we come now to support the latter against Persia.

We were most kindly received by the heir-apparent, Ghulam Hydur Khan, and have an exceedingly nice house made over to us, with every luxury the *sirdar* can think of sent for our table daily, lots of the choicest blanched rhubarb and fruits; and have free leave to run about the country as much as we please, the only restriction being that we have to take a military escort with us. We shoot quail and are altogether in clover, while we get the credit of being surrounded by every danger which the imagination of good friends in the provinces, who know nothing of the matter, can conceive.

All I hope is that we may never be in worse quarters, and that those wise-heads in Paris, who apparently have taken upon themselves to arrange matters of which they know little, may not go and make a mess of the whole business by giving Herat to any son of Yar Mahomed; for the whole pack are as much Persian in Herat as the *shah* himself, and the result would be that Russia would have Herat before we were ten years older. Have not the good people in Parliament enough work at home, that they insist on playing pranks here?

We have only received one post since we left Peshawur on

13th March, and are consequently far behind the world, having only just heard that Persia has given in. I have proposed to Lord Canning, in the event of this report being true, that our mission move on and see Herat given over, and take the opportunity of feeling the extent of Persian influence in those quarters, and seeing with our own eyes and inquiring for ourselves what we can only now receive sifted through Afghan mediums. I think such a trip might be useful to the Government.

All the world are in love with the rifles I brought out from home with me, from Lancaster. I can make it very uncomfortable for man or beast at 1100 yards. The *sirdar* has promised to get me a master who can train hawks to catch deer, and won't I astonish the *"chickára"*[3] about Murdân when they next get the pleasure of my company amongst them!

The famine now is awful here; the poorer classes live entirely on boiled clover, while some even eat it raw. The country is dried up, and everything at famine prices.

The state of Candahar city at that time can hardly be better depicted than in the words of Dr. Bellew.[4]

In our passage through the city, for our morning ride in the open country, we often met dead bodies exposed in the streets by their friends, who loudly clamoured for contributions from the passers-by for the burial of the corpse of one of the "faithful"—an appeal which few who were in a position to aid with their mite could resist Apparently this proved rather a profitable calling, and dead bodies were conveyed about the crowded thoroughfares on beds, till their advanced state of putrefaction was more than the showmen could bear. We were told that the sums thus collected by the carriers of the corpses were spent in food for themselves and their starving families.

The sufferings and privations endured by the Candaharis during this famine were really terrible. According to the current rumour, the famine was in a great measure produced by the grain-dealers, who were accused of hoarding their grain under the impression that the mission was only the advance-guard of a British army about to visit Candahar, and from which they expected to realize much greater prices than those current in the country. It was even asserted that the heir-apparent coun-

---

3. Gazelles.
4. Bellew's *Mission to Afghanistan.*

tenanced this nefarious proceeding, and himself turned grain-merchant, and realized a handsome profit by importing grain from Ghuzni, on the one hand, Sabzarvar on the other, and selling it in the city at famine rates.

Be the truth of these rumours as it may, there is no doubt but that the preceding season was one of drought throughout the province. In this case the grain-dealers were justified in regulating the price of the grain according to the supply, so as to make it last until the next year's harvest came into use; otherwise, had they yielded to the clamour of a short-sighted and uncalculating public, the stock of grain in the country would have been consumed long before a fresh supply could be hoped for, and nothing short of complete starvation would have been the fate of the whole population.

This explanation is necessary in defence of the grain-dealers (who are all Hindus), a greatly abused and persecuted class in this country, because a proceeding such as that alleged against them above would produce results injurious to their own interests, apart from the severe punishments they would incur, were they to attempt such a thing.

With respect to the heir-apparent, less can be said in support of his conduct during this crisis. Had he the welfare of his subjects at heart he would have imported large supplies into the city, and, selling the grain at cost price, foregone the wealth he accumulated at the expense of his subjects, and thus had the satisfaction of alleviating their sufferings and securing their attachment. But, alas! philanthropy is not known amongst Afghans, who, as a rule, act up to the saying, "Each one for himself, and God for us all"

The heir-apparent fed his own troops at the rate of 32 lbs. of flour for the *rupee*, and deducted the price of the quantity supplied to the troops from their pay; but in the city he sold grain at the same rate as the grain-dealers, *viz.*, 4 lbs. of flour for the *rupee*. At such price the poor could get no flour at all, and for several months subsisted on clover and lucerne, wild herbs and mulberry leaves, which they as often ate uncooked as cooked.

At this time the Lumsdens could only obtain information from such persons as it pleased Ghulam Haidar Khan to admit to their presence; for whilst they were permitted to ride about the country with an escort, there was no disguising the fact that all who approached them were watched with extreme jealousy.

Amongst the most interesting of approved visitors was Akhundzada Nur Muhammad, a Sayad, formerly confidential agent to the late Candahari Sirdar, Kohandil Khan, who had entrusted him with a mission to Teheran. Nur Muhammad was a particularly shrewd man, and more than usually well-informed. He had visited Calcutta, Madras, and Bombay, and his memory was well stocked with all he had seen and heard. Lumsden learnt from Nur Muhammad that the late Sirdar Kohandil Khan, when at Candahar, independent of Cabul, and including Herat in his domain, was sincere in his desire for alliance with the British Government; but finding his overtures repulsed, had no alternative but to throw himself into the arms of Persia to save himself from being swallowed up by Cabul. With this view, he at first deputed his own son, and afterwards Nur Muhammad Khan,[5] to represent him at the court of the *shah*, where he was received with the greatest cordiality. The chief object of that mission was to secure from Persia the acknowledgment that Herat and Seistan were portions of Candahar.

A reminder of the uncertainty of events, and that the position of the mission might at any moment become exciting, presented itself on the 2nd May. An Ichakzai horseman of one of Ghulam Haidar's cavalry regiments managed to pass through all the outer sentries, and was only stopped at the entrance to the heir-apparent's bedroom by a Hindustani soldier on duty, who, not understanding what a common trooper could have to do with the *sirdar* at that time of night, refused to let him pass and took him prisoner.

On examination a sabre was found concealed in the man's clothing. Ghulam Haidar, aroused by the uproar, sent for the prisoner, and promised him his life on condition of fall confession and disclosure of the instigator of the attempted crime. The man at first pleaded starvation, and that he had only come to ask for pay, but eventually he admitted that he had received a promise of 4000 *rupees* from Muhammad Sadik Khan, son of the late Sirdar Kohandil Khan, to assassinate the heir-apparent. Muhammad Sadik Khan was immediately placed under a guard, whilst the Ichakzai trooper and eight of his clan were discharged from service and ordered to quit the country.

---

5. Nur Muhammad Khan was subsequently in the year 1877 deputed by the Amir Sher Ali to meet Sir Lewis Pelly in conference at Peshawur. Nur Muhammad died at Peshawur before the negotiations were completed.

CHAPTER 17

Afghan Troops at Candahar

From this time the Lumsdens were daily employed in the inspection of the troops at Candahar, and in searching out every detail of the state of the army, of the strength of the regular troops, and of the available contingents which the chiefs throughout the country could bring into the field. The resources of Afghanistan as regards carriage, ammunition, stores, and the like, were fully investigated. The non-commissioned officers and some selected men of the escort of the Guides were employed in drilling and instructing the Afghan non-commissioned officers and soldiers, and in a few months the improvement in the regiments at Candahar was very marked.

The total regular Afghan force was calculated at sixteen regiments of infantry and three of cavalry, with an artillery park of one mortar, five heavy guns, seventy-six field-pieces, and six mountain train guns. The infantry of this army were as fine a body of men, in point of physique, as was to be found in Asia, and seemed, at first sight, capable of undergoing immense fatigue. They were generally recruited from the mountain districts, and the best men were said to be Ghilzais, Warduks, and Kohistánis. The system of recruiting was very bad. It depended neither on conscriptive nor voluntary enlistment, but on the forcible seizure of able-bodied men from each district, who had no choice but to serve. Failure to do so entailed their personal imprisonment, and the utter ruin of their families.

The pay of a foot-soldier was nominally five *rupees* a month, with two months' deduction annually for clothing and half mounting. The distribution of pay was very irregular, and a considerable portion was paid in kind, or what amounted to the same thing, by remission of a certain amount of taxation due by the families of the men. The soldier consequently found himself without means to secure the necessaries of life, and was driven to recruit his finances by plunder and highway robbery—crimes at which their officers had to wink, and they not infrequently shared in the booty.

Military punishments were severe; pay was sometimes forfeited for months together, while soldiers were stripped, laid with their faces on the ground, and beaten with sticks until they became insensible or died. In cases of desertion their families were seized and sold as slaves, whilst they themselves, in event of capture, had either to serve in chains or were put to death. Men were hanged for selling a Government musket. Fear alone prevented mutiny, the slightest symptom of which was punished by instant death without a shadow of a trial

Most of these troops were armed with old British flint muskets and bayonets, or imitations of them, made at Cabul. A few companies had two-grooved rifles, constructed from models carried off by deserters from our own regiments. The accoutrements were of the very worst description, and had been generally picked up at auctions of condemned stores in our frontier stations, whilst some were made in Cabul. They were seldom cleaned, and never fitted to individual soldiers. The clothing was also obtained from similar sources.

Officers of all grades, even in the same regiment, presented themselves in every imaginable British costume, from a naval uniform to a whipper-in's hunting-coat, a general's full-dress, or a civilian's tall beaver hat Notwithstanding such drawbacks, however, the corps were very fairly drilled, and appeared rough-and-ready serviceable soldiers. The reason given for their being so fantastically dressed, in preference to their own picturesque costume, was not that the Government had not the money to expend on better clothing, but that the British uniform carries with it in Afghanistan a prestige which it is vain to look for under any other garb. The beards of the soldiers were also shaven, in imitation of our custom, and in order to render the recognition of a deserter more probable.

These troops were never brigaded together, and their officers knew little or nothing of their duty. They could go through a few parade manoeuvres, but confessed their total ignorance of their practical applicability. Blank ammunition was never served out, and, except when they were on actual service, the men never fired a shot of ball cartridge. With the exception, perhaps, of a few *shikáris*, who had handled their weapons from their youth, none of the men had the slightest idea of using their arms with precision, and there was scarcely a decent shot among them.

Each *sirdar's* contingent of regular soldiers was commanded by a General, who exercised the powers of life and death and was responsible for their military training, and also for the more difficult task of keeping them contented on the least possible amount of pay. His life was continually at stake, for, in case of mutiny, he had not only to quell spirits that could no longer endure, but also to soften the temper of an all-powerful Afghan ruler, whose Semitic proclivities induced him to attribute every appeal for arrears of pay to want of tact on the part of the General. When these officers proved themselves energetic, active soldiers, who contrived to keep matters tolerably straight, it generally happened that they secured great power and influence, and became so useful to their masters that, in case of accident or death, there was no one to replace them.

Such a man was the late Sher Muhammad Khan, formerly an officer in the E. I. Company's service, of the name of Campbell. Campbell had served under Ranjit Singh in the Punjab, and he came up to Afghanistan with Shah Shuja-ul-mulk in 1838. He was conspicuous for gallantry, integrity, and judgment; but being severely wounded, and taken prisoner in the battle lost by his master near Candahar, he renounced his faith and declared himself a Muhammadan. He subsequently took service with the Barukzais, for whom he laboured long and faithfully, but later he gave himself up to drunkenness and debauchery. Campbell commanded Sirdar Muhammad Afzul Khan's troops in Balkh, and died there in 1856.

Of somewhat similar character was General Firamosh Khan, who commanded the heir-apparent's contingent of troops, and became the most conspicuous soldier in Afghanistan. Firamosh Khan was a native of Weigall, one of the divisions of Kafiristan, and was, in 1857, about thirty-five years of age. He was originally a slave, the property of the late Wazir Muhammad Akbar Khan, at whose death he was transferred to the late Sirdar Muhammad Akram Khan, whom he accompanied to the Punjab with the Afghan contingent, which joined the Sikh forces in opposing us at Goojerat in the campaign of 1848. Firamosh Khan was, in all military matters, the adviser of Sirdar Ghulam Haidar Khan, and had more influence with him than most of his chiefs.

If Firamosh Khan had received any education, and his lot had been cast in a sphere not among Afghans, he might have been a very superior character and leader of men. He was clear-headed, intelligent, and possessed of great energy, with an aptitude for picking up and retaining all sorts of information. He had been instructed in the rudiments of military art by Sher Muhammad Khan (Campbell), and had mastered the subject sufficiently to be able to manoeuvre a regiment of infantry or cavalry. He had caused every detail of drill, as set forth in our military manuals, to be translated into Persian, and had learned them thoroughly. Of war Firamosh knew nothing, nor, as he said himself, was he ever likely to require the knowledge; for when Afghans engage in fighting amongst themselves, they rely more upon diplomacy and intrigue than on military strategy.

When actually driven to fight, the natural courage of their race is ever to the fore, but every petty chief supersedes the general, who is but a *"ghulám,"*[1] and has little voice in the matter; and, as may be expected on these occasions, the result is that in a multitude of such counsellors there is not much wisdom. In mountain warfare against the hill tribes Firamosh Khan had displayed that personal courage for which the inhabitants of Kafiristan are noted. Afghans declared that, being a slave, he dared not commit a serious mistake, which might have cost him his head. He nominally received 100 *rupees* a month for his expenses, with horses and arms supplied by his master.

Although naturally Firamosh Khan's disposition was anything but cruel, the associations of his life had engendered traits of cunning and revenge, said to be the inevitable result of the conversion of the *Kafir* to Muhammadanism, of which the following instance is a notable example. When the Wazir Muhammad Akbar Khan went up with a force to Kunur (the valley which runs down from Chitral towards Jellalabad), he sent Rustam Khan, a converted *Kafir* slave, with a company to occupy Chagar Serai, a village on the Afghan side of the border.

On arrival Rustam Khan sent a message to his relations in the village of his birth, that he was at Chagar Serai, full of anxiety once more to meet his own kith and kin, and begging them with affectionate entreaty to come down to welcome him. Some forty of his relations gladly responded. On arrival they were conducted into the village. The company of soldiers, by order from Rustam, fired a volley into them, killed six *Kafirs*, and took the remainder prisoners, who were sent off by Rustam Khan and sold for his own profit as slaves in Cabul. General Firamosh Khan related this diabolical tale as an instance of the acumen of his race under proper tuition.

Besides the regular army, the *amir* looked to the *jezailchis*, or militia, which were formerly the only infantry, for the defence of the coun-

1. Slave.

try. These light troops, armed with the *jezail*,[2] were perhaps as fleet of foot on their mountain-sides and as good skirmishers as are to be found in Asia. Good judges of ground and distance, with an almost instinctive scent for an ambush, they prided themselves on the fact that they could secure cover even behind a pair of their own grass sandals. They were of two descriptions— firstly, those in Government pay, on a nominal salary of five rupees a month (paid chiefly in grain), and armed by the State; and, secondly, the clansmen of the different chiefs, who were bound to give military service in return for land granted revenue-free.

In our intercourse with Asiatic races, none of the institutions of western civilization have been more appreciated than charitable dispensaries, and the opening of one of them at Candahar by Dr. Bellew had the happiest effect of drawing patients of every grade and race. Whilst Bellew's zealous and assiduous discharge of what was to him a labour of love was a godsend to the people, it secured for the mission an opening for intercourse apart from the ordinary channels which were carefully and jealously watched by the immediate followers of the heir-apparent. No one, however, appreciated the value of competent medical advice more than Ghulam Haidar Khan himself, and no one more frequently, on the slightest excuse, appealed for Dr. Bellew's assistance. Under what difficulties that advice had to be tendered, and what trials that master of his own profession had to undergo from the multitude of Persian and Afghan *hakíms*,[3] who were also invariably called in for every consultation, cannot be better described than by himself.[4]

On the last day of the *Roza* (or Muhammadan Lent) the heir-apparent sent the General Firamosh Khan over to our court with compliments to me, and requesting I would favour him with a visit, as he was not well. Though he was not a hundred yards from our residence, he sent over a saddled horse for my conveyance; but I preferred walking over, and at once did so, much to the disappointment and evil forebodings of the groom and other attendants, who had fastened a multiplicity of charms on all parts of the horse—tail, mane, and legs—in the hope that they would operate to render my visit an auspicious one,

---

2. A heavy rifle, resting on a forked iron prong.
3. Physicians.
4. Bellew's *Mission to Afghanistan*.

had I mounted the animal so highly favoured and protected by them.

Entering the heir-apparent's public audience hall, I found him stretched on a bed placed in its centre, and surrounded by a dense crowd of courtiers, physicians, and household servants, whose respective condolences, controversies, and sobs, mingled together, created a dreadful confusion and noise that quite drowned the deep groans of the *sirdar*. My approach was quite unheeded till close at the *sirdar's* side. I greeted him in the usual manner, and expressed sympathy for his sufferings. He at once seized my hand with both of his, and, with an anguished and terror-stricken countenance, implored me to relieve him speedily of his sufferings, or he must expire. In a few minutes I ascertained that he had an attack of gout, which had settled in the great toe of the right foot, and was now very hot, red, and swollen, and most intensely painful I at once assured the *sirdar* that I recognized the disease, promised him speedy mitigation of his sufferings, and explained the treatment necessary to be adopted.

On every point I was met by some objection on the part of the three attendant *hakíms*; one of them, rushing to the window, declared that the atmosphere was disturbed in its equilibrium, and that the stars were not in the conjunction favourable to the application of leeches. Another announced his belief that, under these circumstances, a further potation of the "*Sharbat-i-bed mushk*"[5] was indicated, and forthwith produced his flagon containing it But to this measure the *sirdar* himself was averse, declaring that its former agreeable smell and grateful flavour were now both alike perfectly nauseating to him. The third *hakím* was desirous to know my opinion as to the nature and probable issue of the *sirdar's* ailment, and, in fact, perfectly bewildered me with a volley of questions as to whether I classed it under the head of hot or cold, dry or moist diseases.

I told him at once that the *sirdar's* disease was decidedly a hot one, and required immediate treatment. But he struck off into a lengthy harangue on the various and multifarious circumstances which combined to produce hot diseases, and, fumbling over the leaves of a bulky manuscript volume, commenced an enumeration of the remedies suited to each, most of which,

---

5. Willow water or tea.

however, on one frivolous pretence or other, were disapproved of by the other *hakíms*, who were jealous of the start their rival had gained In the midst of all this wrangling amongst the *hakíms* (which certainly had the effect of diverting the *sirdar's* attention from his own sufferings), there was a constant moaning and groaning in all parts of the room, produced by the spasmodic and lugubrious ejaculatory prayers and forebodings of the crowd of attendants and court officials who were gathered round their master.

Matters had now reached a crisis beyond my endurance, and proved the necessity for determination on my part. I accordingly addressed the heir-apparent in quiet but firm language, and told him that if he was really desirous of my professional services, he must allow me to have my own way entirely, or else permit me to retire from the scene. He at once ordered silence, but without effect, and begged me not to go away, declaring his willingness to submit to anything I proposed. Leeches were accordingly at once procured and applied round the inflamed part, amidst a perfect shower of *"Lahouls," "Tufáns,"* and *"Kiamats"*[6] from the bystanders, mingled with the gloomy hopes, fears, and prophecies of the *hakíms*. The leeches were followed by hot fomentations, which in a few minutes produced great relief, or as the *sirdar* pithily expressed it, *"Tafáwut-i-zamin wa asmán"* (the difference of earth to heaven).

Presently he sat up on his bed, and ordered a *"chilam"* [7] and a cup of tea to be brought for my refection. I took a few alternate whiffs and sips, while the *sirdar* was occupied in abusing his physicians for their want of skill and unanimity.

On the occasion of one of the heir-apparent's visits towards the end of May, His Highness, after the usual inquiries regarding health and welfare, produced for inspection a bottle said to contain *"Roghan-i-balasam,"* Balm of Gilead (literally, the oil of balsam), and which, he quietly observed, had been presented to him by a merchant just arrived from Bombay as a sovereign remedy for rheumatism. The bottle, however, had a very suspicious resemblance to a French brandy bottle, and its contents to the liquor usually found in one. On nearer inspec-

---

6. Exclamations:—*Lahoul*, an Arabic word uttered to drive away evil spirits. *Tufáns*, tempests. *Kiamats*, days of judgement.

7. A *hookah*.

"Doctors differ." Dr. Bellew and the Heir-Apparent.

First *hakim*: "Give him cooling things." Dr. Bellew: "Don't eat sour things."

Second *hakim*: "Rub almond oil on his navel."

Afghan orderly: "By God they will kill him."

tion the stamped seal of "Champagne Cognac" was found on the glass, and on further investigation, by extracting the cork, the contents were at once recognized as the veritable *eau de vie*. It was amusing to mark the air of assumed innocence with which the heir-apparent broached the subject and watched the examination of the "*Roghan*."

On being plainly told that the supposed Balm of Gilead was nothing more than genuine brandy, he raised his eyebrows in mimic astonishment, expressing great horror at even having handled the mere receptacle of the forbidden liquor and, at the same time, motioning with his hands to close the bottle, lest the fumes of its contents should contaminate the surrounding air. He begged that it might be kept, as perhaps it might prove of some use. The Lumsdens were nothing loth to this proposal, as their own supply of such stimulants was limited to two bottles of brandy and two of port wine, all of which it had been agreed should be strictly reserved as "medical comforts" in case of sickness. In adopting this shallow pretence and round-about way of presenting a bottle of brandy, the possession of which he was ashamed to own, though he must have known that all were well aware of his regular indulgence in such spirits, the *sirdar* was influenced by a kindly feeling, for he often expressed his astonishment that his guests should feel so little the deprivation of a liquor which he knew most Englishmen were accustomed to, whilst at the same time he lauded their moderation in its use.

Afghans have an idea that Europeans indulge immoderately and universally in strong drinks, and they even urge this as a reason for despising them, as amongst themselves those who do yield to the temptation of drink—and they are a large class, including almost without exception all the chiefs located in cities—do so simply for the purpose of intoxication, and cannot understand the advantages of a moderate use of stimulants.

CHAPTER 18

Outbreak of the Mutiny in India

The last few pages afford, it is believed, a sufficiently accurate view of the peaceful and uneventful life which Harry Lumsden and his companions passed at Candahar from the time of their arrival to the end of May, 1857. There was nothing in their surroundings which could in any way cause them to suspect that they were living just beyond the range of a cyclonic storm of mutiny and rebellion, which had burst over India since they crossed the border into Afghanistan. On the 4th June, however, flashes of the distant lightning and echoes of the far-off thunder manifested themselves in a most unexpected manner. Lumsden, riding out in the morning with General Firamosh Khan, was told that the heir-apparent had just received an urgent express from his father, the *amir*, informing him of the outbreak of the native army at Meerut; the disbandment of two native regiments at Barrackpore; the destruction of a native corps by the British regiment at Ferozepore; the disarmament of the native troops at Lahore; the murder of Europeans at Delhi, and the fact that the mutineers had placed the old king, Bahadur Shah, on the throne of his ancestors. The next morning a post-runner arrived from Cabul with the weekly mail from Peshawur, which confirmed generally the substance of the news sent by the *amir*.

Sirdar Ghulam Haidar Elian received the Lumsdens at a private audience, told them that his father looked to them for advice in such a crisis, and would act in accordance with their suggestions. His Highness forcibly depicted the anxiety and excitement of the Afghan people, and the difficulties his father had to contend with, but he expressed his undeviating faith in British power, and declared that the *amir* and himself were bound by a special friendship towards the British Government.

Nothing was more cheering to Lumsden than the conduct of his escort of Guides. They bore themselves like men; avowed to him their implicit confidence in the absolute loyalty of their comrades in the Regiment to the Government and to himself and their resolve, for weal or woe, to stick to him to the death.

Excitement ran wild among the Afghans. *Mullahs* in the mosques added fuel to the fire, and preached a *jehád*, whilst green rags began to wave in unusual places. Day by day passed, but no letters arrived from India. Colonel Edwardes, the commissioner, was believed to be absent from Peshawur. The position of the Lumsdens was not an easy one. The mission at Candahar, six hundred miles from the nearest British post at Jacobabad, represented the only Europeans who had been in Afghanistan since our withdrawal in 1842. The treaty between the Governor-General and the *amir* was not approved by fanatical Afghans. Lumsden felt that the safety of himself and his companions entirely depended on the caprice of the *amir*, and the conduct of his son, the heir-apparent.

Evening after evening was spent in close conclave with the latter, regarding events both in India and Afghanistan, as they followed on in successive waves of good or bad omen to the re-establishment of British supremacy in our Indian Empire. Harry Lumsden, however, never for a moment doubted our ability to overcome all difficulties, nor did he deviate from his rule to set clearly before the *sirdar* what he believed to be the actual state of affairs, giving his honest opinion as to future possibilities, and the best course to be adopted by the Afghan Government.

In Candahar itself there was at once a marked difference in the bearing of the people towards the British officers. Scowling looks and muttered execrations of bigoted *mullahs* and their disciples followed them as they rode through the streets. News from India was eagerly looked for by the Afghans as well as by the Lumsdens. Eventually genuine and authentic tidings came and continued to come with wonderful regularity, the news-writer being none other than that master of the pen, Herbert Edwardes, the Commissioner of Peshawur, who had returned from leave in the end of April It is our privilege to be able to present in print, for the first time, a most interesting and graphic series of letters which Edwardes addressed to Lumsden, writing between the 8th May, 1857, and the 20th April, 1858.

These letters were preserved and treasured with the utmost care, and it may rightly be said that the relief and satisfaction—too often, alas! greatly dimmed by pain and sorrow—derived from their perusal materially alleviated the agonizing strain of remaining inactive and idle at Candahar while such stirring events were taking place in India—to say nothing of the fact that the beloved Guides were pressing forward to honour and glory under a new commander. However that may be, the tripartite situation suggested by these letters is a grand one. Edwardes, on the watch at the most important strategical point of the frontier, gathering in the details of the struggles taking place at Lucknow, Cawnpore, and Delhi, flashes them like a master of the heliograph in his own picturesque words from Peshawur to Candahar.

No apology seems necessary for the many extracts from these letters which we now give. The officers of the mission, obliged by the turn of events to remain patient and passive as best they could, may be said to have lived at this time upon the news they received from India. The chief source of information was Herbert Edwardes, and what he wrote to Lumsden even now, we think, possesses a double interest, objective and subjective. It is interesting to reflect upon the effect produced by the letters upon the exiles in Candahar, and it is perhaps even more interesting to read the story of the Mutiny of 1857 as it presented itself from day to day to Edwardes at Peshawur.

The first of the letters is as follows:—

H. B. Edwardes to H. B. Lumsden.

Peshawur, 8th May, 1857.

My dear Lumsden,—Your note of 9th April was lying here for me when I arrived on 3rd May, and I am glad to see from it and the diaries . . . that your party have got on so prosperously, and had reason to be so satisfied with the authorities. It looks as if the last negotiations had really made some impression on the Court, and convinced them that we do not wish to take their country, but only to help them to keep it. The peace with Persia will confirm this feeling, unless Lord Palmerston and Mr. Murray put a Suddozye into Herat, which would be a sad blunder. I myself want it given to the *ameer*, and I believe the G.-G. also. Thank you for your kind enquiries about Mrs. Edwardes. I have heard of her as far as Aden—suffering awfully from heat, and a small steamer overcrowded. However, please God she is now in England, . . . and I hope to get a happy account of her ere long. I made a regular holiday of it. Took general leave after I had used up the sixty days; stayed eight days at Lucknow with

Sir Henry, two at Mynpooree with Arthur Cocks; ran up to the Lawrence Asylum and my corps at Dugshaie. . . . Altogether . . . I enjoyed the holiday greatly, and did not write one public letter for ten weeks.

. . . Sir Henry is better in health than I could have expected, but nearly white-bearded; looking very aged, poor fellow. He is much subdued in spirit, and a dear old man; everybody likes him, and he has come like oil upon those troubled waters.

. . . Good luck to you all. I wish I had time to write you a long stave, as it seems a long way off to send a scrawl like this.

Ever yours, very sincerely,

Herbert B. Edwardes.

H. B. Edwardes to H. B. Lumsden.

Peshawur, 16th May, 1857.

It is all very well of you ambitious youths, on pretence of enterprise and perilous adventure, to go off to Candahar, and expect C.B.-ships and promotions for the pluck of it. But next time you go, please take the native army with you, and send us the Afghans and *Shytâns*.[1] These mild and inoffensive Hindoos have been trying to drive the English into their ships. You know, of course, that the 19th N.I. mutinied about cartridges, and were disbanded. The 34th N.I. followed suit, and have been disbanded too. A new regiment at Lucknow has tried to mutiny, and been dispersed. At Meerut the whole native brigade went into open mutiny, and put the Europeans on the defensive—so the *Telegraph* says—but I should say it means General Hewitt on the defensive! A body of the mutinous 3rd Cavalry *koonch'd*[2] over to Delhi as a good fat place, looted both city and magazine, and killed many Europeans, I'm afraid. At Umballa great smouldering excitement, but no fire; and at last confidence is there restored by withdrawal of obnoxious cartridges.

A fire in Hallifax's cook-house there has been put out by the native soldiery, and is announced with triumph; but the value of the incident depends on whether the fire was in the *choolah*[3] or the chopper![4]

At Ferozepoor the 45th N.I. mutinied. . . . The 10th Cavalry

1. Devils.
2. Decamped.
3. Kitchen fireplace.
4. Thatched roof.

staunch; the 57th N.I. laying down their arms to avoid suspicion of being disaffected. The Queen's 61st seem to have settled this job sharp.

At Mean Meer the brigadier put all native troops out of mischief by taking muskets and sabres away from them.

These tidings having reached us here, where some of the ablest military men were residing, a council of war was called, and (fact!) General Reed was declared to have assumed the chief command in the Punjab, and proceeded to lay out the campaign!

A movable column of H.M.'s 27th from Nowshera, H.M's 24th from Pindee, that noble corps the Guides, Coke's Rifles, Kemaon Battalion, 16th Irregulars, European troop of horse artillery, etc., etc., were ordered into the field, to move down the Punjab and punch the head of any station that says knife!

The alacrity with which these troops moved beat anything of the kind I ever witnessed, and I only wish the same energy had been shown in the North West Provinces.

. . . I do believe we have saved the mutiny from spreading in the Punjab.

I have told you all this in merry strain . . . but the crisis has been, and perhaps still is, a serious one. It has passed like a white squall over the good ship British India. When the clouds clear off, I fear we shall see many a melancholy wreck left behind. There must have been terrible bloodshed, and murder of poor Europeans here and there about the country, and many a good friend may any of us have lost—many a fine soldier may have been thrown away. Out of evil comes good sometimes; nothing short of this would have got us Army Reform.

I am glad to hear that you have arrived safely at Candahar, and are so well satisfied with all you see. Goodbye. Kind regards to your brother, and *salaam* to Sirdar Hyder Khan.

On the 23rd May the *sirdar* sent Lumsden a letter from Surwar Khan at Furrah, intimating that the Persian troops in Herat were—agreeably to instructions received from Teheran—collecting carriage for the immediate evacuation of the fort, and in forwarding the same to Government Lumsden expressed his opinion that this was a very critical juncture in Herat affairs; for if the Persians retired without nominating someone to the charge of the province, or making it over to some competent authority, the country would become a scene of anarchy and bloodshed among Afghan aspirants, with "Sirdar Sultan Jan & Co." coming from Persia to add fuel to the fire. He strongly deprecated the acceptance of Sultan Jan, if nominated by Persia, because he regarded him as a mere slave of the *shah*. He thought that such a course would virtually nullify the treaty, because Herat would, in effect, remain as much at Persian disposal as if it was a conquered province. Lumsden considered that the *amir* should be encouraged to nominate a ruler for Herat, and so make it practically what it already was theoretically, an integral portion of the Afghan kingdom.

The same *kossid*[5] who brought the news of the intended evacuation of Herat brought the intelligence of the blowing-up and abandonment of Ak-Musjid by the Russians. The increasing activity of the *mullahs* and certain of the followers of the late Candahar chiefs, together with the continued excitement regarding the issue of events in India, induced the heir-apparent to summon to his council his nephew, Jelaludin Khan, Governor of Zamindawur. He was the second son, by a Barukzai mother, of the late Sirdar Muhammad Akbar Khan. He was about twenty-four years of age, active, shrewd, and intelligent, and was of great assistance to his uncle.

Lumsden wrote in his diary on the 15th June:—

We have for some days, from several quarters, received friendly intimations to be on the look-out for squalls when we move outside the city gates, and today have realized the usefulness of the hints. We never go anywhere unarmed; even when out shooting we are, by the heir-apparent's order, accompanied by a company of infantry. We had gone several miles out on the Herat road to shoot snipe. The *jheel* [6] was a large one, and the Afghan soldiers had formed a loose cordon round it at some distance off. Towards evening there was a cloud of dust on the road, and a bunch of spears came galloping down from Candahar. There was a gathering into knots of our infantry escort, and presently a few shots induced the horsemen to keep at a safer distance. They manoeuvred about for some time, and presently broke into small bodies and fled towards Furrah. The cause was soon evident by the appearance of a more powerful body of horsemen, who, we afterwards learned, were led by Jelaludin

---

5. Express messenger.
6. Marsh.

Khan, in pursuit of Sarfaraz Khan (Achakzai).

Sarfaraz Khan, it appeared, had conceived the idea of organizing a party to attack our citadel in Candahar, seize the British representatives, and carry them off towards Herat, with the object of securing a ransom for our lives, or else killing us as *infidels*, and thus secure for himself the blessings of paradise. His plot, however, was discovered in time, owing to the suspicions aroused by his known large purchases of lead. The trade in ammunition in these parts is no bad political barometer, and at once indicates to the authorities the possible contingency of stormy times.

Sarfaraz Elian, it appeared, had had too much of a start, and although pursued as far as Girisk got safely away. This chief was supposed to be friendly towards the heir-apparent, but apparently fond of change, as he had acted somewhat in the same manner years before to his master, Sirdar Kohandil Khan. In fact, a man must be something more than a prophet in these parts to accept anyone as a trusted friend under all circumstances.

It was at this critical time that, for several weeks, there was no *kossid*, no post from India, although scraps used to come through the Bolan from Sind. Lumsden was anxious, now that Herat was no longer his objective, to be recalled and allowed to join his Guides in the field, but no summons came from Lord Canning or from the Punjab Government, whilst the excitement amongst the Afghans continued to increase, and pressure was being brought to bear on the *amir* to induce him to raise the "green flag," and to muster his strength for a holy war against the British.

Days and weeks were passed in anxiety. Lumsden was in constant commutation with the heir-apparent. Expresses were continually passing between the *sirdar* and his father the *amir* at Cabul. Their attitude to the mission so far seemed to be satisfactory, while the receipt of the monthly subsidy in hard cash had the happiest effect. It was not until June was well spent that Herbert Edwardes' letter of the 30th May reported the further progress of events in India:—

H. B. Edwardes to H. B. Lumsden.

Peshawur, 30th May, 1857.

By your letter of 10th May to me (in a cypher of which you never gave me the key, but which that man of great linguistic

167

attainments, James, has faithfully interpreted), I perceive that you want both letters and money.

What can I say for myself? Will a mutiny of the whole native army—and British India up a tree—be the least excuse? If not, I beg pardon.

Before the messenger of your indignation had got far on his road, I trust you received one or two *dawks*[7] I sent you, with letters, papers, and details of about 3000 *rupees'* worth of guns which I sent up to Cabul for you, along with three *lakhs* of *rupees* for the *ameer*.

I also wrote you some account of the state of the native army. Just after that I was summoned to Pindee to consult with Sir John and Chamberlain, and was there for two or three anxious days. The horizon was very black indeed throughout India . . . only here and there a chap like MacAndrew[8] coming out and *acting* as assistant-residents once knew *how* to act, in the merry days when you and I were young. Nicholson then reported that the troops were going wrong at Peshawur; so I hurried back here, and found a general apprehension of a row at the Eed.[9] Intercepted letters were quite unpleasant reading—that's a fact!

At last the mine blew up. The 55th N.I. at Nowshera broke out, plundered the magazine, fired on 10th Irregular Cavalry, and got off to Murdân, where their headquarters were.

This reached us at midnight. Nicholson[10] and I packed up three shirts and visited the Brigadier. We advised taking the initiative and disarming the brigade, all but 21st N.I., 7th and 18th Irregular Cavalry.

The Brigadier [11] concurred, but not so some of the great commanders. . . . They had "implicit confidence in their men"—they *had!* It was a shame, and all the rest of it. We were youngsters who had seen nought of war, and "knew nothing of these Chutree races!" . . . Nevertheless the brigadier stuck like a man to his decision, and at 7 a.m. we just told the 24th N.I., 27th

---

7. Poets.

8. Afterwards Colonel George MacAndrew, Inspector-General of Police in Punjab.

9. Muhammadan feast.

10. John Nicholson, at this time Deputy-Commissioner of Peshawur under Edwardes.

11. Sydney Cotton.

N.I., 51st N.I., and 5th Light Cavalry to lay down their arms, which they very prudently did, and were much applauded by the above-named colonels. The officers of 5th Light Cavalry gave in their own swords, and in some instances, I believe, *spurs*; and all were injured innocents. The air cleared at once! The day before levies were not to be had for love or money. The old *wuzeer* (Oosman Khan) gravely and sorrowfully opined to Nicholson that this was a crisis in which we must rely upon—whom do you think?—*ourselves!*

As we came back from the disarming parade, *khans, shahzadahs, haramzadas, mullicks, moollahs,* horse and foot, swarmed like vermin. They seemed to come out of holes in the ground. Next we sent a small force to reduce the 55th N.I. to surrender. As the dust of the column was descried, the main body of the regiment marched off in open mutiny, towards Swât. Only 120 men remained with their officers. Poor Colonel Spottiswoode committed suicide—unable to bear it! Nicholson on his big grey horse, with the cavalry, pursued. The mutineers had gained too great a start for entire defeat; but many were brought to bay—100 carcases left upon hill and plain, 150 taken prisoners, and about 400 made good their retreat across the border. They fought desperately, and I hear Nicholson slew about a dozen himself. He was twenty hours in the saddle, and rode seventy miles. I fear the gallant grey will be long before he does such a feat again. Next Ajun Khan[12] threatened to come down, and then was sent for (by the Swâtis) to take command of the 400 at Swât! Fancy the 1st Swât Infantry, and their nemesis the paymaster.

A small force, with Nicholson, is now out on the Aboozye border, and will stay there till one Bahâdur Shah, the last and vilest of the Great *Moghuls*, who has seated himself on a Bareilly chair, and calls himself King of Delhi—anointing his coronation with the blood of fifty poor English women and children who took refuge in his palace, and the circumcision of innumerable Hindoos—shall be tried by a drum-head court-martial and hanged at the jail door.

The followers of the Prophet were quite aroused at this Imperial turn of affairs, and so were the Hindoo *rajahs*. They bethought them of the tolerant rule of good John Company, and the in-

12. See chapter 12.

tolerant one of Aurungzeyb, and they poured in contingents to the rescue. Pattialah handed in an autograph letter from His Majesty of Delhi. The headquarters of the army are now about Paneeput. The mutineers are scuttling. Bahâdur Shah is probably making up diamond pills to take when it comes to the fighting.

As if the above were not enough of wonderful events, the commander-in-chief's death of *cholera* is announced. General Reed commands the army, Sir Harry Barnard the field force against Delhi, Brigadier Cotton the Peshawur division. . . . We hanged the *soobahdar* major of 51st N.I. yesterday morning before the garrison, for mutiny and desertion. The people of the Peshawur valley, with natures entirely changed by a mild and paternal rule, brought the old gentleman back alive, and as far as is known, still a Hindoo, with 900 *rupees* and a gold necklace round his neck. Let this fact be chronicled.

We are now trying no end of others, and there will be a large number of executions, I trust, for however sad it is to think that many of the *sepoys* have been sincerely alarmed as to their religion, yet the history of such a tremendous mutiny must record on awful punishment, or it will all come over again. I don't know how it is that my pen always will make light of things, but I can tell you, Lumsden, that we have passed (I trust I may use that tense now, though we have all many labours and anxieties still left) through the greatest danger that ever threatened our power in India. Ferozeshuhr was a joke to it.

It now remains to reconstruct the broken army of a century! The Irregulars, of course, will get the benefit of it all. The Oudh provinces will feel the loss. Sir Henry, thank God! is safe and well, and has done great things. He made a grand English speech in Hindoostanee to the soldiery at Lucknow. They ought to make him commander-in-chief, Neville Chamberlain military secretary to Government, and John Nicholson adjutant-general Then I think we should get an army. I feel so confused, and weary of multifarious *chits* [13] that I don't know whether I have told you half. Let me gather up a few more fragments.

The 9th N.I. robbed the Boolundshuhr Treasury of two *lakhs*. The 74th N.I. surrendered in a body to the Lieutenant-Governor of Agra. . . . The Guides are at Lahore. All is quiet in the

---

13. Letters.

Punjab. Flocks of European regiments are coming to India. . . . General Cotton lives in the Old Residency. Treasure in the fort. Several Hindoo deserters from the 51st N.I. have been brought back Muhammadans. . . . So much for cartridges and *caste*.

Give my love to Sirwur Khan. Tell him his son, Atta Mahomed Khan, is here with his *ressalah* along with Nicholson, and very glad we were to see some old *tried* friends again! A thousand times I have felt how valuable would all of your party—yourself, Peter, Sirwur, and Foujdar—be to the State at this crisis here. But I also thought for the *ameer* as well as ourselves, and determined not to recall one of you. It would have given a shake to everything in the Cabul territory, and perhaps have spread to Persia the lie that we were retreating on the sea. But these were just the times for you all.

. . . Goodbye. I have given sixteen thanks[14] to your messenger with the arrow-headed characters.

The next communication (in order of date) was brought by an express messenger. It arrived a few days before the long letter of the 30th May, just quoted. It was written in the arrow-headed characters referred to by Edwardes, and being translated, ran thus:—

1st June, 1857.

My dear Lumsden,—*Dawks* went to you on the 16th, 17th, and 18th May; we have had great anxiety with native army at every station in Bengal; *sepoys* at Peshawur disarmed, militia raised, mutiny subsiding; Delhi not recovered yet, but force gone against it; Commander-in-chief dead of cholera; quiet gradually being restored.

---

14. *i.e.* sixteen *rupees* or a gold *mohur*.

CHAPTER 19

Effect of News from India
on Afghan people

Exaggerated reports of events in India continued to excite the minds of the people of Candahar. A deputation of the priesthood waited on the *sirdar*, and requested to be informed whether the *amir* intended to avail himself of the present crisis to strike a blow for the benefit of *Islám*. The heir-apparent was reported to have sent them away with the promise of an answer, as soon as he himself had been placed in possession of the *amir's* views.

So long as Dost Muhammad Khan ruled in Afghanistan such demonstrations were of little importance, further than that they showed the temper of certain classes, for his hold on the people was sufficiently strong to enable him to do what he pleased. No one of his sons, however, could possibly remain equally unfettered. An example of the *amir's* method of silencing uncalled-for reflection on his actions was afforded by the case of Ghulam Khan, ex-*Kázi*[1] of Candahar. This functionary had been the leader of parties in the time of the Candahari brothers, but not long ago he had ventured to state that "the newly-formed alliance with the British savoured of infidelity against *Islám*." The *amir*, on hearing of this, immediately caused the holy man to be arrested and kept in custody until he should pay a fine of several thousand *rupees*, and had enjoyed ample leisure for the discovery of more palatable texts for future discourses.

On the 2nd July the mission received the welcome news of the arrival of our troops before Delhi on the 9th June, and the capture of the Flagstaff Battery. At this time daily expresses were passing between

---

1. Judge.

Cabul and Candahar, and every conceivable rumour regarding the destruction of the British in India was promulgated throughout the length and breadth of the country. The wish was father to the thought in rumours of this kind, and it required all the powers of the heir-apparent to restrain the people.

Nothing but the treaty so happily entered into with the *amir*, and the fact that by that treaty the minds of the Afghans were, to a certain extent, prepared for Dost Muhammad Khan s non-interference in our affairs, saved India at this juncture from the extra strain which would have been put upon her had the *amir* raised the green flag of *Islám* and, at the head of thousands of Afghan and Turkoman hordes, marched into Hindustan. [2]

Throughout the Candahar country the extra demand for horses, farriers, and horseshoes suddenly became very apparent. Not only so, but every available beast, even to brood mares from distant summer pastures, and every mule and beast of burden, was requisitioned from every direction and by every chief—a symptom that all were anxiously scanning the political barometer and getting ready for squalls.

Later on, however, the fickleness of the Afghan temper was amusingly illustrated by the sudden change in popular feeling which took place when the news arrived of our first success before Delhi

H. B. Edwardes to H. B. Lumsden.

Peshawur, 12th June, 1857.

Herewith another batch of papers and letters. You must not be surprised at the scantiness of letters, for the post office has been non-existent between the two ends of the empire.

Since I last wrote to you things got worse and worse by delay in marching on Delhi. Regiment after regiment fell away, and at last they seem going in brigades. Happily the army has reached Delhi, and on the very day of its arrival given the mutineers a defeat and taken twenty guns. On 8th June, at 8 a.m., General Barnard reached Delhi, and found the mutineers had got an outpost established on the flagstaff mound; went into it at once, captured about twenty guns, and put the garrison of it to the bayonet. We lost about 150 killed and wounded; Colonel Chester, adjutant-general, and Lieutenant Russell, of 54th N.I., among the killed. H.M.'s 75th chiefly suffered. The affair de-

---

2. Sir Herbert Edwardes, writing to me in 1864 regarding the effect of the treaty, said: "With what benefit to India, let 1857-58 declare!"—G.R.E.

scribed as brilliant Our troops afterwards encamped in the cantonment, and the heavy gun battering to begin next day....

Since writing to you we have disarmed the 64th N.I., which they pretend to be quite astonished at; but this is not the place where we can afford to show "implicit confidence."

We are raising new irregular regiments as hard as we can go.

The China troops will be intercepted, but cannot be at Calcutta till middle of July. The European regiments of Persian expedition have been brought round, and others from Ceylon and Rangoon, and pushed up to Cawnpore and Benares in *dawk* carriages.

We may reasonably hope now soon to hear of complete success in Delhi, and then the worst will be over. The broken army, however, will infallibly retreat to their homes in Oudh, and Sir Henry will get the end of the storm. He is said to have done splendidly throughout, and Government may be thankful that they had appointed him in time.

The Guides must have been up with the army, I think, when it reached Delhi ...

Never were such times! The Muhammadans have tried hard to turn the Hindoo mutiny to account, and certainly it is Providence alone that has saved us. I am so busy that I can only send a few lines. Nicholson sends his kind regards to you.

Sir John Lawrence, writing to Lumsden from Rawul Pindi on 17th June, thus describes progress in India:—

I hear you are irate against me, and doubtless it was not unnatural that you should be; but had you been so sick as I have been, and had half my work to do, you would not have written to your own "*báp.*"[3]

I have been very unwell for the last two months, until the row in India broke out, and since then we have been in a constant turmoil of hope, anxiety, and task-work.

Such a bother you can scarce imagine. In the Punjab alone sixteen regiments of infantry and three of regular cavalry have gone wrong. There are yet twelve of the former left, and they are not to be trusted; the irregular cavalry are also tainted. The sound birds are the eighteen Punjab and police regiments; they are all right The Punjab Cavalry have done no harm, but with

---

3. Father.

so many Poorbeas in them we do not feel comfortable.

In the north-west all has gone wrong—not a regiment is staunch, and most have broken out, and nearly all been collected and are fighting desperately at Delhi The Guides are down, behaving gloriously. Poor Q. Battye was mortally wounded on the 9th, the day they arrived. The men, both cavalry and infantry, have behaved famously. Muhammad Khan Resaldar killed a *Pailwan*[4] of the 3rd Cavalry, fighting hand to hand, and carried off his charger in triumph. He was made a "*Sirdar Bahadur*" on the spot

The Guides and Gurkhas and a few Sappers were the only native troops with the Europeans, but we are now sending down a considerable levy of Punjabis and more European troops. Rothney's Sikhs, Coke's Rifles, a corps of Punjab Cavalry, Green's Rifles, and Hughes' Corps will also go, the first sometime hence; but for Peshawur we should have sent both Vaughan's and Wilde's Rifles, but they have had to go there.

The troops intended for the China expedition have been summoned, and great reinforcements from England called for. By God's help we shall hold our own until they arrive, but it is all we can do. The mutineers make desperate sallies. On the 12th they left 400 dead behind them; Daly counted sixty in one heap who fell before the 60th and Guide Rifles.

All of this has been caused by almost a perfect delusion. The men have got into their heads that the Enfield rifle cartridges were rubbed in pigs' feet and cow grease, yet none of the ball cartridges had been issued to any of the corps in the north-west nor in the Punjab. General Anson died of cholera at Kurnal; Pat Grant came round as commander-in-chief; Cotton is made a brigadier-general, so is Nicholson, as a temporary measure; Neville Chamberlain acting as adjutant-general.

Few officers have been killed in the fight, but many have been assassinated—none in the Punjab. All our chiefs [5] have behaved famously; those of the Cis Sutlej beyond all praise.

We have told the *amir* to give you all the money you can ask for, and that it shall be paid down on demand along with his monthly *lac*.

---

4. Strong man or wrestler.
5. *i.e.* native chiefs.

H. B. Edwardes to H. B. Lumsden.

Peshawur, 20th June, 1857.

In reply to your letter of the 20th May, I send you a humble apology from the chief-commissioner, who promises to write to you once a month. Things have gone on badly since I last wrote. The force, after arriving at Delhi and opening with a splendid dash, taking twenty-six guns, was unable to do much. There were not enough men or guns or gunners for a siege; and European soldiers too valuable for a *coup de main*, in General Barnard's opinion; so they sat down and screamed for reinforcements as we did at Mooltan in 1848. So the enemy comes out and attacks them, and gets jolly well thrashed, and loses hundreds to our one in every affair; and then goes home to dinner. . . . A reinforcement of 3600 men (more than General Barnard has now) is on the way from the Punjab, and will all have dropped in before the 1st July, when they will be able, I trust, to storm Delhi and strike the first great blow for the pacification of the country. Great disorganization has taken place in the north-west provinces. The Supreme Government is active, and pushing up European regiments as fast as they come. The Guides seem to carry off the palm from all the troops at Delhi; and I hear that the mutual cheering between them and the Europeans on their arrival was a sound to be heard.

Alas! poor Battye has fallen, and Kennedy is wounded. Soobuhdar Major Mirwan Sing is killed. Muhammad Khan Resaldar of Peshawur has defeated the leader of the 3rd Cavalry in single combat, plundered his carcase, and ridden off with his horse. He has been made a *Sirdar Bahadur*. It is evident that our troops are animated by the greatest enthusiasm, and I believe it would be impossible for any amount of rebels to lick them.

But I begin to doubt whether we shall get Delhi before the rains, and then we shall have to hold on till reinforcements arrive from England in September; and it is probable that the state of the country will not improve meanwhile. Here at Peshawur we are strong, and confident, not in Jack Sepoy, like . . . . and other great generals, but in our resources. I have raised a good lot of levies, and that has done good in several ways, and I have got 700 Mooltanee horse (here and close by) from the Derajat, and more coming; and every day patches up the rents in our garments.

The 55th, who fled to Swât, were deemed unconstitutional by Lords and Commons, though the king wanted them; so the quarrel ended in the 55th being walked out *via* Boneyr, *en route* to Cashmere, as they say, but more likely to piecemeal starvation and death. Also the king is turned out; and the Akhoond left alone with his *mooreeds*.[6] The Punjab is very quiet as yet.

The most astounding pieces of common sense have lately been enacted:—

Sir Patrick Grant to be Chief in Bengal

Chamberlain, officiating Adjutant-general.

Cotton, Brigadier-general.

Nicholson, Brigadier-general in command of movable column in Punjab....

Are not these glorious appointments? The one better thing would have been Sir Henry as Commander-in-Chief.

Oudh is said to be in a state of disorder, but we know of two new European regiments having reached Cawnpore.

It will just be as much as we can do to hold India till the reinforcements come from England; but I have no doubt that it will be done—and then, hurrah! for a new army and new ideas....

Your diaries are exactly the right sort of thing, and would have elicited rounds of applause at any other time than this, when we are fighting for existence.

Crawford Chamberlain has got great credit for the way in which he disarmed the Mooltan brigade.

McAndrew, Ricketts,[7] and Ouseley[8] are the civil officers who have come to the front in this affair from the ranks of the "unknown men."

I cannot think that the English diplomatists have concurred in the appointment of Sooltan Jan at Herat, because I see he leaves a hostage at Teheran; otherwise I don't think it a bad go. He is a Baruckzye, and, say what he may now, must be an enemy to Persia in his heart, more or less. I have always, however, said with you that the best thing would be to leave the nomination to the *Ameer* of Cabul.

P.S.—I have heard of Mrs. E.'s safe arrival in England in greatly better health.

---

6. Disciples.

7. George Ricketts, C..B., at that time Deputy-Commissioner of Loodiana.

8. Gore Ouseley, Deputy-Commissioner of Shahpore.

In the midst of his anxieties nothing pleased Lumsden more than the receipt about this time of a letter from Lord Dalhousie, who had always been a constant friend since their meeting at Peshawar.

FROM LORD DALHOUSIE TO H. B. LUMSDEN.

London, 6th June, 1857.

I commit this sheet to Sir John Lawrence (doubting the regularity of the *Dost's* post office) in the hope that he will be able to convey it safely to you, so that you may not suppose me insensible to your remembrance of me, or ungrateful for your letter of the 3rd March. I would have replied before now, but I have been in such poor condition for some months past that I was not able to write to anybody.

The Government paid you a high compliment in selecting you for so difficult, so confidential, and so unsafe a duty as that on which you are employed. It showed its good sense in the selection, and I have not the slightest doubt that you will fully justify their choice.

The conclusion of peace with Persia will probably have the effect of curtailing your mission.

I shall be glad to hear of you all back again; for though nobody is more able to make his hand take care of his head than you are, I don't think our dear friends the Afghans are just the folk "to ride the water wi'."

My long illness and my lameness together keep me so completely out of the world that I know little of what has been going on even in Indian affairs. My interest in them, however, can never cease, and as long as my interest in them lasts the Guides will have a foremost place in my remembrance.

Remember me kindly to Quintin Battye when you get back to them, and convey my good wishes to the corps.

Good luck go with you, my dear Lumsden, and

Believe me always, sincerely yours,

Dalhousie.

No pen can record the feelings of Harry Lumsden as time went on. He had applied to the Governor-General to be relieved, but before his letter could arrive communication between Calcutta and the Punjab had been cut off, and postal organization was totally disorganized. The Governor-General, however, and the Commissioner on the frontier, considered that, valuable as Lumsden's services would be with the

Guides, his retention in Afghanistan at such a crisis was absolutely necessary in the interests of the empire.

"*Kismut*,"[9] as Muhammadans would say, was the only term Lumsden could apply to his position, though he accepted the ruling of an all-wise Providence. But as comrade after comrade amongst the officers—European and native—and the men of the Guides fell in the service of their country, the constant strain was almost too heavy to be borne by the man who had raised them.

Edwardes, on the 30th June, thus continued the tale of 1857:—

> Your diary of 5th to 11th June just in, and I shall send off the budget of papers accumulated for you, though I had hoped to be able to tell you in this despatch of the fall of Delhi
>
> It soon became apparent to Generals Barnard and Seed that their force of about 4000 men was insufficient to take Delhi. It might get in, but would be lost in the city afterwards, so they did not attempt it . . . and called for reinforcements. . . .
>
> Sir John sent 4000 more men, more guns, and more gunners. Meanwhile the miscellaneous stations of the country contributed their little mutinies to the general disorder, so that the N.W.P. became disorganized as a civil government, and passed chiefly under military law. The rebels in Delhi got reinforcements from all these sources, and amused themselves every other day with a skirmish, and a general action once a week on *bhang*[10] and opium days.
>
> The results have been uniform—a most disproportionate loss to the enemy, a trifling one to us. Our troops have been in high spirits, but hottish and overworked. . . . The Punjab reinforcements began to arrive on the 23rd, and were all to be at Delhi by the 1st July; and we suppose that after that they will close in, batter the wall for a day, and storm the place. Very earnestly I hope that it will be successful, and have no doubt it will; if not, I have advised Sir John not to make bad worse by sending more men from the Punjab, but recall the headquarters to the Sutlej, and drop the curtain on the summer campaign No. 1.
>
> It is of more consequence to keep the Punjab all right than to recover Delhi It will help the Government more when the troops arrive from England. For the same reason the General

---

9. Fate.

10. A preparation of the hemp plant..

(Cotton) and I refuse to give any more men from here, for we know well that this is the anchor by which the ship rides.

All this constant skirmishing at Delhi could not go on without loss of officers as well as men, and deeply grieved will you be to hear of poor Quintin Battye having been killed He was mortally wounded in the groin, and died in a day, I believe. Poor lad, he must have a quotation:

> *Dolce et decorum est*
> *Pro patria mori.*[11]

Daly also has been wounded, but not badly, and will soon be up again. . . .

Chamberlain reached Delhi on the 24th, and has got fever. Kennedy of the Guides likewise wounded. Daly bears witness to K. being a first-rate officer.

The Guides have done constant deeds of valour, and reached a pinnacle of fame. Coke's Corps must now try to catch them up.[12]

Ditto Rothney's 4th Sikhs. The Jheend *rajah's* small force has behaved as well as any of our own; and that McAndrew, who heads them, ought to be knighted. But they work him to death.

Unfortunately this delay leads fools astray. The Gwalior contingent has, we hear, mutinied; but it does not appear whether they are negatively rebellious at home, or actively coming to help the mutineers at Delhi.

Today we have heard that all was well at Lucknow and Allahabad up to the 22nd June, which is a great blessing. I fancy that many of the native troops at Lucknow have mutinied; but two or three European regiments had arrived from Calcutta, and enabled dear old Sir Henry to hold his own. . . .

The China four regiments will be in Calcutta in a fortnight The English reinforcements not till the end of August, I fear.

The next two or three months will be very anxious ones to us all; but I believe that with all our shortcomings in India our countrymen have been doing good, and will not be abandoned by God in this pinch Our empire was unsafe, resting on rotten piles, and it was necessary to unroof and unfloor us to show where we were. This has been done, and though we shall suffer

---

11. Referring to Battye's well-known love of quotations and the fact that he died with these words on his lips.
12. *Cf.* chapter 9.

a good deal, I have no sort of doubt as to our ultimate triumph. Here at Peshawur all is very quiet and satisfactory. As usual, I have enlisted the country! Nothing is more surprising than the strength of this frontier in the crisis, yet there are not wanting men who doubt its real advantage to the empire.

Goodbye. Don't be over anxious. It is a stiff storm, but, please God, we shall come safe to port.

CHAPTER 20

Letters from Edwardes, 21st July to 9th August, 1857

After a lapse of three weeks Edwardes again writes to Candahar:—

H. B. EDWARDES TO H. B. LUMSDEN.

Peshawur, 21st July, 1857.

How I wish I could tell you that Delhi has been taken! It still holds out; nor have we made an attempt even to take it. Our army still sits before Delhi, and the mutineers have continued coming out offering battle, being beaten with vast loss, and offering battle again two or three days afterwards with the same result It seems to me that this is providential It very much resembles Sebastopol. The lamented "delay" there was the means of exhausting the resources of all Russia. So with Delhi; all the mutinous brigades concentrate on Delhi as a drain concentrates filth, and we destroy them in hundreds and thousands, as in no other way probably could we ever have done. Meanwhile in the north-west provinces all the native army has gradually gone wrong, and betaken itself to Delhi as above described. . . . In the Punjab, one by one, every native Poorbeah regiment has been disarmed, except the 21st N.I. and Kilát-i Ghilzyes at Peshawur. . . .

At Sealkote the 46th N.I. and 9th Cavalry broke out before called on, and had a tremendous flare up; did many brutal things; wonderful escapes occurred; kind things also were done to ladies and children in the most contradictory manner, and in the end after some days Nicholson destroyed them on an island in the Ravee.

So this brings us to the end of that stage of the revolt—there are hardly any more to rebel! ...

It is quite wonderful—incomprehensible—that such a vast army so highly organized and so splendidly armed should have rebelled in the worst spirit, and been able to do so little. God has certainly brought them and their designs to nought, and probably the grand intent of all is to let the Hindoo and Muhammadan do their worst, and fail for good.

You will be sorry to hear that Neville Chamberlain is slightly wounded in the arm; also little Walker,[1] of the Engineers—all doing well.

Swât is quiet and neighbourly; and Mokurrum Khan and his *Kluk Spors* to join a troop I am sending down to Delhi with *our* green flag and a gold-fish on it!

Peshawur is cutting up *nimak-hulâl*[2] in the most astounding manner. You would not have expected the citizens to subscribe five *lakhs* to the Punjab 6 *per cent* Loan, I suppose? But they are doing it Kazee Gholam Kadir, with a saddle-bag of *boodkees*,[3] led off! It is true one banker fled to the hills, and died of a *coup de soleil* on arrival; but everyone says he was a misguided man. There are some troublesome intrigues going on between the Khyberies and some of our soldiery, which give me a little anxiety, but otherwise the frontier has turned out a trump.

---

1. Lieutenant J. T. Walker, Bombay Engineers, afterwards General Walker, C.B., Surveyor-General of India, was at one time a member of the Guides mess at Murdân. He was always attended by dust-coloured Guides, as he indefatigably laboured to map our newly-acquired territory, and pushed into every valley of the surrounding hills, seeking for the frontier.

In such employ, in securing vantage points for observation, the whiz of a *juzail* or matchlock bullet was so unmistakable a notice to quit, that he and his men had not unfrequently to shoulder the theodolite or other instrument and make themselves scarce.

In every military expedition this keen soldier turned up as a sapper, ready to construct swing or other bridges, blow up towers, or any other work allotted to him.

In the course of time, on the completion of a great portion of his invaluable work, he improved the appearance of his map by a pretty scarlet line along his frontier. No sooner, however, did the penetrating eye of Dalhousie fall on that line, than an official document asked the pertinent question, "Who authorized this lieutenant to define the limits of the British Empire?"

2. Faithful to its salt.

3. Gold pieces.

Sir John has gone to Lahore. Sir Henry all well up to the 21st June.

The whole of the troops here are dressed in *khâkee*. All the world's pay is to fall three months into arrears, except such chaps as you.

Heat frightful, 95° at night

As to your coming back, my idea is that you should not move till the *tide turns,* and then we can announce either Delhi fallen or grand reinforcements, and prestige all up again, etc., etc; and there can be no mistake about the movement *Then* I would have you come down gracefully, and take part in the *tamashah* of the next winter. Depend upon it, your premature withdrawal would be very prejudicial even to the Cabul Government

Whenever we get you safe back we shall give the *ameer* a "*Shookuránuh*"[4] of two or three months' allowance probably.

Two or three water-melons have turned up with queer seeds, with white marks like writing on them, and they are selling for three *annas* each, as miraculous documents bearing on the present crisis. . . . May I be able to give you more decisive and victorious news next letter.

Most thoughtlessly just now have I torn open a fat letter for you from Kennedy, without seeing the direction. As soon as I got to "My dear old Joe!" I shut up, as no one calls me by that good old Scotch lover's name! Pray excuse.

H. B. Edwardes to H. B. Lumsden.

Peshawur, 27th July, 1857.

Since I wrote last to you the clouds blackened terribly, and Brigadier Wilson, commanding the army at Delhi, began to threaten a retreat Sir John once more began pouring down reinforcements from the Punjab, and sent them off with Nicholson, who by this time is at Loodianah. . . .

Things looked very dismal. The old story, *Man's necessity is God's opportunity*. Up came a letter from Sir P. Grant to Lieutenant Boisragon, dated July 11th, Cawnpore, saying all was well, and he had reached that far with six European regiments, and was marching on Delhi after sending help to Lucknow! This was like a sky of brass opening and pouring down rain. We could not imagine before what had become of all the European regi-

---

4. A thank-offering.

ments between Delhi and the sea. Now we know that they are setting towards Delhi with a strong spring tide, and I feel that the corner is turned, for soon the English succours will come rolling in, and only fighting remain. Fighting is all well enough when you have men, but it is dreadful to find you have to fight *without*.

Your letter of 8th came in on 25th, which is better than formerly, but still slow as a top. I think my last letter broke off just as James and Vaughan were *going* to attack Narinjee. Well, they went in and surprised it, and killed fifty men dead on the spot, and seven more have since died, and only lost four dead themselves and eighteen wounded. The result was better than any other affair I remember, and as report says James killed three Princes of Orange with his own hand, we propose to recommend him to the Queen for next Field-marshal. The *Molvee's* standard was taken, with a lot of *Koran* embroidered on it. The *Molvee* himself, with the whole *Koran*, escaped up the hill.

In spite of all this the *Molvee* has returned to Narinjee, and it is not convenient to go there again just now, because we have been obliged to subscribe Wilde's corps to Delhi So I daresay the old General, when he goes larking about Yusafzai, will take a shy at the place *en passant*. Several 55th NX fellows were among the slain. Nothing very new at Delhi or anywhere else, except that poor Chamberlain's wound turns out to be a broken arm instead of a slight cut General Seed obliged to go off sick.

The Calcutta *Gazette* of 18th June announces the exchange of ratified treaties with Persia at Baghdad on 2nd May, "and the entire withdrawal of the British forces from the soil and the waters of Persia awaits only the fulfilment of the conditions of peace which were accepted by the plenipotentiary of Persia on her behalf." So that's how *you* stand!

A telegram just in says that some "*Nana Sahib*" (I fancy an officer of the Gwalior Court who heads the rebels against us . . .) has been jolly well defeated, and lost twelve guns and seven *lakhs* of *rupees*, which our people took. This was on 12th July. . . . As soon as ever things get triumphant, I shall get you down. There will be a world of good things going, in the shape of roving commissions, for the next cold weather; and I hope you will be in time to put in your trenchant blade, and Peter too. . . .

The English mail as yet thinks little of the mutiny, and we shall get their storm when we are getting into smooth water ourselves.

Sooltân Muhammad Khan and the other "Peshawur *sirdars*" have been trying to stir up the Akhoond of Swât against us, but without effect

I don't think there is anything more to tell you, and I am as tired as a dog. I don't know what to do first, or when I have done the last All functions seem to belong to my unhappy department, and I am very weary of the whole whirl and worry. As soon as it is over I shall go and take a rest for two years, for I am dead sick of work in this unreasonable quantity. Whoever wants the commissionership of Peshawur may have it with my blessing.

Still, I am glad I was not anywhere else in this row. I should have been sorry if I had been on furlough. It is well to be of use to poor old John Company in his "last campaign." Depend on it, this finishes his career. Crown ministers may now try their hands. Will they do as well?

H. B. EDWARDES TO H. B. LUMSDEN.

Peshawur, 4th August, 1857.

I am still unable to tell you that Delhi has fallen; on the contrary, there is some little anxiety for our small force there during the few days that can now intervene till Nicholson can arrive with reinforcements from the Punjab (about 10th or 11th) and Grant from the eastward (about 15th, I calculate). The Sacrificial Eed of the Muhammadans fell on Sunday, the 2nd, and it was expected that either then or soon after the rebels would make a grand effort to crush our force, which has been literally reduced by victories and some sickness to a low pitch. The mutineers on the other hand have been reinforced by the Neemuch troops. Sir John is evidently very nervous about the crisis, and has rather overdone himself in sending succours accordingly. However, *that* is a fault on the right side perhaps, and I have myself no fear of our force being obliged to retreat

It has all the impetus of knowing that friends are near, and coming from both sides. Grant brings six regiments, and Nicholson 4000 men, and so I suppose their arrival will be the signal for an assault, which with the blessing of God will demolish the mutinous army. It is clear to everyone that the delay which we have been so lamenting has been made by an overruling Providence the greatest thing in our favour. One after another the rebel regiments have been attached to the vortex, and got themselves gradually buried in successive fights. It is no longer every station that we have to recover, but Delhi alone. The future peace of the country would have been much more remote if we had had to hunt brigades over Bengal.

The incident of the last week has been the outbreak of 26th N.I. at Lahore. Tired of doing nothing, and having no arms, they killed their C.O. with a hatchet and then took to the bush. They were pursued, and out of 600, 500 have been killed. Also the Syuds of Kahgan have bagged the remaining 250 of 55th N.I. and sent them in to Becher. . . . I have heard from Chamberlain, who is getting on well, and hopes to sit up in ten days. This morning has brought James's report of attack No. 2 on Narinjee. It took place yesterday. The *Molvee* had received large succours from Ghinglai and Punjtar, and great preparations had been made to receive us on this occasion. But that astute fellow James found out a back road and sent one column up it; column No. 2 advanced in front as usual.

The Ghazees see their victims approaching, as they think, like fatted calves. They rejoice mightily in their small numbers; they leap, they howl, they curse, they wave their thirsty scimitars in the morning sun, they glory in the cheap and easy "martyrdom "which is theirs today, they split the air with Púshtú yells and—*hilloa!* what sounds are those? A British cheer! The peak above the "martyrs'" heads is swarming with smock-frocks and rifles! "The mountain path's betrayed! Fly for your lives!" The *Molvee* runs like ordinary men; the flags fold up like pocket-handkerchiefs; the breastworks are abandoned with a scream of fright—and the Ghazee army bolts without a blow! Our chaps hadn't a chance to catch them. Twenty who were run over by their friends were taken prisoners, and more than that number fell to rifle shots.

The elephants were then brought up, and levelled every house; the trees and wells were blown up, and the place left at noon a miserable spectacle. The Narinjee army showed no more. No one knows where or when they stopped. It's said they are running still with fanatical devotion—doomed to be never out of breath or danger! We had one *sepoy* killed and three wounded by random shots; not a European touched. Really it was quite a mercy. This affair will do the district good.

Goolab[5] is sending 5000 men to help at Delhi The *ameer* is anxious to do something of the kind, and perhaps some cavalry would be acceptable; but when all is over, and the "little bill" comes in, I should not like to pay Peshawur for it Any little pecuniary consideration would not matter.

...The position of the Persians at Herat is rather unaccountable. I wish they would be off.

H. B. Edwardes to H. B. Lumsden.

Peshawur, 8th August, 1867.

Maharaja Goolab Sing died on the 2nd instant after an illness of only two days, so I have just learnt by a telegram from Lahore. I had heard before of his son having been suddenly summoned.

This event *may*, or may not, prove inconvenient to us. The young prince is supposed to be inimical to us, but I think he will find himself in difficulties, and will be glad of our friendship.

How can I now tell you the dreadful loss we have all suffered? Our dear Sir Henry was wounded on the 2nd July, and died on the 4th July at Lucknow. There is no room for doubt or hope. We have all lost a friend, a master, an example—a second father.

The Punjab, India, England has lost the noblest of public servants. Anything so distressing as this I have not yet heard, though Heaven knows there has been no lack of bloodshed. Thousands, black and white, will mourn him. *For* him indeed we cannot grieve, for he was a humble and sincere Christian, prepared to die at any time, and he has died at last for his country. But, for ourselves, we must lament all our lives, for never shall we see his like again. Now and then only, like meteors, such men are born, and those who happen to see and know them are most fortunate. It is a standard of public and private worth, which elevates our own while thinking of it I am sure you will be most dreadfully grieved. There is no getting over it; it remains a lifelong regret....

Daly writes that their own position at Delhi is quite one of ease and security. They have made their pickets and out-posts and batteries all as snug as can be, and suffer little annoyance, while

---

5. *i.e.* Maharaja Gulab Sing of Cashmere.

the enemy is disheartened and bolting in large numbers, plundered by every village of Goojurs and Goalas as they pass. Nakedness is not believed; they are turned over and over for some hidden copper that has yet escaped. Norman writes the same. On the *Eed* the priests roused the mutineers to a grand effort, and the firing lasted from sunset of the 1st to sunrise on the 2nd; but the rebels never once had the pluck to come close, and were shelled and graped and rifled till they own they lost 500 dead, while our casualties were only 46 killed and wounded. In short, all accounts agree that the rebels are worn out, and that our fellows are just comfortable. The Europeans play leapfrog whenever the rain stops, and not a faint heart in camp.

Nicholson would soon arrive and raise the mercury still higher, and I should not wonder if they go at Delhi without waiting for Grant (whose approach, I fear, was prematurely announced), for Havelock's must have been the leading column, as he speaks of Sir P. Grant "soon being in the field." Altogether I feel quite easy about Delhi now, and only turn my thoughts to this sad loss of dear Sir Henry. God grant it may yet turn out untrue.

You will be sorry to hear that poor Travers of Coke's corps was shot through the head on the *Eed* day, and died in a few hours, leaving a young wife at Lahore.

our brother[6] has been recommended for the second in command, and Norman writes to Sir John that "Chamberlain and Coke have both begged me to urge that Lumsden be at once appointed second in command in poor Travers' room. I assure you he is a good specimen of one of the best of families." Strangely enough, I had a few days before recommended Sir John to give your brother not half but a whole regiment, on the same ground of reliance. This is complimentary to two of our friends at Candahar, whose names I withhold to spare their blushes.

I don't think I have anything more to tell you. All in the Punjab is quiet. I wish I could hope to be able in any future letter to contradict this mournful news of Sir Henry's death.

The reports you have heard of our leaving Peshawur were all false, and I hope will never be realized. Goodbye, and God take care of you all.

---

6. William.

CHAPTER 21

Position of the mission at Candahar

A fortnight later Edwardes again writes:—

H. B. Edwardes to H. B. Lumsden.

Peshawur, 19th August, 1857.

Doubts are still entertained by some people of dear Sir Henry's death, but from a letter of Lord Canning's to Sir John I see that the news came *in a letter from Lucknow* to General Neill at Allahabad, who sent it to Calcutta, so I do not venture to entertain any hope. The feeling of sorrow is universal from one end of the country to the other; and, indeed, not merely public life, but the world, seems no longer the same thing to those who had so long been wont to look to Sir Henry as their chief. General Havelock had another fight between Cawnpoor and Lucknow, and took twenty guns; but he must have found it a stiff job, for he was waiting for reinforcements from Cawnpoor before going on to Lucknow. [1]

Sir John has a rumour that General H. reached Lucknow "too late," and all Europeans massacred. But I believe it was impossible to have got this news in the time, and hope we shall soon hear either of his having brought away all Europeans to Cawnpoor, or else of his being able to leave them with fresh troops, plenty of provisions, repaired defences, and raised spirits, and then push on to Delhi Nicholson has reached Delhi, and writes

---

1. For further reading on this subject, *A Lady's Escape from Gwalior*, republished as *The Memsahib and the Mutiny*, by R. M. Coopland, *The Cawnpore Man* by Mowbray Thompson, (one of the only four survivors), *Ladies of Lucknow* by G. Harris and Adelaide Case and *Reminiscence of the Indian Mutiny 1857-59* by William Forbes-Mitchell are also published by Leonaur.

that the tide has turned there very decidedly in our favour, and that as soon as a siege-train arrives from Ferozepoor they will assault Delhi at once, unless the southern reinforcements are so near as to be worth waiting for. Chamberlain is doing well.

All is quiet in Cashmere, and no sort of excitement seems to have followed Goolab Sing's death. The Kookeekheyls have come in and given security for their fine of 3000 *rupees* for the murder of poor Lieutenant Hand, and are now busy in politely expelling from the Khyber one Syud Ameer Badshah (a tadpole of the Koonnur spawn, hatched at Acheenee in Peshawur valley, and for many years a wandering enthusiast at Teheran, Cabul, Constantinople, and Mecca), who has come down from the Shinwaree country with a flag and a *Koran* and a suit of clothes, and expects people well off to kick up a row to please him. The Kookeekheyls say they don't like killing him, as he is a Syud . . but they don't mind kicking him out of the pass.

It seems to me that the religious spirit of these parts has become overlaid with a love of money, and that it would really take a great man and a powerful to raise a crescentade against us. The *ameer* might do it, for instance, but not Peter the Hermit! There is hardly any crime in the district or cantonments. As yet the health of the troops here is unusually good. The English soldiers here are much excited at the reports that have come from Cawnpoor of the brutalities practised on the poor European women there in the massacre of Wheler, etc. . . . . Steamers are bringing up troops and landing them at Cawnpoor, and it was expected that a division would move from thence towards Delhi on the 8th or 9th.

The Gwalior contingent is the only body of disciplined troops which has not yet joined the rebels, so that the material of the rebellion has been well-nigh used up, and all accounts agree that the Delhi rebels are melting away. The police-magistrates will have to pick the bones of the mutiny. I am puzzled about these Persians at Herat, and can only suppose that the Persian Prince, hearing of our Indian troubles, has taken on himself to wait for fresh instructions. . . . .

You are evidently very anxious to return, but I do not think it could be prudently done till our star is more in the ascendant again than now. Under the smoke of the fall of Delhi you might be gracefully withdrawn.

H. B. Edwardes to H. B. Lumsden.

Peshawur, 28th August, 1857.

I was very glad to get your letter announcing the evacuation of Herat, at last, by the Persians, as their movements were getting rather suspicions. . . . Fever has at last overtaken me, though not badly, and I cannot write you much of a stave; but am happy to tell you Nicholson went after a force of mutineers at Nujafgurh, twenty miles west of Delhi, on the 25th, and gave them a disastrous licking, taking twelve guns. Well done, our man! Sir John has been to Julundhur to review 3000 Jummoo troops, who started afterwards for Delhi in good spirits. At this point of the game they are probably to be trusted. 14,000 men were leaving England for India, which, with 5000 China troops, gives us 19,000. . . . All is quiet in the Punjab, thank God, and the siege train expected at Delhi from Ferozepoor about the 1st September, when probably they won't wait for down-country reinforcements.

Sickness much on the increase here, and chiefly among the Europeans, unfortunately, so that in a day or two I expect we shall have to put a black regiment or two in irons, of which the General is making up 2000 on speculation. His activity of mind and body, his vigilance and determination, are great; but either his high qualities are not known at the Horse Guards, or he has no friends. . . .

We have no further news from Lucknow, and are very anxious about Havelock. I know you are all tired of Candahar, and want to return; but you will agree, I think, that Delhi should first fall before you move, so that your march may be a triumph—not a retreat. Did I tell you that the Kookeekheyls turned out the "*Badshah*" after feeding him respectfully for five days?

I had written this much when *bundooks*[2] began going, and we all scuttled to our respective posts. The 51st N.I. being ordered to encamp on the parade in front of the British regimental barracks, didn't like it, and when the new Sikh regiment was at dinner made a dash at Khalsa's[3] arms. Khalsa drops his curry and goes in at Pandy; kills fifty in the ring at once; 51st bolt to the country; pursuit in every direction; number of Pandys killed and more made prisoners, and old James still riding about

2. Rifles.
3. Meaning the Sikhs.

the *mehrah*[4] with a flock of Mooltânees. None of our people hurt The cantonment magistrate and some young officer were mobbed by the Pandys, who tried to drown them in a pond, but fat saved them—they floated! This is a good job (unless it brings back my fever), for we have got rid of a corps, and shall put another in irons.

Sic transit gloria Pandi.

What a dull life you fellows must lead at Candahar!

And how accustomed one gets here to a row like this of a morning, which a year ago would have startled India.

Goodbye; all health to you and a quick return to the bosom of the native army.

P.S.—The co-operation of chiefs and people was instantaneous and cheerful, particularly after hearing that Pandy had no muskets!

Drumhead courts-martial sitting now on the prisoners. Sharp's the word with Cotton.

Edwardes was right in saying that the life of the Lumsdens at Candahar must be dull. It was so in truth in comparison to that of British officers at Peshawur, or in the disturbed parts of India. There was something, however, stirring in the air of Afghanistan that might lead, at any moment, to excitement enough, a something which cannot perhaps be described in words, but which, in trying times, has been felt by most men. The prolonged operations before Delhi were creating want of confidence in our supremacy.

Rumours of disasters to our arms were following each other quickly, and were being spread far and wide. The Persians, instead of retiring on Mashad, halted on the banks of the Heri-rud, giving out their intention of attacking the Turkomans at Merve. The heir-apparent placed no reliance on Persia, and was ready to believe that the state of affairs in India might lead to the reoccupation of Herat, regardless of treaty obligations.

News came from Cabul that the *amir* was being urged by the priesthood and others to seize the opportunity of our being in difficulties to declare a *Crescentade* and sweep down the Khyber. All this made Ghulam Haidar very anxious. Despatch after despatch was hurried off by him, and every argument was pressed on his father praying him not to be carried away by popular feeling, but to maintain his treaty with

---

4. Plain..

the British Government. Fortunately, just about that time a payment of three *lakhs* of *rupees* (three months' subsidy) had been received by the *amir*, and this fact no doubt materially assisted in keeping the vessel of state steady.

Ghulam Haidar himself was rapidly failing in health. Dr. Bellew was in constant attendance, and considered there was much ground for anxiety. Lumsden had made up his mind as to how he would act under the various emergencies which might arise. In the event of the closure of the Cabul and Quetta routes, he had secured promises of assistance from more than one of the disaffected chiefs on the Herat and Seistan borders.

Meanwhile news was received that a *kossid*, carrying the post from Peshawur, had been attacked and murdered by robbers near Mukkur. The delay was most tantalizing, as tidings of the fall of Delhi were hourly expected, as well as an order recalling the mission; but the mail-bag eventually reached Candahar on the 20th September, bringing news from Delhi up to the 1st. One of the letters was from John Nicholson.[5] It will be seen that it conveyed to the Lumsdens the announcement of the death of their well-loved brother William! who was killed in action at Nujufgurh, before Delhi, on 25th August.

JOHN NICHOLSON TO H. B. LUMSDEN.

Before Delhi, 1st September, 1857.

My dear Lumsden,—It is with great grief I have to communicate news which will be a sore trial to you and Peter. You will not have been wholly unprepared for it, for you know that hard fighting has been going on here for some time.

Your poor brother was killed at the head of his regiment in action on the 25th. He died nobly doing his duty, and sincerely regretted by the whole army. His last words, as he fell dying to the ground, were ones of encouragement to his men and officers. He was in command of the corps at the time, Coke having been wounded and Travers killed in previous actions.

We shall assault before the 10th most probably, and I hope that his and other losses will be amply avenged. Give my love to Peter. You have my sympathy with you more than I can express. Ever, dear Joe,

Yours very sincerely,   John Nicholson.

No letters were received at this time, nor by the next post, from

5. The last received from him by Lumsden.

194

Edwardes, who had hitherto written regularly. The following was from Sir John Lawrence, dated Lahore, 9th September:—

Your poor brother William's death will be a great blow to you and Peter. He was a fine young fellow, and a very promising soldier. These are sad times. There is not one of us who has not lost some near and dear relative; many who have lost several How it is all to end God only knows. The crisis at Delhi seems now to have arrived. Within the next two or three days the assault must come off.

By this day month troops from England will be pouring in, and Pandie's time will have come. It is sad to think how much misery might have been saved if we had had 10,000 more European troops in India, though 30,000 will scarcely now suffice to make all straight I have written twice to Calcutta, proposing the return of the mission, but it takes a weary time to get a reply; nothing under three months. At one time messages came round by Madras. I hope, however, when Delhi falls that the direct route will be clear. There will then be nothing of importance to stop communication.

Nicholson has done well He is the only officer who has done great things up here. He cut the 46th N.I. and the wing of the 9th Light Cavalry to pieces, and it was he who intercepted the Pandie force in their attempt to get round and intercept the siege train. He defeated some three or four thousand of them, and took all their guns.

General Havelock, however, has apparently done the most. He is said to have won nine actions, taken upwards of seventy guns, and killed several thousands of the insurgent soldiers.

He is now waiting for reinforcements to advance on Lucknow, which still holds out bravely.

CHAPTER 22

News of the Attack on Delhi on 14th September

On the 7th October the heir-apparent casually mentioned to Bellew that, in a letter just arrived from the *amir*, he had received the intelligence of a successful attack by the British on Delhi on the 14th September. Shortly afterwards Lumsden received the following letter from Edwardes:—

H. B. EDWARDES TO H. B. LUMSDEN.

Peshawur, 12th September, 1857.
I have delayed this *dawk* several days in hope of telling you of the fall of Delhi, the attack of which was fixed, as I heard from Nicholson, for the 10th instant But no news has yet come, and I can only conclude that the engineers miscalculated their time, and that the batteries could not be opened so soon. So I will begin writing, in the hope that before Monday (this is Saturday) I shall hear about it God grant that we have been successful, and that Nicholson and other props of our army may have been spared

What grief my last letters must have brought you. These blows are hard to bear. But what family of Englishmen can hope to escape without some such loss of relative or dear friend from a nation's calamity like this revolt? Happy indeed if only one life have to be mourned. I have heard of many people who have lost five or six—brothers and sisters and wife. The disasters in Cabul in 1841-2 were as nothing in comparison to the wholesale murders and butcheries which have been committed in this bloody '57. . . .

Monday, 14th September.—Still no news of the fall of Delhi; but all private letters speak of the assault as certain about 13th, 14th, or 15th. Our anxiety is intense—and the whole country feels the influence of it. Rebels and blackguards hover round the frontier in flocks like vultures to see what comes of the battle. There is nothing new in the state of Hindostan. The troops are crowding up, and in slow process of time will, of course, be seen by those who now disbelieve in their existence. Our Lucknow people still hold out, and will, I hope, be able to do so till Havelock can advance to relieve them. Sir Colin Campbell is pressing up the country, but I hope the imperial city will have given its mural crown ... long before he can approach it. There have been numerous and circumstantial reports that Sir Henry Lawrence was still alive. But Sir John says they are quite unfounded.

15th September, 1857.

Last evening, at 7 p.m., at last arrived the long-expected news that Delhi had been assaulted, and our troops were in, but fighting is still going on. This message was fired off by General Wilson at 10 a.m. on 14th, and got to us *via* Lahore in nine hours. You may imagine our intense anxiety for further news! It is now noon, and the second message has come from Lahore. It runs thus:

> It is now 8 a.m. Yesterday at 7 p.m. we had from the Cashmere to the Cabul gate; fighting inside was still very severe. Many officers killed and wounded. Both the Nicholsons severely—the latter has lost an arm. The 1st Fusiliers charged a battery four times, and at last took it.

Thank God, then, that the battle has gone for us, and that the lives of those two glorious Nicholsons are spared to their country.

We could not hope to take such a fortress with such a small force for nothing. And many lives of fine fellows will yet be lost in completing the victory; but I trust the victory is now assured, and that at last, after four months' paralysis, we have rolled back the tide of rebellion with our own resources—by the strength of the Punjab—without a man, or a round of ammunition, or a *rupee* from Calcutta, or England. It is much to be *humbly-proud* of; if I may use such a phrase.

I can write no more; this is what I waited so long for, and fear you have been under anxiety at the long delay. It was worth waiting for.

P.S.—By the "latter" Nicholson I understand Charles, of course.

H. B. Edwardes to H B. Lumsden.

Peshawur, 21st September, 1857.

I am glad to be able to tell you that yesterday the palace of Delhi fell into our hands, the king and what they call the royal family having got tired of being shelled day and night from our mortars. We had also possession of the city up to the Ajmere Gate, and only the fraction from the Toorkuman to the Delhi Gate was still unoccupied. The rebel forces were broken and flying in every direction, and doubtless while I write the whole of Delhi is in British hands again. Royal salutes have been fired today throughout the Punjab in honour of this victory over mutiny. The tide of rebellion is at last effectually turned.

I cannot tell you in what direction the king has fled, but there seem only two courses open: either to repair to Oudh and hoist the flag in the plain, and flourish the scimitar and *Koran* for another month or two; or the rush to Agra and surrender to the first *chupprassee*,[1] and take his chance of being believed innocent. There is no lack of credulity in the present day. Old, unaccustomed to exercise or fatigue, without resources, without a capital city, without prestige, and encumbered by a troop of women too divine to be seen, too mortal to do without meat and drink, I daresay the last of the *Moghuls* will prefer imprisonment to martyrdom or a long march.

I have repeatedly urged your recall as soon as Delhi should fall, and Sir John tells me he has written several times to Government about it, but he will not recall you on his own responsibility. To relieve us of the appearance of keeping you against the stipulations, I have told the *vakeel* here to ask the *ameer's* wishes as to jour recall Your despatches of 3rd August are just in, and you appear to think the heir-apparent wishes your departure! in order that he may operate against Herat But I should think that, on the whole, the *ameer* would like to keep you as long as he can for the sake of the subsidy.

---

1. Bailiff's officer.

If our representatives at Teheran have concurred in the nomination of Sooltan Jân, it would not do for the *ameer* to act against Herat for the object of reinstating the family of Yar Muhammad.

H. B. Edwardes to H. B. Lumsden.

Peshawur, 23rd September, 1857.

It now appears that the *whole* city of Delhi was ours by the evening of the 20th September, and I send this off with the new and important item below:

Captain Hodson has brought in the king a prisoner to Delhi.

So ends the tragedy of the "Great *Moghul*." . . .

Sir John has relaxed his grasp on the treasuries. We are all to be two months instead of three in arrears.

There is nothing else to tell you, except that the fall of Delhi has sensibly cleared the political atmosphere, and the citizens of Peshawur propose to illuminate for two successive nights.

Government 6 *per cent*. Paper was selling at 25 *per cent*, discount a week ago, and is now risen to 10 *per cent*. On hearing of the king's capture it will perhaps come to par.

H. B. Edwardes to H. B. Lumsden.

Peshawur, 29th, September, 1857.

And now I have to tell you another dreadful death—poor dear John Nicholson! He died at 10.30 a.m. on the 23rd September. To the last I had hoped he would live. But he is really gone. We shall never shake his hand again. You can understand all I feel about it. Henry Lawrence and John N. were the father and brother of my public life. Both are gone.

General Cotton published a most feeling order about John Nicholson. . . . Everyone says the same, that even Delhi was dearly purchased at this price.

There is a little row in the Gogaira district. . . .

Otherwise the fall of Delhi seems to have had an instantaneous effect in tranquillizing the public mind. . . .

All here is quiet.

I put the question to the *ameer* as to his wishes, and he said he did not object to your staying a little beyond the agreement, if the subsidy staid too, and if it remained discretionary with him to give you all *congé*.

CHAPTER 23

Death of John Tower Lumsden
at Lucknow

Rumours from Cabul brought information to Candahar that at a *durbar* held by the *amir* in the early part of September, the Hafiz Ji,[1] supported by a gang of fanatical *mullahs* instigated in their turn by Sirdars Sultan Muhammad and Pir Muhammad, pressed upon Dost Muhammad the necessity of undertaking a religious war against the British. The moment was a critical one; the fate of Delhi was uncertain; the resolution of the aged ruler seemed for an instant to stagger. Sirdar Muhammad Azim, his second son, however, stemmed the torrent. He reminded his father and the chiefs of the power of the British Government, of the storms which had harmlessly burst over it; and he pointed out that failure might once again cost the *amir* his kingdom. He declared that self-aggrandisement alone had induced his uncles, the Peshawur brothers, to urge the *amir* to action.

The step was a bold one. The *durbar* was broken up. There was temporary estrangement between father and son, but after due reflection Muhammad Azim was reinstated in favour by the *amir* and his counsel accepted. Influenced also by the cool and determined bearing of Edwardes at Peshawur, the *amir* weathered the storm, which, indeed, entirely subsided on the fall of Delhi The glorious news of the success of our army, and the favourable turn of affairs in India, cheered the spirits of the British officers at Candahar and increased their hopes of early recall

Unfortunately Dr. Bellew, on the 23rd October, met with a bad accident, caused by the collapse of a vineyard wall while he was in the

---

1. High priest.

act of climbing over it. The outer bone of his left leg was broken and the ankle joint partially dislocated. The Lumsdens set the broken bone in a most artistic manner, as they thought, with the aid of Bellew's instructions. In the course of time, however, when it appeared that the junction was not quite straight, it was suggested that it might be well, according to the precepts laid down in a certain work on surgery, to rebreak and reset the leg, as the owner would certainly have done to one of his own patients. To this proceeding, however, Bellew altogether objected, and eventually, after about six weeks, he was able to walk again.

H. B. EDWARDES TO H. B. LUMSDEN.

Peshawur, 10th October, 1857.

Only time to tell you that Lucknow was relieved on the 25th September, and garrison rescued, place recovered, etc.

General Neill, alas! killed. Sir J. Outram slightly wounded.

Troops arriving in shiploads at Calcutta, Bombay, and Kurrachee.

I have been all day replying to some designing questions of the *ameer's*, or would have written you a long letter as usual, but there are so many *chits*[2] in this *dawk*[3] for you all that it does not matter.

H. B. EDWARDES TO H. B. LUMSDEN.

Peshawur, 24th October, 1857.

England is roused effectually, and we shall have enough troops to hold India while we reorganize the N. Army.

The item that strikes us in the mail is that three officers are sent *via* Persia on a mission to Herat. These are the commissioners, I presume, who were agreed on in the Treaty of Peace. But how exclusively the Persian politics are conducted by the *Home* Government, without consulting or even informing the Indian Government. At first sight one would think your mission had better have gone to Herat; but as Persian commissioners had to go along with the English ones, it could only be done from the Teheran side.

All this, however, will show the *Ameer* of Cabul the impropriety of his undertaking any hostilities against Heart. There can be

---

2. Letters.
3. Poet.

little doubt that any quarrels with Herat will be liable to English and Persian mediation, and the Cabul Government, being "friends of our friends" must abide by that arrangement How thankful the *ameer* ought to be that we have expelled Persia from Herat. . . .

You will be glad to observe, from the going on of fighting at Lucknow, that Havelock has not retired to Cawnpoor with the garrison of Lucknow, as many advocated, but is just regaining and holding the city, preparatory to reoccupation of Oudh. . . .

Lord Canning has published nice orders about the death of dear Sir Henry, the recovery of Lucknow and Delhi, and the services of Sir John. They are not so well *composed* as Lord Dalhousie's used to be, but they have more feeling and earnestness. . . .

Charles Nicholson is going on well at Meerut, thinking nothing of his lost arm, but all of his dear lost brother. He is a fine, noble fellow, so manly and yet so tender. He writes well with his left hand. . . .

The *Ameer* of Cabul is carrying on a diplomatic war with me about the hill tribes here, whom he claims as his *subjects*, and wants me to make no arrangements with them except through him. Fancy the Khyberees his subjects! I tell him he ran away from them last January, and his giving them *mowajibs*[4] without taking *revenue* is just "blackmail," and proves that the Khyberees are independent, as they say they are themselves.

H. B. Edwardes to H. B. Lumsden.

Peshawur, 2nd November, 1857.

Sir John, in reply to my entreaties that he would recall you on his own authority, says:—

> I would gladly see the mission back again in India, but cannot recall it myself. Having no idea of the Government's views and intentions, I may only do mischief. Our officers therefore must stay where they are, unless indeed the *ameer* should write, clearly showing that he desires their return.

So you see I have done all in my power. It only remains now to see if Government will answer our numberless applications and hints.

---

4. Allowances.

Meanwhile, if Hyder says he is astonished, you must say that, "*bumoojib ahid-namuh*,"[5] the mission was to stay till the war was over with Persia, and the war will be reckoned quite over only when the conditions of peace are quite fulfilled; to ascertain which a commission has gone to Herat to see if it is empty of Persians, and till that ceremony is over the Bombay troops do not retire from the Persian soil, but defile the "*Khâk-i-Pâk-i-Irân*"[6] at Bundur Busheer, and so you can only suppose that you are to retire from Candahar when the "Ducks"[7] retire from Busheer.

This is the only way in which *I can keep the treaty for Government*, and officially it's all correct; but in common sense I think your mission should have returned when the Treaty of Peace with Persia was duly ratified.

All goes well in Hindostan. The condition of things now may be summed up as a pursuit, except at Lucknow, where Havelock has had his hands full, but stuck to the place like a brick. The Delhi movable column must have got down and joined him about now, after thrashing the rebels at Agra.

Reinforcements too are now arriving thickly at Allahabad from England, so the Oudh province will soon be reconquered and disarmed. . . .

The Punjab troops seem to have gone to the front at Agra wonderfully. Watson[8] and Probyn[9] with the cavalry . . . are highly praised.

H. B. EDWARDES TO H. B. LUMSDEN.

Peshawur, 10th November, 1857.

. . .The Guides are about to be relieved, and come up to Murdân again. . . .

H. B. EDWARDES TO H. B. LUMSDEN.

Peshawur, 17th November, 1857.

I am still unable to say "Return!" No answer yet from Calcutta. It seems unaccountable.

---

5. In accordance with the treaty.
6. *i.e.* the pure soil of Persia.
7. Meaning the Bombay troops.
8. Afterwards General Sir John Watson, K.C.B.,V.C.
9. Afterwards General Sir Dighton Macnaghten Probyn, G.C.V.O., K.G.B, K.C.S.I. V.C.

I send you in compensation Mrs. Stowe's *Dred*, to amuse you in prison. The moment orders come I will send you an express, and I have no doubt myself that you will be allowed to return. The Afghans will, I hope, understand that the mission to Herat is only a formal ceremony to see the treaty completed. But our Government certainly should have communicated to Dost Muhammad Khan the details of that treaty, and I have repeatedly stated that in a highly bumptious manner.

There is little new in India. The crowding in of troops is at last satisfactory, and as it has pleased God to save us without their assistance, it is certainly all the better they didn't come sooner, for we have shown the world a spectacle they little expected. The "Indian officers" have gone up again in public estimation, and the home papers are full of nothing but desire for the severest punishment to the mutineers. I send you a *Friend of India* on these points. . . .

Please God, much good in many ways will come out of this awful crisis; but our lost dear friends can never be replaced!

H. B. EDWARDES TO H. B. LUMSDEN.

Peshawur, 2nd December, 1857.

Sir John still tells me he has received no orders from Government about your recall, and cannot recall you on his own responsibility.

There is no public news that you will not see in the newspapers. Sir Colin Campbell has put the finishing stroke to the Lucknow struggle, I fancy; and there must have been hard fighting, for the casualties are heavy.

Roving bands of the broken native army are all over the country, not knowing whither to go, but disturbing everything. . . .

H. B. EDWARDES TO H. B. LUMSDEN.

Peshawur, 14th December, 1857.

Still no orders from Government about you. I have received letters from Taylor at Herat up to 13th November, and from what he says it is clear that the present ruler there was appointed with the concurrence of our representatives, and has a mind to take hold of our garment rather than that of Persia. He gives a deplorable account of the destruction worked by the Persians in Herat, and this looks as if the Persians never expected to come back again. By the same *kossid* came letters from the Herat *sirdar*, offering no end of friendship and service.

It is just as well we stopped the heir-apparent's projects against Herat, for I am sure it would have been in the teeth of all arrangements from the other side.

Here there is nothing new to tell you. There is no doubt that vast numbers of English troops have arrived in the three Presidencies, but they get slowly up country; and the interior of India is disorganized by the broken fragments of our old native army wandering about it and plundering with no plan, and no hope of any further success. Thus our communications are not yet re-established with Cawnpoor. Futtehgurh is still held by *moofsids*.[10] The Gwalior contingent which was careering about is, we hear, at last nearly destroyed....

I have just drawn up an epitaph for dear J. N.'s grave at Delhi, and will try and send you a copy. It is most difficult to do justice to such a man.

Meanwhile Lumsden had received letters from Colonel Taylor, dated Meshad, 18th September, 1857. Colonel Taylor, along with Lieutenant Hardy, Bombay Artillery, and Lieutenant Clerk, Madras army, were then proceeding to Herat to acknowledge the *de facto* Government there, to witness the withdrawal of the Persian army, and the fulfilment generally of the terms of the treaty which had been entered into between the British and Persian Governments.

Colonel Taylor's mission remained in Herat until the 1st March, 1858, but even at that date the Persians had not completed their obligations. The Jews and Hazaras, subjects of Herat, who had been forcibly carried off to Meshad, had not been given up. Lash Juwain was still retained by Persia, whilst Sirdar Sultan Jan continued to acknowledge the sovereignty of the *shah*, by causing the *Khutbah*[11] to be read in the mosques and coin to be struck in his name. On Colonel Taylor's departure Sultan Jan gave out that he had dismissed the mission, as he could have nothing to say to *kafirs*.[12]

Before Lumsden left Candahar, however, the aspect of Persian affairs on the Herat border had considerably changed. The Persians having occupied Sirrukhs, left Shah Doulot Khan, a fugitive Afghan

---

10. Rebels.
11. The prayer for the king or ruler of a country.
12. *Infidels.*

sirdar, as ruler of that district, pushed on to Merve (*Shah Jehan*), the Turkoman capital, and sat down before the place which they had not the means to subdue. Shahzada Sultan Murad Mirza, in command of the Persian army, was reduced to extremities; provisions ran out, the troops were starving, and forced to eat their own baggage donkeys. In attempting a retro-grade movement, they were surrounded and cut to pieces by Turkomans, or taken prisoners and sold into slavery, whilst their leader at the outset secured his own personal safety by flight.

H. B. EDWARDES TO H. B. LUMSDEN.

Peshawur, 9th January, 1858.

Truly vexed am I not yet to be able to send you any news of your recall. Not a word has come from Government. All is going on well in Hindostan. Sir Colin seems making a battue of Oudh; drawing a cordon of columns round it, and bringing down the Nepalese at the back to prevent escape. He is now about to drive Futtehgurh and Rohilkund rebels all into Oudh, and there finish with a grand crash. The Grand Trunk Road is at last open from Calcutta to Peshawur, and letters, etc., are coming direct. Chamberlain's resignation has been accepted, and he returns to the Punjab force with great joy.

We have had as dull a Christmas as you may suppose. It is painful to think of the friends we had *last* Christmas Day, and shall never see again in this world.

You will be deeply interested in Inglis's Lucknow despatch. It is the best I ever read in my life, and is a most affecting and wonderful recital of human bravery and endurance. Every man of them was a hero, and every woman a heroine. There never was anything like it in history.

The Guides are approaching Peshawur, and are to have a grand military reception in the general's first style.

I shall claim the honour of addressing the corps and of entertaining the officers. The men also are to have a feast. I so regret that you could not be present.

It was in January, 1858, that Lumsden received the news of the death of his cousin, John Tower Lumsden, son of Henry Lumsden, of Auchindoir and Clova, Aberdeenshire, who, after a distinguished career in the Bengal army, was attached as interpreter to the 93rd Highlanders, and fell at the storming of the Secundrabagh. They had been brought up together as lads, and Harry delighted to relate an anecdote of Adam Ledingham, the old gamekeeper at Clova. He had educated them both in sporting pursuits, and, like old Scotch servants, treated them as his own children.

When Jack Tower was leaving Aberdeen in the steamer for London and India, old Adam turned up, having walked in forty miles to bid the lad God-speed. With his hand on the boy's shoulder and tears in his eyes, Adam instilled into him his last precepts: "Noo, Johnnie, gin ye gang to the wars, mind me, and haud weel ahin the dykes." How well he "haud ahin the dykes" is told by General John Alexander Ewart, Colonel of the regiment, in his *Life*, vol. 2:—

> On reaching the breach I found it to be only a small hole about a yard square and about the same distance from the ground. I was soon in, and as I jumped down a man of the 93rd was killed close to my side. I also noticed Captain Burroughs bleeding from a bad sabre-cut over his head. The interior of the building was full of very tall grass, a path running to the left and another to the right I chose the latter, and as we ran, Cooper, of the 93rd, who had got through the hole just before me, was displaying great gallantry. Captain Lumsden, who had been attached to my regiment as interpreter, was also with me. He was a fine fellow—an Aberdeenshire man—and as he dashed forward he waved his sword high above his head, cheering on the Highlanders, and calling out to them to fight for the honour of Scotland. As we turned the corner, a large body of the enemy appeared in sight. They did not apparently like the look of us, but they instantly bolted through a passage to our right which led into a sort of inner court In a moment we were at them, but poor Lumsden was killed, and Cooper got a cut across the head.

H. B. EDWARDES TO H. B. LUMSDEN.

Peshawur, 23rd January, 1858.

The Guides are coming in here in a few days, and I have a dinner-party of *forty-eight* in honour of the officers! no slight undertaking at the close of an exhausting crisis. How I wish you were here. Meerut and Delhi are going to be thrown into the Punjab; ceded by the Governor-General to Sir John, who conquered them! . . . The *dawks* between Peshawur and Calcutta are going as usual, as if there had never been 1857. . . .

The whole border is in commotion about the wealth of the Guides, who have brought countless fair ladies, and splendid *bylees*[13] with red curtains and fat bullocks from the precincts of the palace. Every Guide is said to be a Croesus. The tales are endless. It is like the return of the Crusaders."

The following documents tell of the return of the Guides from Delhi to Peshawur:—

Extracts of Divisional orders issued by Major-General Sydney Cotton, commanding Peshawur division.

Peshawur, Tuesday, 2nd February, 1858.

No. 82. Major-General Cotton makes known throughout the division under his orders that the troops of the Peshawur cantonment were paraded under his personal command this day to receive and welcome the "Corps of Guides" on its arrival in cantonments from the siege of Delhi.

A royal salute was fired in honour of the Guides on their approaching the parade ground, and the troops saluted, when the major-general delivered the following addresses to that corps and the Peshawur Force. A *feu-de-joie*, with an accompanying ordnance salute of twenty-one guns, followed the addresses, after which the Guide cavalry and infantry, joining their comrades, marched past and saluted the major-general at the head of their respective arms.

Address to the Guide Corps:—

Captain Daly, officers European and native, and soldiers of the Corps of Guides,—I have invited you here as brother soldiers of the frontier this day to welcome you on your return from the siege of Delhi, and to acknowledge in the most public manner the high sense we entertain of the value and importance of the services rendered by you to the State during the progress of the present insurrectionary war.

In the name of Colonel Edwardes, our commissioner, on my own account, and on behalf of my brother officers, I warmly greet you on your return amongst us.

We respect, we honour you, and we feel proud on being re-associated with men whose deeds of daring have earned for yourselves and for our noble profession never-dying fame.

We deeply lament that so many brave men—our comrades of

---

13. Bullock carriages.

the frontier—should have fallen in the rebellion; the names of Nicholson, McBarnett, Battye, Murray, Travers, and Lumsden are with sorrow deeply impressed on our hearts and minds.

Address to the Peshawur Force:—

Officers, non-commissioned officers, and soldiers of the Peshawur Force, the gallant band, horse and foot, now before you are "the Guide Corps." I have invited them to meet you here this day, and I have paraded you to welcome and honour them on their return to the frontier from the siege of Delhi. This is a public demonstration of respect due to men who, as comrades, well deserve at our hands the highest honour we can bestow. Like ourselves, the corps serves, in ordinary times, in a place of great responsibility, guarding the frontier of British India in its most vital point Our feelings as brother soldiers are well considered and consulted when we meet together to do them honour, and by a public demonstration to acknowledge, in a manner beneficial to Government and on its behalf, the value of great services performed in such times as these by particularly true and loyal men.

Of all the passions of the human heart there are none with which we, as soldiers, so readily sympathize and with so much sincerity, as the valour or honourable devotion of brave men who fight and die in their country's cause.

The object of ambition of every real soldier is to be engaged with the enemies of his country.

This is a noble ambition. Some are more fortunate than others in obtaining opportunities to display the noble qualifications of the soldier; many brave and gallant men pass away unknown to fame and unheeded, their qualities as soldiers remain concealed. "War alone," as Napier said, "is the coppel[14] by which their qualifications are tested."

Great and important to the British Government have been the services of the gallant body now before you during the progress of the present war.

---

14. This word was unfamiliar to us, but a learned friend has given as the following explanatory note:—Coppel, or, as it is now more usually spelt,, cupel, is a vessel used in assaying gold or silver with lead; but is also used figuratively in the sense of test, as in Disraeli's *Tancred*, "Money is to be the cupel of their worth." It is from an old French word, *coupelle*; med. Lat, *cupella*, a diminutive of Lat *cupa*, a cask.

I will briefly detail them for your information, and for record. The faithless Hindustani *Sepoys* mutinied at Meerut on the 10th May, 1857, and at Delhi on the 11th; the news reached Peshawur on the night of the 11th. On the 12th a movable column was resolved on to keep down mutiny in the Punjab. It was necessary to have picked troops, who could be relied on, not merely to fight, but to fight on the right side. All thoughts turned first to British soldiers, and H.M's 24th and 27th Regiments were warned.

But next to British soldiers the men who, in the hour of doubt and danger, stood highest in the public confidence were "The Guides." They were then cantoned at Murdân. Their commander, Captain Daly, received the order on the 13th May, marched that very evening, and reached Attok (thirty miles) next morning. It was soon seen that Delhi was the centre of the mutiny, and to Delhi the Guides were ordered to push on. They did push on; they reached Delhi on the twenty-fourth day after leaving Murdân, three of which days they halted by order. The distance was 580 miles, or fifty-seven regular marches achieved in twenty-one, and during these twenty-one days they turned off their road twelve times, burnt three villages. No soldier can hear of such a march without admiration, and their "deeds of arms" were equal to their march.

Within three hours after reaching Delhi the Guides engaged the enemy, and every one of their officers was wounded, and for nearly four months both men and officers were constantly in action, sometimes twice a day.

They took 600 men to Delhi, and received 200 recruits during the siege. Not one man deserted to the enemy; 350 men were killed and wounded, 120 fell to rise no more.

I need not dwell upon their repeated deeds of valour, their general actions, their skirmishes, or their single combats, and now we receive back these "Gallant Guides," covered with glory. The plaudits of their British comrades have followed them from Delhi; our hearty cheers, British cheers, shall welcome them home again to Peshawur.

CHAPTER 24

Order Recalling the Mission

At Candahar, in the meantime, the health of the heir-apparent had become a source of anxiety. Dr. Bellew considered his state to be very critical, and it grew from bad to worse with the development of severe winter weather. The *sirdar* determined to go to Cabul, not only for change of air, but also to secure from the *amir* the revenue contract of a certain portion of the Ghilzai district. But such a journey could not be undertaken until spring; so, Afghan-like, Ghulam Haidar set to work at the beginning of the year to squeeze the last copper out of his Candahari subjects. On the 24th January, 1858, for the fifth time since the previous April, he called in the whole of the copper coinage at half its value, and within a few weeks reissued the same at full rates. Disaffection was the natural result, and soon began to show itself in the city and neighbourhood.

Typhus fever raged in the town, where sanitation of any description was quite unknown. The native doctor attached to the Guides and one or two of the men were among the first victims. On the 16th January Bellew was fired at from a window of a house adjoining the courtyard of the temporary dispensary, where he daily received crowds of patients. The bullet just missed him and lodged in the wall. Immediate report was made to the heir-apparent, who ordered inquiries, which led to no satisfactory result. The police surmised that a boy might have been amusing himself by firing at sparrows, but as Lumsden remarked to the *sirdar*, "boys don't usually handle rifles, and when they do Afghan children are not ordinarily supplied with bullets to waste on sparrows."

There were symptoms of mischief in the air, and a few days later the storm burst. It was said that someone had overheard a young Hindu lad repeating the Muhammadan profession of faith, which, under priestly interpretation, was tantamount to the renunciation of idolatry and the acceptance of *Islám*. The *mullahs*, therefore, insisted on the immediate circumcision of the boy, who was in their hands. The parents, hearing of his position, rushed with a number of other Hindus to the mosque, and demanded his restoration. The *mullahs* refused, a tumult ensued, the police interfered, carried off the boy in custody, and referred the case to the *Kázi*.

All this caused a great commotion in the city. The Hindus sought justice from the *sirdar*, and at the same time facilitated judgement by a *douceur* of some 3000 *rupees*. The lad was released during the night, and at once hurried off by the Bolan route to Shikarpore in Sind. Next morning the anathemas of the priesthood were hurled against the careless jailors, the Hindu population generally, and the fugitives in particular; but in the course of a few days, when it was rumoured abroad that the heir-apparent had been bribed, and was accessory to the escape of the idolaters, the wrath of the *mullahs* against their Ruler knew no bounds.

The officers of the mission, when riding through the *Charsu*[1] were grossly abused by the chief priest, an *Akhundzada* of note, who denounced them, the heir-apparent, and the *Kázi* as *infidels*. No reply or retort of any kind was made, and the officers rode on as if nothing had happened. The *sirdar*, however, on hearing what had taken place, became very angry as well as alarmed; he sent a military guard to the *Charsu*, and ordered all the *mullahs* to leave the city.

Fuel was thus added to the fire. The *mullahs*, with their disciples, to the number of some five hundred or more, stormed the *Kázi's* house, and smashed the door with stones, the *Kázi* himself escaping with difficulty. They then proceeded to the shrine of the Kiulka Sharif (or repository of the prophet's cast-off clothing), the lock-fastened door miraculously flying open, as they asserted, at their approach. The *mullahs* then brought out the holy banner, and swore upon it that they would neither eat nor drink until they had taken the blood of the *infidels*. This done, the priests marched off in triumphal procession, followed by the scum of the people, to the shrine of Huzrat Ji, without the walls. There they planted the flag, and called upon all true believers to join in a holy war.

The heir-apparent becoming alarmed, detachments of troops were ordered to hold the city gates, while the remainder were kept in readiness for further action. A day or two later, when it was evident that

1. Central market-place.

a crisis had arrived which must be faced, Ghulam Haidar began to temporize. He sent out an emissary to ascertain from the *mullahs* the cause of the uproar, asking them to depute two of their most influential leaders to explain their grievances. No deputies, however, could be found enterprising enough to respond to such an invitation.

Meanwhile Lumsden had ascertained from his Guides, who, in their private clothes, had mixed amongst the soldiery, that all the men of the Afghan infantry, with the exception of one Cabul regiment, had sided with the *mullahs* and people of Candahar, and could not be depended on. The Artillery, fortunately, remained staunch. In this crisis the heir-apparent summoned 2000 Durâni *jezailchis* from Zamindawur, and retained them about the palace. They were men of his own clan on whom he could rely.

After the lapse of two days the *mullahs* found difficulty in maintaining their vow of abstinence, for when the people of the city—including, it was said, some of the *sirdar's* own followers—sent out cooked provisions for their sustenance, the holy fathers, totally forgetting their oaths, scrambled for food like a pack of hungry dogs; so much so, indeed, that some of the faithful ventured to hint "that such lovers of flesh could hardly aspire to be martyrs in spirit."

The death of a Hindu took place in the city, but when his relations attempted to burn the body at their usual place of cremation, the *mullahs* seized the opportunity of showing contempt of existing authority. Followed by an excited mob, they snatched the half-burned corpse from the fire, fastened a rope to it, and dragged it in malicious triumph through the city. The whole affair had a bad effect on the heir-apparent, who developed feverish symptoms, and a restless, nervous temperament The state of tension became even more trying on the return of the express horsemen, who had been despatched to report matters to the *amir*. These men declared that they had found the passes closed, and the roads blocked by snow.

Ghulam Haidar Khan then began to negotiate with the malcontent leaders. He placed the father of the Hindu lad, who had escaped to India, in confinement, directing that he should be kept in custody until the boy returned. He also agreed to allow the *mullahs* to visit the prisoner, and verify the fact of his continued confinement. The *sirdar* further opened communication with the *Akhundzadas* (high priests), who had led the people, and, assuring them of the immediate payment of handsome rewards, and promising gifts of lands and *khillats*[2] from

2. Dresses of honour.

213

the *amir*, succeeded in breaking up the gathering.

On the 25th February Lumsden recorded in his official diary:—

We have no connection with either party, but at the same time it is easy to see that a breath is all that is required to turn the popular cry from the Hindus to the *Feringhees*.[3] I am therefore quietly watching events, and should symptoms appear of this unwholesome excitement running higher, I shall consider it my duty, in accordance with the spirit of my instructions and the interest of Government, to take leave of the heir-apparent, and quietly withdraw the mission to India by the Bolan route, before we may actually be driven to ride for our lives, as General Ferrier, under like circumstances, had to do from this place.

On the 25th March the heir-apparent, leaving Sirdar Futteh Muhammad Khan in charge of Candahar, bade the mission farewell, and began his march. The *Akhundzadas* to whom, as stated above, lavish rewards had been promised, had meanwhile been sent on ahead towards Cabul, accompanied by an escort, the commanding officer of which returned, after a short space of time, to Candahar. When asked how he had managed to accomplish the journey so quickly, he replied significantly that the saints had, in a miraculous manner, disappeared on the road. He inferred, therefore, that they would give no further trouble, nor require any further reward.

Towards the middle of April the long-looked-for order permitting the withdrawal of the mission was received. It was contained in a letter from Sir John Lawrence, sent *via* Sind and the Bolan. "The Governor-General now authorizes you using your discretion, and leaving Candahar, whenever you may consider it expedient to do so."

Since the departure of the heir-apparent the state of affairs had not improved. Chiefs, at all times difficult to manage, were not inclined at once to respond to the orders of a young and less powerful Governor. Lumsden lost no time, therefore, in making all necessary preparations for departure by the Ghuzni and Kurram routes, as already settled with the *amir*. But now that the Afghan authorities had become satisfied that the British Government had no sinister motives in keeping the mission in their country, they realized that they might lose a *lakh* of *rupees* a month by the return of the officers to India. Every difficulty was therefore thrown in the way. It was the *Ramzan*, the period of fast, when men could not travel, camels could not possibly be procured,

---

3. Foreigners.

and so on. Even at the last moment, when camels had been obtained through Ghulam Sarwur Khan Khágwáni, a border chief attached to the mission, the animals were stolen, and the thieves could not be discovered.

Such an incident, in Afghanistan, could not have happened without the cognizance of the ruler. Lumsden, however, notwithstanding every trick to prevent his departure, eventually secured the requisite camels by purchase, and, on arrival at Peshawur, reported the matter and sent in the bill to Government. Sir John Lawrence was not a ruler to be played fast and loose with. He forthwith directed that the value of the camels stolen at Candahar should be deducted from the *amir's* next monthly allowance.

It was interesting to learn afterwards that the *amir*, on ascertaining the facts, was much annoyed. He, however, not only recovered the amount of the price of the camels from Sirdar Futteh Muhammad Khan, but took the opportunity to mulct him heavily by a fine for having brought discredit on his master, and for dishonouring the rules of hospitality due to his guests.

H. B. EDWARDES TO H. B. LUMSDEN.

Peshawur, 13th February, 1858.

Concerning the Bombay plan for keeping a mission always at Candahar, I wish you would kindly give me your views, formed on experience. The only advantage is to get reliable information, otherwise it would be better to have no connection with the country. The Guides have been received here in a most enthusiastic way. Grand parades and feasts of every kind. They are all gratified, and a good example has been made of our ability to praise as well as blame. . . .

The Governor-General is at Allahabad by this time. The Commander-in-Chief was to be before Lucknow on the 10th.

They will have stiff fighting there, I suspect; but all arrangements have been well made, and all is now going right throughout the country.

How do you feel now that you are a Queen's officer? The fun is now to hear the Queen's officers "apprehend they'll have their pay cut down!" It is quite astounding what sighs are now heaved from unexpected bosoms over the grave of that much-abused old chap, John Company. . . .

Peshawur, 2nd March, 1858.

Herewith a lot of letters and papers for you all. Still not a line from Government about you. The G.-G. is at Allahabad, and the Chief Commissioner at Delhi; so perhaps they will soon meet, and sparks fly out. We are in the daily expectation of news from Lucknow, as the Commander-in-Chief has been for many days pouring troops across to Alum Bagh, and for weeks drawing a ring of columns round Oudh. The weather is getting warm there, and all the officers seem anxious to begin and finish whatever there is to do. The enemy are in great strength, but so are we; and there is, please God, no doubt as to the issue, but much loss must be expected, and I hope Sir Colin will take care that divisions of the enemy do not cross the Ganges on his flanks, and again break up the communications of the Grand Trunk Road.

Peshawur, 18th March, 1858.

The news from Lucknow yesterday was that "we have got possession of the Furreed Buksh Palace, Residency, Muchee Bhâwun, and Emam Bârah, with little or no opposition. A number of rebels bolted this morning over the stone bridge, and Lucknow is well-nigh rid of them. They are believed to have taken a roundabout road to Fyzabad."

So I daresay that during today we may hear that Lucknow is finally ours. The struggle there has not been so great as was expected and, I may add, desired; for if the rebels go running all about Oudh, our columns must go running after them, and this is not pleasant in the hot weather. It will take a long time to settle India down again. The papers describe the natives generally as being more insolent than formerly, though they have been defeated You see they got a glimpse of the possibility of expelling us, and will remember it The only thing is for us to rise to the occasion, recognize our own position, and draw the teeth of the nation. I would systematically commence to destroy every fort in India now held by natives, and build forts of our own at strategical points, and disarm the whole population of the continent; but I do not hear that there is any great change of policy in the Supreme Government, and we can only hope that in that case we may get a change of men.

I coincide in all your views as to the impropriety of retaining your mission so long after the specified time in Afghanistan, also in "the less we have to do with them the better," *i.e.*, that we are more likely to remain friends *without* any permanent political missions than *with* them. But it is of no use to express opinions to a Government that gives no answers!

In a recent letter there was just a scintillation of hope for your return. I had recommended that all the information in your diaries should be selected and published by Government, to which, oddly enough, they promptly replied that it should be done at the conclusion of your mission. So they *do* contemplate a conclusion. I began to think they *didn't*.

You must live on this for a month or two. I daresay that after Oudh is smashed the G.-G. will think it safe to recall you....

I am looking very anxiously to see what is done in Parliament about the government of India, for I believe that a minister without an Indian Council will soon lose the empire for us.

The *Army* would, perhaps, be improved under the Crown....

P.S.—H.M's 81st marched in here this morning 1100 strong with "a stunning band!" There is something very stirring in a military band, certainly; and I thought this morning how little *impression* on the mob would comparatively be made by a regiment marching *silently* through them. That regular time—*throb, throb, throb,* like a giant's heart—makes something superhuman of the body which it moves and animates, and when the big drum comes in with his gruff voice I don't wonder at the nursery-maids bolting, and the brats in the street getting run over.

Peshawur, 22nd March, 1858.

Your diary of the 25th February has at length elicited a reply from the Governor-General, and I have received the following telegram: "Send an express to Major Lumsden to say that he can leave Candahar should he consider it expedient to do so. The Governor-General leaves it to his own discretion. I shall send an express to Jacobabad, and by Derah Ghazee Khan." Perhaps, therefore, the Chief Commissioner's express will have reached you before this, which I shall send by the shortest cut, if I can find anyone to take it ... The inability of the heir-apparent to resist the ecclesiastics is a melancholy sign of weakness, significant of the future.

As for news, Lucknow is, I believe, entirely taken, for the last telegram says, "About 120 guns taken in Lucknow. Mrs. Orr and Miss Jackson are safe." . . . I send you the outline of the new India Bill, in case you may not have got it Mr. Brunton, the manager of the railway, is here taking a cursory survey of the line from Lahore to Peshawur.

Peshawur, 25th March, 1858.

Now my way is clear for a holiday, and, please God, I will go home this autumn and have two years of rest

I shall not be idle, for I mean to write down Sir Henry's life, and give a sketch of all the staff that stood around and loved him. (*At least of all who send me any letters or reminiscences.* Any who do *not* must expect me to be cross—and ugly.)

Peshawur, 20th April, 1858.

Things do indeed look queer with Persia, and I must say I admire Mr. Murray's pluck and pertinacity . . . in sending to stop the fleet and troops at Karrack till Persia fulfils her pledges at Herat. No doubt Persia is put up to it by Russia to aggravate our difficulties in India; but just see what an ass Persia is— to secure her footing in Toorkistan, which is only valuable for Russia, she is wasting an army at Merve.

I am inclined to agree with you that it would be wise for us to occupy the Bolân. It is a greater strategical point I think than the Khyber, for it commands two lines of operation, to Herat or Cabul, and would enable us either to meet Russia or turn the Afghans. You would see, however, that it would be opposed by Sir John with all his might I am myself strongly opposed to taking Afghanistan (unless Providence positively thrusts us upon it, which is not now the case at all), but I see great advantages in holding the Bolân. We ought to get over our absurd contempt for fortresses, and create a few at great points like the Bolân, Peshawur, Mooltân, and some other point in Sindh. . . .

CHAPTER 25

Lumsden's Return to the Guides

On the 15th May the mission left Candahar, and, after paying a visit of three days to Muhammad Azim Khan, Governor of Kurram, arrived, without incident worthy of record, on the 17th June, at Thul-biland-khel. There they found Major Boswell, of the 4th Sikhs, with other officers and a party of the Punjab Force, waiting to escort them to Kohat. That day was ever to be remembered. Lumsden and his companions rejoiced in being once more with their own people. Hour after hour they talked of friends lost, deeds achieved, and all that had happened in India during the eventful period of their absence. Before reaching Kohat Lumsden's brother received orders to join without delay the appointment of assistant quartermaster-general to Sir Hugh Rose's force operating in the central provinces. The mission soon broke up, and Harry Lumsden with Dr. Bellew rejoined the Guides at Hoti Murdân.

Lumsden's opinions with regard to the policy which should govern our relations with Afghanistan were set forth by him in letters to the Government of India. He considered that the exaggerated reports of the effects of the mutiny which had spread through Central Asia might prove adverse to our interests. Politicians of other countries had not failed to make use of them for their own purposes. Russian influence weighed down the scales against us in Persia. Furthermore, Russia now held Mongolia under her sway, and she was, in fact, pushing forward towards China. Afghanistan alone seemed still to be independent, and to keep it so should be our aim. Friendly and intimate intercourse should be maintained with the *de facto* Government of Cabul. The internal administration should not be interfered with, the Afghans being left to manage their home affairs in their own way without interference by Persia or by any other power.

Thirty years afterwards, when Russia had swept over the *steppes* of Central Asia and reached the banks of the Oxus, and when her network of intrigue had embraced Cabul itself, Lumsden fully admitted that the problem had changed, and that new considerations in regard to the military defence of the frontier must influence the Indian Government. But in 1858, when the embers of the mutiny were still smouldering, and our permanent European garrison in India was comparatively a mere handful, the whole of our native army being in a state of reorganization, Lumsden looked upon the field of possible operations in a very different light. The Bolan Pass with Quetta had not then been occupied or opened out. The invasion of India by that route would have been a very hazardous undertaking, inasmuch as from Ferozepore to the sea, along the southern banks of the Indus, the country was a desert which from want of water could not be penetrated by any large force.

An invader could only advance on India from the north between Ferozepore and the Himalaya, across the line of the Sutlej. Lumsden considered that our then existing frontier, covered by rugged and barren hills, through which there was but a limited number of passes for the approach of an invading army, was the best position for defence. Situated as we were on our own side of these passes, we were prepared to fall on any force debouching on the plain, but were bound to strengthen our position by every means in our power, and especially by connecting by road the whole of the frontier posts. He was strongly in favour of pushing on lines of railroad, and of completing by steamers the chain of communication with our true base, the sea.

Lumsden strongly advocated the carrying out of a friendly policy towards the border tribes which separated us from Afghanistan, but he thought we should never forget the fact that the touch of money renders Pathans more and more rapacious, and that they are a people who will only respect authority which can punish with one hand and reward with the other. He specially dwelt on the military quality of the Afridi tribes, who enlisted so readily in the Guides and other frontier regiments, and who, when caught young, made good, obedient soldiers. These tribes looked upon our service as the great field for all the aspiring spirits of their clans, and day by day they were being drawn closer to us. It was worth remembering that, whilst the *Amir* of Cabul tried to claim them as his subjects, the Afridis entirely repudiated him as their ruler, and, referring to the allowances received from Cabul for the management of the Khyber, pointedly inquired, "Do we pay tribute to the *amir* or he to us?"

In forwarding to Government his report on the mutiny of 1857, at Peshawur, Colonel Edwardes thus summarized the work of the Candahar Mission:—

> And here I would beg to acknowledge the very great services of our officers in Afghanistan during the late crisis. At Candahar, with the heir-apparent, were Major Harry Lumsden, Lieutenant Peter Lumsden, and Dr. Bellew, accompanied by Ghulam Sirwar Khan Khigwanl. It was thought to be a service of great enterprise for the English officers, especially when they set out for Candahar, even in a time of peace; and their situation became one of decided peril when India was in a blaze with a Muhammadan struggle. But these officers and *khans*, by a soldierly equanimity, by a fortitude equal to the occasion, by a calm trust in the cause of England, by the good feeling which their previous demeanour had created, and by keeping the Cabul Government candidly and truthfully informed of real events and thus disarming monstrous exaggeration of our disasters, preserved the confidence of the *amir* and his best counsellors, and were largely instrumental in maintaining those friendly relations which were of such vital importance to our success.
>
> For these unusual services I would venture to solicit for all these officers and *khans* some mark of honourable distinction from Government.

From Sir John Lawrence, Chief Commissioner Punjab, to Secretary to Government of India, with the Governor-General, dated Lahore, No. 332 of 21st October, 1858:—

> In conclusion, it remains to submit the Chief Commissioner's very strong recommendation that the services of the officers composing the Candahar mission, Major H. B. Lumsden, Lieutenant P. S. Lumsden, and Dr. Bellew, may meet with the favourable consideration of the Supreme Government Major H. B. Lumsden himself is one of the ablest and best military officers in the service. He has distinguished himself in the Afghan war, both the Punjab wars, and in most of the border fights on the Peshawur frontier during the last ten years. He raised, organized, and commanded the famous Guide corps. While he was absent at Candahar, the corps performed excellent service

before Delhi Therefore, in undertaking the Candahar mission, Major Lumsden missed the opportunity of commanding his corps and of winning rank and distinction before Delhi; while on the other hand he gained little but honour and risk in the interior of Afghanistan.

From Secretary to Government of India, with the Governor-General, Allahabad, 29th December, 1858, to Sir John Lawrence, Chief Commissioner Punjab, No. 5462, pars. 2:—

I am directed to acknowledge the receipt of your secretary's letter, No. 332, dated 21st October last, submitting report on Candahar mission. The Governor-General has read these papers with the deepest interest, and with a very high appreciation of the clear, sound judgement and admirable temper of Major Lumsden, who has shown no ordinary qualifications for the discharge of a very difficult duty. His lordship desires to acknowledge the great and lasting good services which that officer has done in the warmest terms. . . . It will be a pleasure to his lordship to place Major Lumsden's services prominently before the home Government, and he may be sure that, though different in kind, they will not be valued less highly than if they had been rendered in the field, at the head of the noble regiment with which he has been so long connected.

The question of appointing an Agent to the Governor-General for the whole frontier from Peshawur to Kurrachi came before the Government of India in October, 1858, and although Sir John Lawrence was entirely opposed to the creation of such an office, he recommended, in the event of his opinion being over-ruled, and Edwardes being obliged to go home, that Lumsden should be invested with the requisite powers, and allowed to exercise them while he still remained commandant of the Guides.

Lumsden was gazetted a lieutenant-colonel on the 15th May, 1858, and reassumed command of his regiment in June of the same year. On the 5th December, 1859, he was nominated a Civil Companion of the Most Honourable Order of the Bath. The long-looked-for return of Lumsden to the Guides was a pleasure not unmingled with pain. It was a pleasure to be once more with the soldiers he had raised and trained, and whose ardent attachment to himself personally had secured their allegiance to the State in its need; yet he could not but regret that a call of duty had taken him from their head in the hours of trial and of triumph. The feelings of the corps itself, and the life of the officers at that time, have been described by one of themselves, Colonel H. C. E. Ward, who joined the Guides as a subaltern before Delhi, and was with the regiment on Lumsden's return:—

Of the early days of "The Guides" and their officers I can tell you nothing, except from hearsay, and that is of little value. I joined the Guides in September, 1857, at Delhi; Lumsden was then absent on the Candahar mission. The only two old officers with the regiment at that time were the late Colonel T. G. Kennedy, C.B., and Lieutenant Herbert Hawes. The latter and I marched up with the Guide cavalry from Delhi to Peshawur; he could never speak too highly of Lumsden, and beguiled many a weary mile of our long marches by stories of his wonderful power over the men, their affection and reverence for him, and his influence, not only over the regiment, but the people among whom the Guides were quartered in all the country round.

The old native officers, too, were never tired of talking about their absent commanding officer—how much he would regret not having been in India in time to take part in that great struggle, and how rejoiced they would have been to have had him with them. In this they had no idea of depreciating Daly, his *locum tenens*, for they had proved how well they had served him, in many a hard-fought field. All this had prepared me to be impressed with Lumsden's strong personality, but I was not prepared for the genial kindness with which he accepted me as the last-joined recruit for the Guides, and laid himself out to teach me how to make myself worthy of the regiment. In a very few months I was as strong an admirer of his as any of his older friends. I was young, and perhaps impressionable, but, be this as it may, I have never ceased to feel how much I owed him for his amiable kindness, and for the persistent encouragement he gave me to study thoroughly the languages of the border, and all that could be of use to me as a soldier or an officer on the frontier. He made life at Hoti Murdân infinitely more interesting than I had imagined possible, for he employed me as his amanuensis, and in that capacity I wrote up whole books of his memorandums[1] on the various frontier tribes with whom he had come

---

1. These papers, referred to by Colonel Ward, had been called for by Government, and were freely quoted in the early gazetteers and papers regarding the frontier by MacGregor, Paget, etc.

LUMSDEN WITH THE GUIDES

in contact, and so I learnt more of the manners and customs of the Pathans, among whom we lived, and their neighbours, than I could have acquired in years of experience.

I had also to write, at his dictation, a series of letters on the then (as now) vexed question of frontier policy. His view then was that there was nothing to gain by pressing forward too hurriedly; that as Russia pushed forward in Central Asia, we might, to some extent, have to follow her example; and until the two European nations met, there would be no permanent peace for either—the tribesmen on either side would always give trouble. Even as long ago as 1858-59 there was talk of obtaining a sanatorium for the Peshawar garrison in Tirah, either by purchase or treaty. Lumsden did not, however, approve of the project, and it never came to anything.

During the years I served with the Guides I rode over most of Yusafzai in Lumsden's company, on military or sporting expeditions, and I used to be much struck with the respect in which he was held by all classes; even the agriculturists would come to him with their troubles, and prefer his decision of their disputes to referring to the civil courts.

They had the same implicit belief in his sense of honour and justice that the men of his regiment had. I never heard a grumble at his verdicts, however much they erred on the side of severity.

He hated red tape, and his one difference with higher powers was his objection to the endless returns which, after the first few years, the authorities found it necessary to introduce. I believe that it was well known that he might have been Commissioner of Peshawur when he pleased, if he could only have brought himself to accept the red tape and returns that were inevitable in such an appointment

A large, powerful man, he was a good and strong rider in spite of his weight, and being left-handed (though he could use his right when necessary) had a great advantage as a swordsman over most men. A perfect shot, and skilful with all weapons, he was always ready to share in and promote the sport or amusement of both officers and men. I think he was one of the first irregular cavalry officers who introduced into the riding-school of his regiment a stiff series of jumps, interspersed with dummy figures, among which the men were regularly instructed at sword and lance exercise. He insisted on his officers making themselves thoroughly proficient in all soldierly exercises, and he used to impress on us the view that the Guide officer should always be able to do everything he took up a little better than the men.

We were all required to be thoroughly acquainted with the whole country up to the border, and be always ready to ride anywhere at a moment's notice. He would say at breakfast-time that "Toorungzie post must be inspected today," eighteen or twenty miles off. He encouraged us to take these expeditions alone. He would see that the horse was in good condition and well shod, and that the arms were in good order, and used to tell us that it was much better to go alone, for an orderly might come to grief, and you could not leave him, so two men might be lost instead of one. His instructions were always so clear that even the first time I visited that post, when quite new to the country, I had no difficulty.

He always insisted on—perhaps I am wrong in using that expression— he always received implicit obedience from all and sundry. No one ever thought of not carrying out his orders. The only time I ever saw any hesitation was once when smallpox appeared in the fort of Hoti Murdân. Lumsden ordered each company to parade for vaccination, as soon as the doctor had the lymph ready. As acting adjutant at the time, I marched up one company to the doctor's quarters. In those days vaccination was new, and not well known, and there was some slight demur when the first man was called up. Lumsden turned to me: "Now then, youngster, off with your coat, and set the men an example." I was vaccinated, and not a man hesitated afterwards. I have no doubt that, had I not happened to be handy, he would have been vaccinated himself. One of his great principles was, *"Never ask your men to do anything you would not do yourself"*—a maxim that has helped me through many a difficulty, not only in soldiering, but in other walks of life.

Personally I should never have thought of disobedience of any order of his, or even of the possibility of such disobedience. When the regiment marched on the Mahsood Waziri expedition, in 1858-59, I was left behind at Hoti Murdân. The evening they were at Peshawur, I got a note from Lumsden at mess, about 8 p.m.

> We march to Kohat the day after tomorrow. If you can
> join before the regiment goes through the pass—come.

He meant me to have come *via* Peshawur. The messenger had
been delayed, so that distance was too great My only chance
was to go *via* Noushera, and across (at that time) a wild and
rather disturbed tract of country, in a bee-line to the hill above
the pass. The distance was about fifty miles, or a little more; road
there was none. The idea of not going never crossed my mind,
so I went, and rode into the Guide camp at sunset next evening.
The only baggage I had on that campaign I carried on my back,
and during the expedition I shared Lumsden's tent.

One morning the force was drawn up to attack a fortified village. Lumsden turned to me: "I must have another troop of
cavalry, ride back and bring up so-and-so with a troop." I suppose he saw regret in my face at being ordered off just as the
fire was about to commence, so he added, "The quicker you go,
the sooner you will be back."

I ought to have mentioned before that not only were the Guide
officers expected to be proficient with rifle, sword, and pistol, but they had to acquire a certain knowledge of farriery.
I learned then how to treat most of the ordinary ailments to
which cavalry horses are liable, and how to shoe a horse—a
knowledge for which I have many a time, in later years, been
thankful to Lumsden when, in the wilds of Central India, I have
been a hundred miles from a farrier, and had to put a shoe on
my own horse.

Such was Harry Lumsden in his bearing towards officers and men
of his own Guides.

Sir Richard Pollock, who, it will be remembered, was one of Harry
Lumsden's companions in the "*burj*,"[2] has recorded his recollections of
him as a political officer:—

> I first met Lumsden at the siege of Mooltan, in Edwardes' camp,
> where I was a political officer. He was there with his Guides
> detachment, and with the gallant and eccentric Futteh Khan
> Khuttuk. I learnt from the first day of our acquaintance to ap-
> preciate him thoroughly. A singular mixture of shrewdness and
> simplicity, absolutely free from selfishness and self-seeking, with
> great originality, a perfect temper, and a keen sense of humour,

2. See chapter 9, *ante*.

he could not fail to be a favourite wherever he went, or fail to be valued as a soldier and leader with special experience, gained while yet a young officer serving in Afghanistan and on the Peshawur frontier.

I think he was a head and shoulders above all his contemporaries in his knowledge of native character (especially Pathans) and his ability to get good and loyal service out of them. He read them like a book, and, while he could be severe on occasions when necessary, his general treatment of them was kind and liberal, and he could make allowance for tribal necessities, clan feeling, etc.

Never was any man who had such high qualifications for administrative work so intensely averse to it I suppose because he hated putting pen to paper. While commanding the Guides he took civil work temporarily to oblige the Government, but deliberately and without hesitation declined to be a frontier commissioner, though he must have well known that the appointment would lead to the very highest posts, such as Hyderabad, or to a lieutenant-governorship of a province.

CHAPTER 26

Lumsden nominated to command the Frontier Force

On the 20th March, 1860, Lumsden was nominated to the command of the Punjab Frontier Force during the absence of Brigadier N. B. Chamberlain, C.B.; but that officer not having availed himself of the leave granted to him, Lumsden remained with the Guides, and served as second in command, under Chamberlain, in the expedition of that year against the Cabul Khel Waziris north of Bannu, and later against the Mahsud Waziris. That expedition was a very remarkable one. It tested the quality of the Frontier Force and its officers to the utmost, and no troops could possibly have come out of the ordeal with greater credit to themselves or to the service to which they belonged.

The following description by the late Sir Henry Daly fully sets forth the causes which necessitated the expedition, the composition of the force, and the difficult nature of the country operated in by the troops; whilst a letter from Camp Pulloseen, in the Waziri country, dated 28th April, 1860, from Lumsden to his father, graphically describes the part taken by him in the attack on his camp on the morning of the 23rd April, 1860. Sir Henry Daly says:—

> Of the fifty fights and expeditions in which the Punjab Force was engaged on the north-west frontier during the ten years Sir Neville Chamberlain exercised command, I will touch on one only, the expedition against the Mahsood Waziris in 1860. This is an illustrative one. The Mahsood Waziris were pre-eminent for plunder and violence; their raids increased year by year in daring, till at last in 1859, after years of immunity, their chiefs brought a body of five or six thousand men into the plains for

plunder.

General Chamberlain, who passed down the frontier at this time, wrote to the Government:

> In the course of my annual tour I see much of all classes, and nowhere do I hear the cry for justice till I come within reach of the Waziris. Then commence a train of injuries received and unredressed. There is no more pitiable sight than the tears and entreaties of a family stripped of all their means. Supposing our backwardness to arise from fear, men and women counselled courage, saying, 'We will assist you; they can't stand before guns and percussion arms.'

This final raid brought their deeds of rapine to a crisis. It was determined to march a column into their strongholds, which no stranger had ever approached—an entangled mass of mountains of five ranges, with their crests rising from 5,500 feet to 11,500 feet, accessible only by the defiles of the Suleyman range channels, by which the drainage from the mountains finds its way to the Indus, varying in breadth from 1000 yards to 80 yards.

The expedition, composed of soldiers of the Punjab Force-no English bayonet or sabre in the ranks—consisted of—

Detachments of the Punjab light field batteries, 3 Royal Artillery British officers, 101 fighting men.

The Peshawur and Hazara Mountain Trains, 6 Royal Artillery officers, 125 fighting men.

Detachments of Guide-Punjab-Mooltan cavalry; 4 British officers, 331 sabres.

Detachments of Sikh-Guide, Punjab-Gurkha infantry, 41 British officers, 4,536 men.

In all about 5,200 fighting men—Sikhs, Afridis, Gurkhas, and Pathans of every clan, with 64 British officers, of whom 7 were staff—led by Brigadier-General Sir Neville Chamberlain, whose presence, to every man of the force, was a guarantee of success.

On the 17th April, 1860, the column entered the Tank Zam defile, a huge ravine rugged with rocks and boulders; the passage difficult in fine weather, impassable even for elephants after a storm of rain, for the watercourses at the base of the towering mountains wind for miles before reaching the plains, but selected as the route which afforded the best means of getting up supplies from the rear.

On the 19th, at midnight, the general marched off with the whole of the cavalry to seize a height, followed by Lumsden with the mountain guns and 2000 infantry.

Now began a series of marches in which miles occupied hours, the safety of followers, supplies, etc., requiring heights on both sides to be crowned until the rearguard came up. In the new ground, day by day, breastworks had to be constructed for night pickets of stones from the hillsides, palisaded to prevent a sudden rush from overpowering numbers. All tents were struck at dusk, half the men slept accoutred, all in uniform, and the inlying pickets were of necessity strong.

The Waziris, with unity which is proverbial amongst men who subsist almost entirely on plunder from the plains, were gathered, perched on crags and heights, ready for every chance, occasionally fighting with desperation. One chief, seeing an English officer with a few men reconnoitring the ground, shouted to his followers, "Now is the time to die for our faith, and to show the kind of men whose country is invaded." There was no lack of enthusiasm, a desperate rush was made; the gallant fellow died, but not until others had fallen.

The first serious opposition burst out on the 25th, The reveille was just sounding, and all was quiet, when a volley from the pickets and the "Fall-in" call startled Lumsden's column of 4 field guns, 100 sabres, and 1200 infantry, which had moved by another gorge. Three thousand Waziris, sword in hand, burst through the pickets; 500 penetrated the camp, where a desperate hand-to-hand struggle ensued. They were driven back, leaving 132 bodies behind them. No wounded were found, though the number must have been great.

The sick and wounded were now sent back. Sixteen days' supplies, four thousand shoes for the men, and shoes for the horses—for struggling over rocks and boulders had destroyed these—were taken, and arrangements made for an advance on Kani Goram, the capital, hitherto considered inaccessible.

At this time a message came from the Waziris that they desired a conference. The chief man appeared in camp. The general told them "there was still time to make terms; we had no wish to meddle with their affairs, but we must have security against their plundering and murdering on the British territory, and that unless this was assured their capital would be captured."

After much discussion the Mallicks said, "Why go further? Our people are rough mountaineers, difficult to restrain. Blood was fresh, and bodies of relations still unburied in the sun; our country is unfit for an army!" The general replied that it was contrary to our custom to show hostility to the dead, and pointed out to them that many of their dead had been honourably buried by our troops, and that the relations might come and bury the remainder. The Mahsoods, who hold it a sacred duty to bury their dead, seemed touched for the moment; but, depending on their numbers, their crags, and mountains, they roughly put aside overtures for peace, and left, warning us of their preparations.

On the 4th May the force moved forward through a narrow cleft in the rock. Six or seven thousand of the enemy were in position; the mouth of the pass was closed by an abattis so strong that guns had no effect on it. Along the crags and ridges were breastworks of stone, terraced one above the other, thick with Waziris. I will not delay by attempting further description of ground, etc, which well might lead the mountaineers to rely on their courage to maintain it.

The force was formed into three columns of attack. The right and main attack had to carry breastworks on a crest, the last twelve or fifteen feet of which were almost inaccessible; the ground below was broken and cut up with ravines. The attacking party, in groups, fired from behind rocks, to shelter themselves from the fire and stones hurled from above. Casualties were thick amongst them. The Waziris, seeing this check, leaped from their breastworks, and with shouts, sword in hand, burst through the leading men and readied the mountain guns and reserve. The ground on which this occurred was visible to both sides; the hills and crags rang with cheers from the clansmen as they watched the glistening swords.

Captain Keyes, now Sir Charles Keyes, was with the 1st Punjab Infantry in reserve. Putting himself at the head of a handful of men, he cut down the leader of the Waziris, already on the flank of the guns. Thus the tide of triumph was turned. The men of the battery, under Captain Butt, never swerved; they stood to their guns and fought The brilliant stroke was over.

The Waziris, leaving the ground thick with dead, retreated up the hill so hotly pursued, that the breastwork was carried and the position won.

Our loss was Lieutenant Ayrton, 94th, attached to the 2nd Punjab Infantry, and thirty killed; eighty-four wounded.

The centre and left attacks were carried with trifling loss, and the stronghold of the Waziris fell into our hands.

During the halt at Kani Goram the soldiers who had won, encamped in order outside the walls, were permitted to visit the town, under officers, morning and evening. A Synd, watching the orderly marching of the conquerors about the city, called out to the bystanders, "Well done, British justice!" It is said that this remark, testifying to the strength of discipline, touched the English general as much as his military success.

On the 9th May the force marched back by another route towards the plains, and on the 19th, with little molestation, reached Bannoo, where the column was broken up.

Thus the force, bearing sixteen days' supplies for 8000 men, led by Sir Neville Chamberlain—of whom it is not fitting to speak in such a paper as this—with a few English officers, marched in triumph through a country which no native power had ever dared to enter—a hundred and sixty miles through clefts, over crags and mountains peopled by desperate marauders, watching and contesting every peak and point Yet such was the force of discipline and system that three camp followers, and as many camels, were the only losses *en route*.

The casualties in action were 450.

Killed: 1 English officer.
               3 non-commissioned officers.
               100 men.
Wounded: 346.

FROM H. B. LUMSDEN TO HIS FATHER.

Camp Pulloseen, in the Waziri Country,
28th April, 1860.

In my last to Belhelvie, I think that I intimated a change in matters on this border, and that Chamberlain could not go home just yet, owing to a row having broken out with the Mahsood Waziris. It appears that these tribes, who have for years been troublesome, took it into their wise heads that as the Commissioner and all the chiefs in the district were away at the Governor-General's *durbar* at Sealkote, they had a splendid opportunity of plundering our border villages. Accordingly some three thousand of them assembled and poured out on to the plains, where they were met by a hundred and fifty of the 5th Punjab Cavalry, under a knowing old *ressaldar*. Our troops retired at first, drawing the hillmen after them, and pretending to be completely disorganized till they got their friends some three miles from the hills and close to what would have been a glorious prize; but all at once the cavalry formed up, faced about, and, with a discharge of carbines and a shout, charged home into the mass of Waziris, killing some two hundred of them before they could get back to the friendly shelter of their rocky hills.

This opened the eyes of the Waziris a little, but as there was a score against them for hundreds of pranks of the same sort committed daring the last few years, Government deter-mined to settle the account A force of 4500 infantry, 400 cavalry, and guns have been sent into the country to make ourselves as agreeable as possible for the next two months. We came in some twenty-five miles into the hills, and then split into two parties, the general taking away the greater portion of the force into an adjacent valley, and leaving me with 1500 men to protect the camp and stores, and with a free hand to do what I could in this part of the country, as well as to keep open our communications with the plains. The Waziris had evidently resolved to fight it out, very confident of success, and had no intercourse with us, nor could we secure any information of their intentions.

I had closed in my camp to make it compact, thrown out pickets, with inlying pickets to support, and made myself as snug as I could, though ready to move at any moment During the night a few stray shots were fired by the sentries at intervals, but all appeared tranquil until just as the reveille sounded at daylight of the 23rd April, the camp was alarmed by a volley fired from the rear picket, and three thousand Waziris overpowered our pickets, rushed on camp, upset some irregular levies of the Bannoo district, and dashed, sword in hand, on the Guides. I had my clothes half on, ready for any emergency, and immediately took my inlying picket out to the ridge, and placed them so as to rake the face of the ridge, down which they were coming, and then returned to my Guides, who, though surprised in their tents, and the half of them unaccoutred, still made a respectable resistance, falling back inch by inch on the guns (two nine-pounders and two howitzers).

Here Bond and Lewis, of the Guides, contrived to get together some two hundred men, and formed them into line across camp, called on them to advance, which the men did with fixed swords and a cheer (which would have done your heart good to hear, for it was an earnest to me that, although taken aback, my lads were far from beaten), bearing down all before them, and clearing the camp. While this was going on on the right, the Gurkhas and 4th Sikhs had time to form, and being brought up on the flank of the enemy by Major Rothney, commanding the Gurkhas, soon turned the enemy's repulse into a complete rout

I took the three regiments for about three miles over the hills in hot pursuit, and did not stop nor give them time to breathe till they broke up and dispersed over the hills.

Our loss was twenty-two killed and one hundred and twenty-eight wounded, while we counted ninety-two Waziri bodies in and around camp, besides what they carried off and their wounded.

Of the total loss, of course, my Guides came in for a heavy share, and I have to regret the fall of sixteen Guides killed and fifty-one wounded; but, at the same time, I am most proud of their noble behaviour, under the most trying circumstances in which any soldiers could be placed.

Taken aback, scattered, and unable to understand what had taken place, they rallied at once and advanced with fixed swords without the slightest hesitation.

You may fancy how sudden the attack was when I mention that I was sleeping with all my clothes on, and, before I could put on my sword, the Waziris were in camp. Out of a picket of a *havildar*, a *naick*, and eight *sepoys* of my corps, both the non-commissioned officers and six men were killed, and the other two left for dead at their post We killed the chief of the clan and most of his bravest men who followed him into camp, and have, I think, taught these gentlemen a lesson which they will understand, and that is, that even under the best of circumstances they have not a shadow of chance against disciplined troops. The general is well pleased with the business, so that is all right! Our fortune, or rather God's mercy, was very great, for not a single European officer was touched. Such a sight I have never before witnessed as the confusion and row of that first quarter of an hour, and I don't much care if I never see it again. Our poor camp-followers were most to be commiserated, having no chance of defending themselves, except by flight; seven of our *dhooli* bearers were killed and six wounded.

We have sent off our sick and wounded into the cantonment of Dera Ishmail Khan, and the general having rejoined, we shall move on to the headquarters of our friends at Kani Goram, the Waziri capital

Chamberlain will not now be able to get home this hot season, nor do I think that we shall return to cantonments much before June.

On the advance to Kani Goram, Lumsden commanded the left column at the successful attack of the Barrera Pass, was present at the burning of Makun, and withdrawal to Bannu, and returned to his quarters at Hoti Murdân on the 1st June, 1860.

CHAPTER 27

Attempt on Lumsden's life

Little more remains to be told of Lumsden's life on the north-west frontier. His distinguished services, both as a military and as a political officer, made his advancement to employment higher than that of the command of a regiment a matter of certainty. The change came in the beginning of 1862, when he was appointed to the Brigade-command of the Hyderabad Contingent.

Only one event of importance seems to have occurred in the interval between the Waziri campaign, described in the last chapter, and Lumsden's transfer from the Peshawur border to the Deccan. This event was an attempt on his life, which was made on the 2nd August, 1860, by a Hindustani camp-follower, a tent-pitcher. British officers, whose duty compels them to serve in a country chiefly inhabited by Pathans, are fully aware that more or less they carry their lives in their hands.

In the early days of our rule on the Peshawur frontier many brave servants of the Queen died, or were severely wounded, by the knives or swords of assassins. Among the former may be mentioned Mackeson, Adams, Mecham; among the latter, John Nicholson, Godby, and Lumsden. Lumsden's assailant, as already stated, was not an Afghan, but a down-countryman who had probably become infected with the Afghan spirit of violence. Herbert Edwardes once wrote: "There is evidently something in the air of the frontier which rouses brutality in every Muhammadan."

Our experience confirms that view. The inferior population on the frontier follow the example of the dominant race: Afghan customs and the Afghan code of honour are the fashion, and are followed in some instances even by Hindus.

Lumsden was attending regimental ball practice in the morning, when his would-be assassin suddenly wrenched a native officer's sword from its scabbard, and attempted with one full swing of the weapon to sever the head from the body. Fortunately the aim was inaccurate, and Lumsden escaped with a severe wound on his left arm just above the elbow.

There was no time to repeat the blow. A Guide soldier wrested the sword from the hand of the assailant, and felled him to the ground with the butt of his rifle. No reason could be assigned for the attack, though it was surmised that as the assassin had recently visited Sitána beyond the frontier, he might have been instigated by some of the fanatical Hindustanis of that colony. Lumsden himself had never punished the man, or given him any cause for discontent The wound was a severe one, but it healed rapidly, not, however, without leaving effects which were felt from time to time throughout the rest of Lumsden's life.

FROM H. B. LUMSDEN TO HIS FATHER.

Murdân, 14th March, 1862.

I must send you a few lines to tell you of my having been appointed to the command of the Hyderabad Contingent.

I can only hold the appointment for five years, but as that glorious fellow, Neville Chamberlain, is as hard as nails, and may possibly be still at the head of the Punjab Frontier Force when I am dead and gone, it is no use, however much I may regret leaving this frontier, where I have spent the best part of my life, to wait for his shoes.

I am told the climate of the Deccan is good; the command all that the most fastidious man could wish for; and, as you will see from the enclosed, the appointment was given me in such a flattering letter and minute of council by Lord Canning that it would have been madness to have refused it

I have to part with my Guides, with all my associations here, and with most of my things, and to rush down to Kurrachee, Bombay and Poonah, and from thence, how I can, to headquarters at Bolarum, near Secunderabad, to take up my command. Only fancy my getting among the Mulls[1] at last, and having to learn Maharatta and Telagu in my old age! Why, I shall be a walking Oriental dictionary by the time my Indian service is up.

---

1. Madrassees.

Government House, Calcutta,
3rd March, 1862.

Dear Colonel Lumsden,—I have greatly desired before leaving India to be able to mark substantially and publicly my high appreciation of your character and services, and to prove that I am not forgetful of the admirable manner in which, in 1857 and 1858, you discharged your duty when on a mission requiring more than ordinary tact and delicacy, and somewhat beyond the ordinary course of a soldier's functions;

The opportunity has presented itself in the vacancy of the command of the Hyderabad Contingent.

Your appointment to this command has been made, and will be gazetted immediately.

I hope it will be acceptable to you, but as it is made without previous consultation with you (for which there is not time) pray understand that if for any reason you prefer to remain with your present corps, you are entirely free to do so.

I will take care that it shall have no appearance of an omission of duty.

Have the goodness to telegraph to Major Bowie as soon as you conveniently can do so.

Whether you accept or not, believe me, I am faithfully,

Canning.

The following extract of a minute by the Governor-General, dated 2nd March, is forwarded to Lieutenant-Colonel Lumsden, C.B., for information.—By order,

C. J. Bowie, Military Secretary.

The command of the Hyderabad Contingent is vacant by the expiration of the term of service of Brigadier Hill. The post is one which calls for the exercise of the highest qualities of a commanding officer; good temper, firmness! and capacity to enforce discipline upon irregular troops, and to deal with the questions which are apt to arise with a native court, are essential.

The officer who, in my opinion, best fulfils these conditions is lieutenant-Colonel H. B. Lumsden, C.B., now commandant of the Corps of Guides.

Colonel Lumsden has not only done much distinguished service, but I have a grateful recollection of the excellent judgement and temper which he showed during his delicate mission to Afghanistan in 1857, at the time of the Persian war, and during the first part of the Indian Mutiny.

Lieutenant-Colonel A. T. Wilde[2] succeeded Harry Lumsden in command of the Guides. He had served with the Punjab Force from its creation. He was an accomplished soldier, and had seen a great deal of frontier service. At the head of his regiment, the 4th Punjab Infantry, he greatly distinguished himself in the operations in Oudh and elsewhere in 1857.

Lumsden, having parted with the Guides, set out at once for the Deccan. Before briefly describing his comparatively uneventful life there, we will attempt to explain the character of the special body of troops he had been nominated to command. The traditions of the Deccan and Central India show that in the latter half of the last, and in the commencement of the present century, European adventurers, such as Lally, Dupleix, Bussey, Perron, De Boigne, and many others, vied with each other in securing alliances, and in developing the interests of their respective countries in Southern and Central India. Before Tippoo fell at Seringapatam, or General Sir Arthur Wellesley and the Marquis of Hastings had crushed the power of the Peishwa, and swept the Maráthá and Pindari hordes from Southern and Central India, the name of the French adventurer "Raymond" was one to conjure with in Hyderabad.[3]

It was not until after the defeat of the Deccan troops at the Battle of Kurdla, when eighteen disciplined battalions under French officers, commanded by Raymond, had failed to stem Maráthá invasion, and the state of Hyderabad was compelled to cede provinces yielding a revenue of £350,000 a year to the conquerors, that Mir Alum, the great-grandfather of the late Sir Salar Jung, induced the *Nizam* to open negotiations with the British Government and to enter into the treaty of 1800. In that treaty the Governor-General, the Marquis of Wellesley, guaranteed the integrity of the Hyderabad state against for-

---

2. Afterwards Lieutenant-General Sir A T. Wilde, K.C.B., C.S.I.
3. The tomb of Monsieur Raymond at Hyderabad is to this day kept in repair by members of the *Nizam's* family, and annually, on the anniversary of his death, is visited by hundreds of devotees, who spread flowers and garlands thereon. It is said, however, that many of these devoted Muhammadans have no real knowledge of the object of their veneration, and on being asked, have alleged that they are presenting their offerings to the memory of a holy saint, "Abdul Rahman" (Raymond).

BRIGADIER GENERAL H.B.LUMSDEN, C.S.I., 1865

eign invasion, secured the disbandment of the French battalions, the dismissal of their officers, and on the part of the Indian Government undertook to keep up a subsidiary force of two regiments of cavalry and eight battalions of infantry with the usual proportion of artillery, to be stationed within the *Nizam's* territory.

At the same time the *Nizam* agreed to maintain, at the cost of his state, 9000 cavalry and 6000 infantry as the Hyderabad Contingent, under British officers, for general service and the requirements of the Deccan. The Hyderabad Contingent soon gained great proficiency, and as an auxiliary to our own army did excellent service in the Maráthá war, and showed itself vastly superior to any of the Nizam's own troops. In the course of years, however, the Government of the *Nizam* allowed their payments for the expenses of the contingent to fall hopelessly into arrears. The pay of the soldiers, however, had been regularly disbursed by the Indian Government. The *Nizam* showed no inclination to make good this expenditure, which amounted to some £800,000.

In 1853 a fresh treaty was, of necessity, entered into by the Marquis of Dalhousie. The British subsidiary force was reduced to one regiment of cavalry, 5000 infantry, with due proportion of artillery; while in 1860 the Hyderabad Contingent was reduced to a force consisting of not less than four field batteries of artillery, 2000 cavalry, and 5000 infantry. The revenue and the administration of the province of the Berars was at the same time ceded to the Indian Government as security for the payment of the accumulated debt, and also to insure in the future the regular payment of the Hyderabad contingent and the cost of the administration of the province. On arriving at Hyderabad Lumsden met with a cordial welcome from all. Sir George Yule, the Resident, and Sir Salar Jung, the Prime Minister, were both most friendly in their greetings. Throughout his career Salar Jung, who had succeeded to the premiership almost by hereditary right, had ever shown himself the staunchest vassal of the *Nizam*, and at the same time the warm friend of the Indian Government

In addition to his position as Prime Minister, he was one of the triumvirate in a regency which, since the death of the Nizam Nasir-ud-Dowlah in May, 1857, had guided the affairs of state for the infant Nizam Afzul-ud-Dowlah. Sir Salar Jung had a presence which would have commanded notice in any assembly. Invariably clothed in simple but becoming attire, of average height and fascinating manner, his masterly intellect was reflected in an almost indescribable expression which demanded attention and secured respect Lumsden delighted to listen to the minister's descriptions of the introduction into the Deccan, by his great-grandfather Mir Alum, of the Arabs who have stood steadfast adherents of his family, and who alone had been able to cope with the Rohilla bands, which had hitherto been maintained by all the principal chiefs. These Rohillas had become a curse to the country, and their extirpation from the Deccan was the constant aim of the minister.

When Lumsden had been but a short time in command of the contingent he discovered that these Rohilla soldiers were, for the most part, hungry Afghans drawn and constantly replenished from Yusafzai and the countries across our Peshawur border. Many of these men soon identified him as the same Lumsden whom they had seen in Murdân, and they were not slow in seeking his assistance in carrying on their numerous suits in our Peshawur courts, or in settling some of their family differences.

The officers and men of the Hyderabad Contingent were a very efficient body, located in the scattered cantonments of Bolarum, Hingoli, Aurangabad, Mominabad, Ellichpur, Jalna, and Lingsagur. The cavalry were as well mounted as any native corps in India, especially the native officers. The men of the Contingent were recruited from much the same-sources as those of the old Bengal cavalry and infantry. The British officers were good, and proud of their service; always ready for duty, and ever responding to Lumsden's slightest wish. The flaw in the interior economy of the force was the power of the native officers and its serious indebtedness. The cavalry especially were overwhelmed with debt. The pernicious system of living on advances from bankers— a custom dating from very early times— in this as well as in other native contingents, had not been eradicated. Lumsden, in summing up his service in the Deccan, pithily recorded:

Found the Hyderabad Contingent in debt, and left it clear.

In a letter to his father of the 10th April, 1863, we find the subject more fully dealt with:—

I have just returned from another round of inspections, finishing my work for this season, and have got off a long and rather healthy report to Government, pointing out my ideas of what is required to bring up this contingent, and proposing some changes which will astound some of the old contingent officers. The fact is this force has too long been a sort of preserve for the private *shikár* of the Resident and his friends. The result is that things have been permitted to go on in the old style, and native officers have had everything their own way, whilst European officers have not been allowed to have anything to say to them.

On one occasion one native officer actually decided whether his regiment was to go on service during the mutinies or not. He was a good man, and did his best for the State, but I think that it is neither advisable nor right that any native should be armed with such power, and I want to make European officers the men in these corps, and the native officers their assistants.

I also want to get the cavalry out of the hands of the bankers, and independent of their influence. What think you of a regiment which owes a *lakh* and sixty thousand *rupees* to its banker? Fortunately for the well-being of this contingent I have not been brought up in it, and therefore have not any local ties or influences to sway me, but can say what I like; and the new Resident, being also an outsider, will be more inclined to let me have my say than the old one was. My only opponent is —— who is one of the old school, and cannot see why arrangements which have worked well for the last forty years should be upset for the theories of an outsider.

I considered it my duty to give the Government my honest opinion of everything, and, having done so, I'm ready to carry out any orders they may please to send me.

Whilst Lumsden steadily pursued his work in the Deccan, he could not sever the ties which had connected him with the Peshawur valley and his Guides. In a letter of the 15th December, 1863, to his father, he says:—

Since my last the Umbeyla war on the Yusafzai border has assumed larger proportions, and resulted in the heavy loss on our side of 14 officers and 194 non-commissioned officers and men, and 14 officers and 139 men wounded; among the latter General Chamberlain himself, shot through the wrist, and obliged to resign his command, to which Brigadier Garvock, commanding at Peshawur, succeeds. Captain James, Commissioner of Peshawur, has now returned from furlough, and reached the scene of action; and it is reported his influence is inducing the hill tribes to give in and to come to terms. I sincerely trust this is not the case, for however much we must deplore the loss of the fine fellows who have fallen in this business, it is my opinion that, once we go to blows with natives, we should not leave off till the latter give in from a conviction of their helplessness.

A treaty made under other circumstances will only prove a source of more trouble hereafter, and leave an idea in the native mind that we gave in to them from want of ability to go on with the war. Once a shot is fired the politicals should retire into private life till called to the front again by the suppliant chiefs begging to be let off Chamberlain, or the officer commanding the troops, is the only man who should now have anything to say to our enemies.

Matters went on for several years in Bolarum and other Contingent cantonments in their usual routine. Lumsden ran home on six months' leave in the summer of 1866. On the 5th September of that year he married Fanny, daughter of the Rev. C. J. Myers, of Dunningwell, Cumberland, and vicar of Flintham, Notts. He returned to India in November, and settled with his wife at Aurangabad. He found everything in the Contingent as he had left it, and he soon began a tour of inspection of the several stations. Lumsden delighted in wandering amongst such scenes as presented themselves throughout the Deccan—Aurangabad, Ellora, Golconda, and the like. He lost no opportunity of indulging in field-sports in a country teeming with large game.

Since coming to Southern India Lumsden had already had a critical encounter with a mortally wounded leopard, who sprang upon him and would possibly have crushed his arm in her jaws had he not, fortunately, given her his rifle-stock as well as his arm for a mouthful. He thus saved the arm, though, as he used to say, the leopard had spoilt its beauty for the rest of his days. An extract of a letter to his father of the 31st March, 1867, thus describes another exciting adventure:—

Leaving my wife with friends at Ellichpur, I and my Brigade-Major Watson started off on a trip to the neighbouring hills to see if we could pick up a bag of bison, which are said to be very plentiful in this part of the country. The season proved too early, as little of the grass in the hills had been burnt, and, after a week's hard work over very hard ground, we came back without having so much as seen a bison. MacKenzie, my host, was put out at the idea that he had led us this wild-goose chase, and to make amends sent out his *shikaree* to the hills below Elli-chpur to see if he could not hit on a tiger. The *shikaree* returned with the report of a tiger all right in a *nullah* close to the camp. So out we three went, and stood shoulder to shoulder in an open spot in the jungle, while a line of beaters drove our friend towards us.

You may fancy our delight, after the beat had come half-way, to see four fine, handsome, full-grown tigers walk out in line into the open space in front of us. Such a row as ensued beggars description—rifles cracking away as fast as their owners could get them laid on, tigers returning the compliment with a roar and a charge which brought one's heart into one's mouth. But the result was that in two minutes we had two of our enemies dead, and another so badly wounded that he could not leave the jungle, while the fourth fairly ran clear out of the place over the open fields rather than have anything more to say to us. It was the finest thing I have yet seen, and one to be remembered for the rest of one's days.

CHAPTER 28

Lumsden starts for England

Early in 1869, Lumsden's period of command of the Hyderabad Contingent having expired, he determined to go home on leave. No immediate prospect of farther employment in India presented itself, Colonel Wilde had succeeded Sir Neville Chamberlain in the command of the Punjab Frontier Force. Lumsden was happy at the fate of his Guides. Colonel Sam Browne,[1] one of his oldest friends, and an officer with a record of brilliant service, had followed Wilde as their commander. Colonel Browne's former regiment was the 2nd Punjab Cavalry, at the head of which he had lost an arm and won the Victoria Cross in the capture of an artillery battery while serving under Lord Clyde at Bareilly in 1853.

Lumsden did not, however, hasten to embark for England. He rested for a few months in the Deccan on account of his wife's health, so that their arrival at home might be in the summer. This delay enabled him to respond to a somewhat unexpected demand for his assistance as an expert in the conduct of our relations with Afghanistan. Lord Mayo, who had just succeeded Sir John Lawrence as Viceroy of India, invited Harry Lumsden to the *durbar* appointed to be held in the spring of 1869, at Umballa, for the reception of the Amir Sher Ali, who had succeeded his father, Dost Muhammad, some six years before. Leaving his wife with friends at Aurangabad, Lumsden started for the north on the 11th March.

Umballa at that time presented a truly Oriental scene as, day by day, trains of elephants and camels came pouring in with their loads of tents and baggage, from which was quickly formed a vast canvas encampment covering hundreds of acres around the cantonment. In

---

1. Afterwards General Sir Sam Browne, G.C.B.,V.C.

addition to the camps of the Viceroy, the Commander-in-Chief, and the Headquarters of the army, there were those of some 12,000 troops of all arms, British and native; while numerous feudatory chiefs and *rajahs* from the Punjab and Cis Sutlej states were also assembled. These native princes and noblemen brought their own soldiers and retainers in great strength and in their most gorgeous apparel. They were not only keen to vie with each other in a royal pageant for the reception of the *Amir* of Cabul, but they did not forget that they were now, for the first time, to make obeisance to a new Governor-General.

It was a very great pleasure to Harry Lumsden to find so many of his old friends congregated at Umballa—Lord Napier of Magdala, Sir William Mansfield, Reynell Taylor, Richard Pollock, and others, as well as old comrades amongst the Sikh chiefs of the Cis and Trans-Sutlej states. He was glad also once more to meet his old Candahar friend Nur Muhammad,[2] who had come down with the *amir*.

> Their camps, (he wrote to his wife), are really a sight worth seeing. The Patiala *Rajah* has a set of tents quite equal to the Governor-General's, and it is amusing to see the care he takes of six guns, which he keeps covered up all day with cloth, to protect them from sun and rain.
>
> All these *rajahs* and chiefs invited to the *durbar* are now arriving, and each of them considers it part of his dignity to give a twelve o'clock gun, as well as a morning and evening one, in each of their camps; so that instead of one cantonment gun now regulating the time, there is a continuous banging of guns from noon to half-past, and so on!

The Amir Sher Ali arrived on the 24th March. Lumsden and his brother, who happened to be driving on the mall, met the royal carriage proceeding under escort to the camp. The *amir* immediately recognized them, called a halt, and entered into conversation. After enquiries for their health, he said he had recognized Harry Lumsden from a photograph which he had seen, but that his brother had become much stouter. The Lumsdens heard afterwards that Sher Ali, like a true Pathan, looked upon that meeting as a bad omen. Afghans are very superstitious. When starting on an expedition, they regard the sight of a hare crossing their path as unlucky, and every possible endeavour is made to destroy the animal. A fox, on the contrary, would be looked on as a happy omen, and its brush viewed with delight.

---

2. See chapter 16, *ante.*

"Did not Lumsden," argued Sher Ali, "meet Muhammad Azim in Kurram, and was not my eldest brother, Muhammad Afzul,[3] his friend when, from Turkistan, he constantly supplied him with deer hawks in Yusafzai? So what good could come from meeting him?"

The arrival of the Viceroy, on the 27th March, was a state ceremonial in which Harry Lumsden was told off to accompany his old friend Richard Pollock, the Commissioner of Peshawur, who had come down with the *amir*. He now, by invitation, left the Army headquarters camp, where he had lived with his brother, for that of the Governor-General. Lumsden considered it a great privilege to be able to make the acquaintance of Lord and Lady Mayo, and to be one of the numerous guests whom they received with such hospitable cordiality and made so thoroughly welcome.

The Umballa *durbar* was Lord Mayo's first great public act in his office of Viceroy and Governor-General of India. The *amir*, governors, chiefs, and people critically scanned the new ruler. No one could suffer such scrutiny more becomingly than Lord Mayo. His stately bearing, nobility of manner, and genial expression, his manifest vigour and power, impressed all who approached him, and secured respect and devotion. His intercourse with the *amir* was carried on with the greatest cordiality, and everything was done that could be done to secure confidence and goodwill. Although Lumsden had no official connection with the matters under consideration, he was greatly interested in them, and was closeted for many hours with Lord Mayo, in whose views as to the advisability of continuing the policy initiated during Lord Lawrence's reign he entirely agreed.

The whole pageant, including the great *durbar*, visits and return visits, reviews, and such like, was carried out with regal splendour. On his departure the *amir* took with him the right royal gift of £60,000, six selected steeds of the best blood of Arabia procurable in India, a richly jewelled sword, gold and silver plate, with a magnificent selection of guns, rifles, pistols, of every description, and last, though not least, on setting out from Peshawar, the entire equipment and material of a Horse Artillery battery. With regard to more substantial benefits to his country, Sher Ali was assured that the Government of India would view with severe displeasure any attempt on the part of his rivals to disturb his position as ruler of Cabul, and to rekindle civil war. And it was promised that, from time to time, the British Government would

3. These were Sher Ali's half-brothers, with whom he had had innumerable disputes and many battles.

try such means as circumstances might require to strengthen the *amir's* government, so as to enable him to transmit to his descendants all the dignities and honours of which he was the lawful possessor.

In the meantime a friendly understanding had been arrived at with Russia by the home Government, by which Sher Ali's sway over all his father's possessions on the south side of the Oxus would be acknowledged so long at least as Sher Ali kept to his own side of the river and forbore from interfering in the affairs of Bokhara. The English Government, for their part, stood forth as sponsors for the Afghan *amir*, promising to use their influence in fulfilment of the pledges offered on his behalf; while Russia undertook the like office for the *Amir* of Bokhara, whose troops were even then raiding across the Oxus.

The *amir* left Umballa on the 3rd April; the Assembly broke up, and the various officials returned to their respective posts. Lumsden rejoined his wife at Aurangabad. They started for Europe on the 12th, both genuinely sorry to leave the many friends they had made in the Deccan.

Sir Harry Lumsden at home

CHAPTER 29

Home

Harry Lumsden's father and mother were still living at Belhelvie, so it was necessary for the younger couple to fix upon a new home. They found the task of making a decision as difficult as many others had found it before them. Lumsden was amused on hearing that, as he had been born at sea, he must regard Stepney as his native parish; he did not, however, feel called on to dwell there. His wife's health necessitated the spending of winter in places of mild climate. The Channel Islands, the Riviera, Southern Italy, Algiers, were chosen in succession. The season invariably found them in London. Grymesdyke, in Buckinghamshire, was taken as headquarters, but visits to Scotland or elsewhere were numerous.

After the death of his mother, in 1873, and that of his father, at the age of eighty-five, in the following year, Harry Lumsden inherited Belhelvie Lodge, and made it his permanent home. The estate is a small one of some seven hundred acres, a couple of miles from the coast and seven from Aberdeen. His father used to delight to describe it to his old comrades as "just a suitable *château* for a worn-out old ramrod to wind up his days in." Belhelvie had home associations which made it dear to Harry Lumsden, as the tent of the Arab to its owner, and his personality attracted to it many old comrades and friends whom he delighted to see around him.

The characteristics of his youth stuck to him in his old age; a more simple, unselfish man never lived. He not only brought sunshine into his own home, but reflected it on all around him. A friend who had visited Belhelvie on several occasions has given us notes of impressions from which we propose to make a few extracts.

Sir Harry was the central charm of the whole place, full of fun and brightness, genial and kindly alike to old and young friends, interested in everything, the most delightful of hosts. He was a picture to gaze upon, dressed ordinarily in a dark tweed suit, which showed off to advantage his marvellously young, open, bright face and kindly eye. His hearty greeting at once set his guests at ease.

His garden, stables, kennels, poultry-yard, workshop which was also his gunroom—together with his pet animals, all presented sources of endless interest In his workshop he had his wood-carving table, his lathe, his magazine of rifles, rods, nets, and hawking paraphernalia of every description, whilst on shelves and in the presses were rows of chemicals, encyclopaedias and practical books on subjects such as agriculture, botany, chemistry, horticulture, the veterinary art, and photography. He settled down to a country life, but so regulated it that no day was ever too long; he read many books, and was happy in the possession of the faculty of retaining and applying the knowledge he acquired; he had endless resources, and he educated himself in his own hobbies: of these none was more fascinating to him than representing flowers and birds in woodcarving.

Gifted as a draughtsman, and enthusiastic as an ornithologist, he threw a life-like spirit into his work. On his annual migration to London he used, with the bashfulness of a pupil to his professor, to submit his works for the criticism of one of the master wood-carvers of his day, the late Mr. G. A. Rodgers, of Maddox Street. That artist appreciated the originality of the work, and used invariably to retain it for long periods on view, superscribed "the work of a pupil." "There is a speciality in Sir Harry's work," he would say, "with feeling, eye, and handling not given to many."

The Military Exhibition of May, 1890, awarded to him a diploma of merit for two panels designed and executed by himself In later years he carved a *reredos*, which has been erected to the memory of his father in St. Paul's Episcopal Church in Aberdeen, where he, as his father before him, regularly worshipped. A font cover for the Guides' church at Hoti Murdân, a lectern in Flintham Church, Notts., in memory of Lady Lumsden's father, who had been vicar there for more than forty years, and an altar frontal in her brother's church, Rushington, Lincolnshire, also attest his skill.

In regard to photography, we may quote from our friend's notes:—

Diploma of Merit, Military Exhibition, 1890
Woodcock and Partridge
Designed and carved by Major–General Sir H. B. Lumsden

Sir Harry was an excellent photographer. His dark-room was at one end of the workshop. He had made a most successful swinging cradle or bath for his negatives, and was much pleased with its success. It was placed near a tap, so that he could turn on a stream of water, which kept the cradle moving. The cool, white china reservoir, however, had its temptations for the inmates of a neighbouring poultry-run. One very hot summer's afternoon Sir Harry had put some precious negatives into the cradle. On going back to see how they were getting on, he found that an anxious old hen had led her foster-family of young ducklings to what seemed to her safe and shallow water. They were thoroughly enjoying themselves in the bath, but the photographs were ruined. He described the scene in a most amusing way, sympathizing thoroughly with the ducklings in their appreciation of his cradle.

Lumsden's old passion for hawking never deserted him to the end of his days, and he always had one or two birds in training. He instructed his keepers in the intricate mysteries of the ancient art as he had mastered it in the East, where every winter he used to import birds that had been nestled in the snow-clad cliffs of the Hindu Rush. These he trained to work with grey-hounds, and bring down ravine deer on the plains of Yusafzai. The education of a hawk[1] is a long process, requiring great patience. Lumsden's feelings on one occasion may be imagined but not described. A favourite trained hawk had been lost for a couple of days. If sighted, the bird could easily have been recalled to the lure. Passing his own lodge gate, he met a neighbour's gamekeeper with a dead hawk in his hand "Eh, Sir Harry," cried the man, "I've just killed sic a hawk," and presented the lost pet for inspection. The jesses on the legs had escaped the notice of the keeper, who really believed that he had accomplished no ordinary exploit.

Again to quote our friend:—

His hawk watched Sir Harry with keen eye. When he saw his master put on his leather glove he knew that his hour of enjoyment had come. The bird knew his voice perfectly, and would come down from the sky seemingly when Sir Harry called him; he was as gentle as a dove on his master's hand, and when there would allow himself to be stroked by anyone standing by.

1. See Appendix B.

No happier employment could be assigned to Sir Harry than to leave him on the banks of loch or stream to handle the lightest of Alnwick rods, and with the finest of tackle to endeavour to land a wily trout. He loved to stand, immersed to his waist, in a river when salmon, grilse, or finnick were on the take, and to work out the problem of their capture. Every autumn he went his rounds to innumerable friends in the north of England or in Scotland, who delighted to receive him, as much for his *bonhomie* as for his shooting powers, which rarely failed to ensure him a full share of the bag. He was one of the twelve guns which, at Mr. Rimington Wilson's, at Broomhead Hall in Yorkshire, on the 14th September, 1872, brought down the previously unrivalled number of 1313 brace of grouse in one day's driving.

He had a great power of attracting wild animals. One summer he reared under a hen a large covey of partridges which, as they progressed to maturity, used to come after breakfast to be fed at the Belhelvie front door. As autumn approached, and the 1st of September came near, these birds seemed instinctively to realize that the close time was drawing to an end. They entirely disappeared, and Sir Harry, who in the season spared nothing when he was shooting, naturally concluded that his pets had been cleared off, or their home party reduced to a remnant of the original flock. When, however, the winter snow covered the ground and Christmas drew near, and "feed" became scarce, great was Sir Harry's delight one fine morning to sec the covey in their entirety back on the lawn calling for their crumbs. A few days later another covey alighted close by, and continued to return daily, but nothing would induce them to approach the doorsteps when anyone was there.

Time was now passing by, and hope deferred of securing further employment in the East had its result on Sir Harry, who used to say in the humblest manner, "I cannot complain, for I have had my share of luck, but kings apparently have arisen in the East who know not Joseph." In 1866 an annual good-service pension of £100 had been awarded, but it was not until the 24th May, 1873, that he was nominated a Knight Commander of the Order of the Star of India. In September, 1875, the offer of a bonus was made to all Indian general officers who would elect to retire. Lumsden, having been unemployed for six years, decided to take the bonus and resign the service. A few months previously he had been invited to accept the command of a division in India, but had declined, as he had become aware that Government was about to invite retirements.

Thus the soldier to whose bearing on many critical emergencies the highest testimony had been borne, and of whom a Governor-General of India had recorded, "A better or braver soldier never drew the sword," retired, having received no mark of military honour beyond the medals on his breast His decorations were granted for political services in employment he never sought for, and which his duty to the State alone induced him to accept.

After his death, more than twenty years later, Lord Roberts wrote to his brother:—

15th August, 1896.

I had a great admiration for him, and looked upon him as one of the best frontier soldiers I had ever known. I always regretted that he did not remain long enough in India to get a high command, and why he was never given the Frontier Force I could never understand.

Another great authority, Sir Henry Norman,[2] who, as Assistant Adjutant-General at Peshawur, had been associated in early years with Lumsden and with Sir Colin Campbell, throughout his command there, also wrote:—

No one mourns his loss or sympathizes in your sorrow more than I do. Almost I think before you came to India I knew him, and you are aware how much we were thrown together in early Peshawur days from the first occupation in 1849.

The notice of his services, though good, is very inadequate, but he was too modest ever to blow his trumpet. I always looked upon him as one of our most distinguished soldiers as well as an excellent political, and why he never received high military decorations has always been a wonder to me.

His splendid conduct in command of a brigade of Sikh troops in Huzara, after the first Sikh war, was little known, and I do not think can ever have been properly represented.

We need not enter fully into Sir Harry's views regarding the twenty years of exciting events which so rapidly succeeded each other after the Amir Sher Ali's return to Cabul. Suffice it to say that on several occasions he was called upon by some of the highest authorities to submit his opinions, which he unhesitatingly did. There are only a few pencil records of those notes now before us, from which it is

2. General Sir Henry Norman, G.C.B., G.C.M.G., C.I.B., late Governor of Queensland.

clear that he continued to the last to look upon the satisfactory solution of the political and military questions involved in the defence of our north-west frontier of India as a very difficult problem. "We must abide the development of events, but be ready for any contingency." As for authorities, he had heard or read most of their opinions, which were founded on European theories, based on a conscription as in Germany or France, with a whole trained and armed population to fall back upon, but were oblivious of the specialities of our military forces in India, and the peculiarities of the zone in which they would have to operate.

He regretted that "The Guides," than which there was no better fighting regiment in the service, were no longer called upon to discharge their special duties as Guides, for which they were originally raised, by the foresight of that good soldier Sir Henry Lawrence. "During every campaign in India," Lumsden wrote, "the want of a good intelligence corps has been more or less keenly felt, and several spasmodic attempts have been made, from time to time, to supply the deficiency by some of the most energetic officers in the country, but only to break down before the inexorable shears of the Indian economists, who have never been able to look beyond the exigencies of their next budget. If I had been consulted how the Guide corps could be most speedily destroyed, and all *esprit de corps* knocked out of it, I should have recommended the abolition of their distinctive non-commissioned ranks, and the edict by which it was in every way to be assimilated to the other corps of the Punjab Frontier Force, of which it should never have formed a portion, but have been attached, as it was originally intended to have been, to the army of India generally."

He deprecated the transfer of the Punjab Force to the commander-in-chief. He thought that the campaigns of 1857 and on the frontier proved the soldiers of that force equal to any demand that could possibly be made on them. He quite allowed that, theoretically, there was reason for such a measure when great mobilization schemes were considered paramount, but that, practically, it was detrimental to the interests of Government, unless some other like body were created on the frontier. He reiterated his opinion, founded on perhaps as much experience as that of anyone, that no regular regiment of the line could secure the men who could be brought into the service by the native officers of a corps in which there were only three British officers, acting as assistants to a political agent.

It stands to reason, he thought, that such native officers have greater responsibility than they would have in regiments where there is a larger number of British officers. Selected as they should be from the sons and relatives of the chiefs or most influential men of the clans, they bring with them a following for whom they are sponsors, and who, for the sake of their home reputation, are bound to bear themselves as soldiers on service. Moreover, in Lumsden's opinion, such an organization secures a political influence of inestimable value, and produces a closer connection between the British officers, the chiefs, and people than is in any other way attainable.

Sir Harry always remained in London each season until after the Punjab Frontier Force dinner, where he met so many of his old comrades, and where, as he used to say, "If there is a Guide at home, I'm certain to catch him." From the commencement of this institution[3] until his death he was a regular attendant, and was always called to the chair. He never would propose any other toast than that of "The Queen," words pregnant with meaning to soldiers, and which in our time touch a sympathetic chord, which vibrates throughout the British race in every part of their dominion, and creates the sparks which burst into flame in the years of jubilee. He felt that in such an assembly there were men who, though perhaps hitherto undistinguished, had a spirit in them which, if opportunity offered, would show them not to be inferior to their more fortunate comrades. Such gatherings were not intended for the praise of the successful, or even of the most deserving, but to keep in memory the days of the boyhood of Joe, Jack, or Bill, who had been to each other as brothers, and who had stood together throughout many an hour of trial and in many an eventful field.

Our friend whom we have already quoted more than once says:—

A young frontier officer, who knew the Guides well, made some remark about them one day at lunch at Belhelvie. Sir Harry's face lit up with one of his brightest smiles. 'Yes,' he said, 'I am going out to Murdân this winter; I want to be with the regiment once more, and keep their jubilee with them.' The young officer said afterwards, 'Fine old man; I understand now why they are all so devoted to him in that regiment still.'

Although blessed with a good constitution, Sir Harry had endured many hardships during his Indian career. In latter years he suffered

---

3. The Frontier Force dinner.

much from gout, which seemed to increase with age. During 1896 he began to show unmistakable signs of weakness. On the 21st April, when saying goodbye to his youngest brother, Hugh David, then returning to Canada, he said: "The chances are that we shall never meet in this world again." And so it proved. He joined his wife in London on the 6th May, and caught a cold which developed into influenza. He was able, however, to preside at the Frontier Force dinner on the 10th June, and to return to Belhelvie on the 12th. During July he appeared to be in his usual health, but he caught a chill at the Highland Society's Cattle Show, at Perth, towards the end of the month. Gradually his lungs became affected; fever and pneumonia followed.

By the 11th August these symptoms seemed to have yielded to treatment. Although he was very weak, the lungs were reported free, and all his friends became hopeful On the morning before his death he talked cheerfully to his brother of the plan he had long cherished of revisiting Murdân during the approaching cold season, and of spending the fiftieth anniversary of their creation with the Guides. But it was not to be. Attended to the last by his devoted wife, he passed away in the early hours of the 12th August, and all who knew him, rich and poor, lost a friend whom to know was to love. Two days later, surrounded by his kith, kin, tenants, and friends, he was buried in the grave with his father and mother in the old Churchyard of Belhelvie.

REQUIESCANT IN PACE.

A regimental order of the 15th August, by Major G.J.Younghusband,[4] then commanding the Queen's Own Corps of Guides, thus paid a soldier's tribute to Harry Lumsden's memory:—

"It is with the deepest regret that the officer commanding has to announce to the corps the death of their first Commandant, the distinguished soldier who raised 'The Guides,' Lieutenant-General Sir Harry Lumsden, To Sir Harry Lumsden's brilliant leadership, splendid activity, and wonderful resources in war, the Guides owe that honoured name they to this day bear.

Whilst deeply mourning the loss of an old chief! let us each and all in our turn endeavour to follow worthily in the footsteps of the brave soldier, genial comrade, and born leader of men, whose noblest monument to all time shall be, that he raised the corps of Guides.

---

4. *The Story of the Guides* by G.J.Younghusband also published by Leonaur.

Appendix A

Recruits.—The first point in raising a regiment is to secure good recruits. Notwithstanding all that has been said about the mutiny in the Bengal Army haying been brought on by the enlistment of high-*caste* men, I am of opinion the mistake was not in having high-*caste* men, but in having all of the same *caste*. Mix your corps, whether in Army or Regimental units, as much as possible with distinct religions and races. Take the best-bred men to be had of each class: that is to say, for your Sikh regiment or company have the mass "Jut" Sikhs, and for Pathans the true Pathan, with his share in the village lands, and not the washermen, sweepers, and fiddlers of the village. It will generally be found that men who have for generations been accustomed to be cuffed and kicked by any particular class will not willingly face them. If you begin with this class of men they must eventually rise to rank and command, and your corps will be shunned by well-bred young men, who would look on themselves as disgraced by being ordered here and there by those whom they have been accustomed to regard as menials. Young blood is always proud, and looks more to this sort of thing than to future prospects.

Class Regiments.—It is useless to lay down rules where so much difference of opinion prevails, but I strongly recommend whole Regiments composed of distinct races and nationalities for our future native Army instead of mixed corps. Such Regiments have distinct associations, are less likely to combine for mutiny, would have great *esprit de corps*, and be always most useful away from their own country. But if mixed regiments are insisted on, I have found it more convenient to

261

have class companies than to mix men promiscuously throughout the regiment The men's baggage in the case of Sikhs, Gurkahs, and Dogras, pots, pans, etc., can be more easily packed where there is no fear of contamination from contact, and any man may touch his neighbour's traps without giving offence. In most instances far less baggage is required, as the men mess together, or can do so on emergency, and at any rate may borrow one another's vessels. A much closer intimacy exists between the native commissioned, non-commissioned officers and men of each company; they have a clearer understanding of each other's ways and wants, and there is a narrower supervision of individual soldiers than can be the case where the controlling grades but half understand the prejudices of many of the men they command.

A strong class emulation is always available for good in a thousand ways; each sect feeling itself isolated and distinct, in a measure looks after its neighbour, and having its own comparative weakness before its eyes, there is less scope for the machinations of designing knaves, for few men will be persuaded to join an enterprise where the chances are clearly as two to six against them, if not more. In caste companies the same principle of admixture should be looked to, that is, have men of different clans or races in each company, thus:—In your Sikh company of Manja and Mulwa Sikhs; in the Afridi company, Mulickdeen Khel, Kookee Khel, Kummer Khel, Kumber Khel, Adam Khel, Jowakies, Bazotis, Sipahes, Zukha-Khel, and so on throughout the regiment.

It is difficult for any European officer, no matter of what experience, to pick out the exact caste of a recruit by looking at or conversing with him for a short time. It is almost impossible, on the other hand, for a recruit to deceive a native of his own faith, and it has been my practice to hold native officers responsible that a recruit whom I have selected is really of the *caste* he represents himself to be. Never allow yourself to be talked out of your own judgement of a recruit by the representations of the men who bring him up, who are sure to try and persuade you that the youth will grow, etc. If you take one indifferent man, a dozen others are sure to be smuggled in, and the general appearance of your regiment will suffer.

Native Officers.— The selection of good commissioned officers is the essence of success in a new corps, for good officers always make good men; the converse is equally true, and a bad native officer will by his bad example play the mischief, not only with his own company, but possibly with half the regiment Select men of family and standing in their own class. Honesty and openness of character are far more essential than smartness and good looks. A native officer who can be trusted to make an honest, straightforward report is in my opinion worth ten smart ones without this quality, although, of course, I would prefer any man who combined smartness with honesty. Next to honesty comes temper and tact in managing men, and this latter is to be gained by experience alone, so that a man who has held some sort of control in his own village or clan, and been in the habit of thinking for himself and others, is to be preferred. A habit of command begets self-reliance, which is a sheet-anchor of an officer in the hour of trial

I am chary of getting transfers from other corps, unless I have an intimate acquaintance with the system and discipline of the regiment from which they come. We are ourselves so prone to look upon the school in which we have been educated as perfection, that it would be hard to hope for better things in a native, and transfers will generally be found drifting into their old ways instead of carrying out a system intended to be introduced into your new corps. Besides, few commanding officers will willingly give away their best men, and it is seldom that a good man is willing to go to another corps if he can see a reasonable prospect of promotion in his own, and a hint of the possibility of his getting the first vacancy will always be sufficient to keep him. The transfer generally proves to be only a middling man, who has nothing particular for or against him.

Cultivate the most intimate intercourse with your Native Officers, study each individual's character and weaknesses, talk with them familiarly on all subjects, teach them to be perfectly at home in your presence, and encourage them to relate to you all ordinary occurrences. It is seldom that a native on these terms can keep a secret long; but, on the contrary, the very fact of his having something on his mind which he would rather conceal will generally make him blurt it out when he least expects it These quiet conversations are the very essence of a knowledge of your corps. Let all officers not actually in disgrace enjoy this liberty of communication equally, but, above all things, beware of backbiting. Never take the slightest notice of insinuations made in private, but compel anyone making them to come forward with his story in public The golden rule with all soldiers is honest, open, fair play, and let the beat man win. The more publicity in everything connected with the men the greater will be the harmony in your corps.

Make your Native Officers feel that they and they alone are responsible for their men, and when a grave slip is made by a man of any company, take care that the native officer feels it in some shape, more or less, as the case may require. At the same time, give your native officers every support in looking after their men, and punish on their representation; but I would on no account allow a native officer to recommend for promotion, or even to hint at a good man when a vacancy exists in a corps. On the contrary, I would have it thoroughly understood that an officer doing anything of the sort is taking the surest mode of preventing the advancement of the individual in question. This is not meant to prevent native officers reporting the good as well as the bad deeds of their men, but simply to guard against favouritism, and to prevent any man thinking that he owes his promotion to the native officer. I would also be very chary of believing half the good reports made by native officers of men who have been on detached command with them without collateral proof. I have frequently seen men brought up for conspicuous gallantry on a particular occasion by a native officer, who after all did no more than his neighbours, but happened to be a friend of the native officer, and a good hand at filling a *chillum*.[1]

These points once understood in the regiment, a great door to favouritism on the part of the native officers will be stopped, without detriment to their authority over the men; and endless jealousies and heartburnings will be avoided, for no native has the slightest belief in the honesty of another, and recommendations of this sort are invariably imputed by men who are passed over to sinister influences brought to bear on the native officer. Look after the native officers, and see that they do not constantly bring up their own pet set of men for temporary short leave, of a day or two, to the detriment of the claims of others. This practice is easily introduced, and invariably leads to jealousies and undercurrents in the company. In selecting a native officer for promotion, take into consideration his former services and any dashing deeds he may have performed in the corps, the estimation he is held in by the men in general, and his standing in the regiment as well as his smartness on parade. It is by no means certain that your smart drill is fit for anything else, although this qualification should be allowed to count so many points. Put great stress on general truthfulness and honesty, and let every man see why each promotion is made,

---

1. Pipe.

as well as the reason why men are passed over, and each vacancy in this grade becomes a lesson to your corps.

Non-commissioned Grades.—Be exceedingly particular in your promotion to the non-commissioned grades, and your selection for the higher ranks will be comparatively easy. Here, again, do all you can to make each *havildar* and *naick* feel his individual responsibility, and, when possible, punish the non-commissioned officer in preference to the erring *sepoy*. If you do this systematically you will seldom have to punish anyone. In promoting men be chary of passing over your old men, if they are good, merely to get a smarter youngster as a *naick*; and remember that the former have been tried under all circumstances, while your youngster may not have been so. In the Infantry I would give a fair share of promotion to lance-*naicks* and *kote-havildars* out of their regular roll, as an encouragement to men to learn to read and write, and to come forward to make themselves generally useful in the regiment I take the senior man if I can with any justice, but if there is anything against him I unhesitatingly go to the next, and never stop till I come to a good man. Let everyone understand why he is passed over, and there will be little room for grumbling. Periodical examinations of native commissioned and non-commissioned officers, by the Commanding officer or second in command, tend to keep up smartness in these grades, and keep you informed of the merits of individuals.

Drill and Discipline.—One of the greatest mistakes is to fancy that the high-bred Irregular[2] soldier will not stand drill and discipline, whereas in fact no man is prouder of both when he has mastered them. The most exacting drill-instructor you can find will always be your Pathan, Afridi, or Persian. The tender point of these men is not in the amount of work taken out of them while absolutely with the regiment, but in the amount of leave they get and the notice that their European officers take of them. So long as a liberal allowance of the former is permitted, and the men know their officers, you may drill and work your corps as much as you please. Never allow a man to overstay his leave by a minute under any pretext short of a medical certificate, and when one does forget himself stop all future leave for an indefinite period. This is the severest punishment yon can give a Pathan or a Sikh, and will engender habits of punctuality in these fel-

---

2. The expression "Irregular" was applied to all troops not of the Regular Army, such as the Guides, Punjab Force, and Bengal Irregular Cavalry.

lows unattainable by any other way.

Religion and Prejudices.—Respect the religion and prejudices of every sect, and establish as a rule that each may do as it pleases in private in its own lines, but that no one is to interfere with his neighbour in word or deed. Punish severely all attempts at proselytizing, invariably turning out a renegade from his creed. "All heathen religions are alike abominable"; and the arrangements of the corps should not be upset by a man who does not know his own mind. The only exception I would make would be in favour of a man turning Christian, who should be allowed to remove to that company in which he feels he can live most comfortably. Never for an instant permit religious discussions, not even between European officers and the men; the former are not here for missionary purposes, and should not be allowed to trespass on the functions of the clergy. In my opinion many laymen, with the best intentions, do the greatest possible harm to Christianity by entering into theological arguments on points which the deepest-read divines cannot discuss, and by getting "shut up" from want of knowledge of their subject, they "make the truth appear a lie."

Punishments.—Punishments are absolutely unavoidable, and as a general rule you cannot punish a good man too lightly, nor a bad one too severely. Admit no compromise, but let punishment follow a fault as surely as day succeeds night Take the greatest care to avoid awarding it while under excitement yourself, for your orders on this head should be irrevocable, and the more deliberately the sentence is given the greater its effect Never forget that the object of all punishment is not revenge on the culprit for his misdeeds, but to deter others from following his pernicious example. "General sternness is mercy in the end." I do not mean by this that a good man may never be passed over a slight fault, but when you show clemency be sure that it is deserved, and the reason unmistakable.

Lay down certain rules privately for your own guidance, so as to make all punishments for the same offence as much alike as possible, only varying them to suit the temper of the recipients. You may give extra work of all kinds, hourly or half-hourly roll-calls, stoppage of leave and all indulgences, the temporary withdrawal of your interest in the man's affairs, and last of all the lash. This latter, so far from degrading a native in his own eyes, is very frequently the only thing which will arouse some characters to a sense of shame, and, as far as I am able to judge, improves nine men out of ten who receive it. Great care, however, is necessary to keep this punishment as a last resource, when all other remedies have failed, for if it does not answer, there is nothing to fall back on but expulsion from the service; and, indeed, I would only trouble myself with the infliction of the lash in cases where the man has shown some decided good points in his character worth retaining in the regiment, such as dash and coolness under fire, otherwise I would rather get rid of a bad man and enlist a better.

Half a dozen floggings in a year should be more than ample for any regiment Petty theft, incorrigible gambling, drinking, and insubordination are the crimes which most frequently call for this class of punishment, but in the first-mentioned case, dismissal from the service would of course be inevitable. Light punishments, which call down the ridicule of his comrades, frequently have an excellent effect on young offenders. Having punished an offence, have done with it, and do not keep haggling at the individual afterwards; this only disgusts the man, and makes him despair of forgiveness, which soon leads to general indifference. Do not turn men out of the service for trivial faults, for then no man will feel safe, and the service will be thought so much the less of. Your object should be to make service in your regiment appear to the world at large a prize not easily to be obtained, and of so much the greater value.

Justice.—In any case, between two men, always listen to both parties, no matter how convinced you are that you know the one who is in the wrong, or how absurd the individual's argument may be. Let the fellow have his say, and then give your verdict This does not appear a very necessary hint, but it is perfectly astonishing how often this most obvious rule is broken by even good officers. You naturally fix at once on the known bad character, but in this one solitary instance he may be in the right, and your character for calm, impartial justice will suffer, and the "*budmash*"[3] becomes a confirmed bad character; besides, a man never considers that he has had justice done him until he has had his say. Do not keep a "lawyer" in your corps half an hour; the instant a man talks to you about regulations and his rights show him the door, if you cannot give him a heavier punishment Such men would spoil the best of regiments.

It has been my constant study to instil into the minds of the Guides that the only stipulations made with them on enlistment are that in ordinary times they are to serve three years, do what they are bid, and

---

3. Rascal.

receive eight *rupees* a month for their trouble. For the Guides I always had some eight or ten men extra per company learning their drill without pay in hopes of getting the first vacancy. All leave, promotion, and other advantages of the service are the free gift of the State, superadded as general rewards for good conduct, but not the *right* of even the best men in the corps, and this I believe to be the secret of the proverbial readiness of a Guide to come to the front whenever work of any sort is to be done; he hopes to earn that which he has no legal claim to. With this belief he is ever on the watch to bring himself to the notice of his European officer by swimming, jumping, running, digging, climbing, or any other means that may offer.

British Officers.—Young officers should take advantage of every opportunity for making themselves acquainted with all the usual forms of petitions in general use in civil courts, so as to understand a *sepoy's* case and be able to put it in proper shape for him; and I would make all doing duty officers hear the petitions forwarded for the men before they are submitted for signature, and occasionally examine them as to the merits of a case being sent on. All the young European officers attached to the regiment should be made to study the religious prejudices of each sect, not for the purpose of turning Hindoo or Mahomedan themselves, but to know exactly what each can do without prejudice to his caste.

General Work.—The men should be accustomed to do anything and everything cheerfully at the slightest hint from a European officer, and every opportunity should be taken advantage of to make them handy with the pickaxe and shovel When a well is wanted I take my own men to sink it; if bricks are required they burn them, and the only reward offered is, when a man has gone through a hard day's work he is excused night duty, and when the work is finished and well done I give all concerned a few sheep or goats and some rice to have a jollification with. I would always let an officer take with him fifteen or twenty men as beaters out shooting, and when opportunity offers, give the men five or six rounds of practice ammunition each to fire with where large game is to be had.

Study your men, and never have to ask what they can or cannot do; give your orders as a matter of course, go frequently to see the work yourself, join in it if possible, and at all times talk of it as good fun, and strive to make the men proud of what they have accomplished. Pit company against company to finish your work in better style, and you can never have the slightest difficulty in getting the men to do anything. Make them feel that regiments who do not work as they do are not to be compared with them, and above all things mark your sulky, morose man, and turn him out.

Power of Subordinates.—I would give my European officers under me almost as much power as I myself possess; they can always consult me when in doubt The more power they possess the greater will be their influence over the men. If a mistake is made you can put it right quietly yourself on the spot, and by giving each officer his "swing" you see how far he has imbibed and understood the principles on which you work the regiment You have him, as it were, in leading strings for command, and when he comes to be chief himself he will not be so likely to get "wind in his head," and run wild after every new "jim" he may see, but he will soberly compare what is new with the old, and then act It is the worst of all plans to concentrate power exclusively in yourself as commanding officer, though it is pleasing to find yourself the mainspring of so large a machine; but you should recollect that you may any day be removed, and all should be so arranged in the corps that the work will go on as smoothly as ever without you. This is a point frequently over-looked or misconceived by irregular commandants.

I need not tell you to be kind, considerate, and sociable with all so long as they do their duty, but stand humbug from no one. Any officer who understands his trade knows how to let this be felt without having to show that he does so, and orders once given European or native must alike obey, and carelessness or slovenly performance of duty be equally noted in both instances. If a young "rip" won't take a hint, it is not worth while disturbing the harmony of your little circle by constant bickerings, but he must be told either to mend his ways or to return for correction to that great mill of discipline for officers—the line. If this threat does not improve him, get him removed from your corps at once. Of course, it he commits himself seriously, the shortest plan is to place him under arrest, and send in charges which bring him up at once, and at any rate give him a lesson which should be lasting.

Standing Orderlies—Do not allow "standing orderlies" to yourself or other officers under any pretext An orderly is your personal attendant for the time being, and as such will give you excellent opportunities of seeing his character, so allow no man to select orderlies for you, but take each man in the regiment as he comes. The native adjutant is very apt to try and keep his own pet clique constantly before your eyes, under the pretext of selecting smart and intelligent men. It is, I admit, a bore to have an orderly who does not understand you at once, but practice is more likely to make him do this than keeping him in the background, and I have often picked up most useful hints from thick-headed orderlies letting out little things which a sharper fellow would have kept to himself. Never excuse a mistake of a sentry. He has no business to be mistaken, for if he does not understand his orders when posted, or is not sure of them, it is his duty to ask.

Pay.—No pay should ever be disbursed in the regiment except in the presence of an European officer, who should briefly note in the acquittance roll-book the date of the disbursement A recent G.O. prescribes that no ammunition is ever to be issued without the presence of an European officer, but of how much more consequence is everything connected with the men's pay. Have all regulations regarding the pay of the men, under every circumstance, carefully and clearly explained to the individuals concerned, and take a special care that ail retrenchments and deductions for clothing, etc, are explained to each man, and do not consider it a bore to give such explanation to a thick-headed fellow who cannot add, but try to convince the man that you really take an interest in his accounts.

Necessaries.—It should be your study to provide everything for your men of the best description, and at the cheapest rate. You should strive as much as possible to save the men's pockets by obliging them to have such things only as are absolutely necessary. These remarks are more especially applicable to the Cavalry, whose half-mounting, *chundah*, and other deductions are a heavy drain on a trooper's pay. The great secret in the management of all these institutions is to collect your money only as you expend it, and let the men clearly see what they are paying for. This must satisfy any reasonable being. But large accumulations of funds on any account are sure, sooner or later, to be misunderstood, or perhaps wilfully misrepresented. I would never set any one man to superintend the procuring or making-up of any articles for the regiment, for he is sure to be accused of making something by the transaction, but let committees of three or four men watch all such work when necessary; for, as I have before said, you cannot have things too clear and above-board in your regiment, but, on the contrary, should invite inspection and publicity.

Ball Practice.—The most important branch of the education of the

soldier is his ball practice, for, after all, what is the object of manoeuvring but to get your men into the most advantageous positions for
shooting down their enemies? And the effect of the most skilful dispo-
sitions must be marred, if men cannot use their arms when they have
gained the vantage-ground. Of course, the first thing in the training of
your men is to make them individually good shots at single targets, at
known distances; but this I hold to be only the A B C of the shooting
art, so far as the soldier is concerned, the finishing of his education in
this department requiring much patience and careful supervision, and
I have reason to know that this part of his training is entirely neglected
in many native regiments.

A regiment should be frequently practised in manoeuvres with
loaded arms, and thus positively taught how little danger there is with
ordinary care in carrying loaded arms. Companies might next be practised in extended order, firing at marks scattered about at all sorts of
distances, elevations, and angles. Skirmishers should be relieved, made
to advance, retire, and incline to a flank, firing, and so on, till they are
perfect Too large marks are not required, as skirmishers in the field
against men who know their work will seldom get a shot at more than
the head and shoulders of a man. Common *ghurrahs*[4] are about the
right size, and can be easily placed. As soon as all the companies have
been thus instructed, they should be drawn up as a regiment, taught to
fire with precision by files and companies and in volleys.

Also file firing in squares and in almost every possible position that
a soldier could be called on to fire. All this appears simple enough,
but let inspecting generals try corps in this way, and I venture to say
that in nine cases out of ten a lamentable failure will be the result In
many regiments the front rank men will be so nervous of the loaded
arms of the men behind them as quite to lose all their senses, and
the Battalion be incapable of manoeuvring. In my humble opinion,
after a recruit has been thoroughly accustomed to fire his rifle steadily
without flinching, he should never be permitted to fire another blank
cartridge, but be kept steadily at ball practice whenever called on to
fire; bad shots must, of course, be taken back to first principles, but the
instantaneous volleys and rapid detonations so admired at reviews are
the very ruin of the shooting of your regiment, and to continue this
ruinous blank hubbub is throwing away the kernel of your nut and
keeping the shell.

---

4. Clay vessels.

Cavalry.—Notwithstanding the united testimony of Napoleon, Saxe, and Frederick the Great, to the value of *light* cavalry, it is a remarkable fact that if we except the *Cossacks*, Europe can scarcely produce a single regiment of really light cavalry. Timour sacrificed weight to speed, and relied upon rapid and successive charges, supported by strong reserves, and such a system has in all ages proved its superiority over that of heavy, cumbrous squadrons manoeuvring at a slow pace, and trusting either to the effect of firearms or to the weight of men and horses. Of all errors none is more fatal than that of imagining that by raising the weight on a horse's back you increase his momentum in a charge. Any weight beyond that of a light man and light equipment fatigues, and finally overpowers the horse, while in a charge it is rendered worse than nugatory by *diminished velocity*.

Your appointments cannot therefore be too plain, or too light, and every ounce which is not absolutely necessary should be removed from horse and man. If the fire of infantry is uncertain, what will be the effect of that of cavalry? Ten carbines a troop are ample for all purposes, and pistols absurd. A cavalry man should trust to his spurs and sword, and have no other weapon; the latter should be light and suited to the power of the individual, but of the very best material procurable.

In the Cavalry, do not for a moment put up with the nuisance of loose horses in camp or quarters, for they are alike dangerous to man and beast, and do more mischief to the *chundah*[5] than would be imagined, so that when you find a man cannot secure his horse properly, make him sit on the beast's back all night, and you will soon find the number of loose horses decrease.

Barghirs.[6]—Break the men of the absurd idea that *barghirs* are the right of commissioned and non-commissioned officers, and make this boon a reward for good service, and a means of bringing men of family into your corps, and take care that low-bred men are not smuggled in as *barghirs*, for they will in time become owners of horses themselves, get promotion, and perhaps own *barghirs* who are of a shade lower *caste* than themselves, and you will thus go from bad to worse. The best way to ensure good *barghirs* is to make the man who brings one answerable for his *caste*, and should he afterwards turn out other

---

5. Horse fund.
6. A *Barghir* is a cavalry soldier, the follower of a native officer, who maintains for him his horse and equipment.

than represented, take away the *"asamee"* altogether, and the eyes of the cavalry will be kept open. Do not allow buying and selling of *"asamees"* in the regiment, but when a man wishes to get rid of his *barghir*, have a committee on the horse and his trappings, and make them over to anyone you choose, who must, of course, pay their value. I look upon the purchasing system as the very worst in the world, for it is calculated to give Tested rights, which were never intended by regulations.

Do not give a *Kote-Duffadar's* place to a man who cannot read and write. It is obviously wrong that he should be responsible for accounts which are kept by another man, while he draws the pay; the man who really keeps the accounts being all the time irresponsible, and drawing but a trifle for doing the work of a highly responsible office. Look well to your horses when passing them into the regiment Take great care to replace *monthly* those which become unserviceable, for if they are allowed to accumulate for a short time, great difficulty may be experienced in finding remounts enough, and the corps may be worst off in this respect just at the moment when ordered on service, whereas four or five horses a month regularly renewed should keep you well horsed. Cabulee horses seldom last long, and are given to knock up in the hot season. Wuzerees are first-rate, but the supply is limited. Hazara horses are liable to ringbone and bad hoofs; and Chuchee breeds do not last, and are impetuous. All other breeds may be taken.

Accounts.—I like our system of accounts in the Guides, for, although it entails a little extra trouble, no mistakes can well occur, as the different books check one another; and as the daily account book checks all the others it should, in my opinion, be kept by the commanding officer himself. If not allowed to fall in arrears, ten minutes' work daily will keep it all right Whatever you do, eschew either making or taking advances, for their adjustment is always troublesome. On service be sure to get all bills for every sort of contingent charges, indents, receipts for stores, etc., passed and countersigned at the time, and sent for adjustment before they are forgotten.

Do not trust even a Governor-General to get them done afterwards, for so long as your services are frequently required any expense will be cheerfully passed by the higher authorities, but, the danger over, it will be found that all sorts of objections are made to charges, and endless vouchers required. Make a rule to get these *passed once a week, all clear,* even if you should let other papers run in arrears for want of time, and you will never repent it.

Bazar.—A really good *bazar* gives a regiment an enormous advantage in the field, where supplies are not very plentiful, and every means ought to be taken to induce men of substance to establish shops with your regiment Especial care must be taken to see all regimental *bazar* accounts settled monthly at the pay table, and no debts allowed under any pretence. While seeing that the *bunniaha* are regularly paid, and fairly dealt with, insist on their providing unadulterated goods, and at reasonable rates, and whenever there is a deficiency in your *bazar* make a point of punishing the shopkeepers. A good *bazar* can never be established without a first-rate *chowdry,*[7] with capital sufficient to ensure respect from his subordinates.

In the Field.—In the field each European and native officer must carry a small pocket note-book constantly about him, so as to be able to send a written order or take notes at any moment With reference to the management of a regiment in the field on actual service I would say, Recollect that discipline and drill have for years been worked into your men for the express purpose of making them handy under difficulties in the hour of danger, and not, as some officers seem to suppose, to be thrown away at the very moment when real work begins. The best troops in the world without these must be little, if anything, better than a rabble; so, when you get under fire, make your men keep their places and wait for orders with the greatest steadiness.

I do not mean by this that men should be bothered out of their lives when hard worked about unimportant trifles, but every officer knows, or should do so, the difference between keeping up strict discipline and habits of prompt obedience and worrying. If regiments are carefully watched, it will be frequently found that there are in each a set of men who constantly fall out of the ranks on one pretext or another, and then straggle into camp at their leisure. Such men are better got rid of at once, for they are never present when wanted, and either drop out on purpose or are physically unfit for soldiers. Two men turned out of a corps on this account will generally cease the disorder.

Commanding Officer.—A commanding officer's place in action is where he can see best and most easily control the movements of his regiment, and not cruising about before his skirmishers by way of

---

7. Headman.

proving his pluck, which should be undoubted and kept for an extreme case, where nothing but example will take men into what looks like certain death, or make them stand against overwhelming odds. He may then go in, and his example will be understood, and be worthy of him. His great object in the field should be to save his men in every possible way compatible with the due performance of the duties of the camp. Get them quickly over their marches, and down to cook and rest as soon as possible after arriving at the ground. Economize sentry and night work, and, in short, keep his men fresh for every possible emergency which may turn up, as on service they do turn up in a most unaccountable way.

Expeditions.—It will generally be found that our border expeditions are undertaken either on a considerable scale for the purpose of thoroughly subduing some particular clan, whose frequent raids have at last roused our Government to necessary action; or, it may be, a sudden drawing together of a small force in a convenient position for a rush on some vulnerable point in the enemy's country, to punish a particular section of a clan before combinations of the whole tribe can be matured for an organized defence on a more extended scale, or for the blockading out of a clan which carries on considerable mercantile transactions in the plain, and teaching it that the hillmen are more dependent on the people of the plain than *vice-versa*, and thus practically demonstrating the advantage of keeping on good terms with their neighbours. Of these three model of bringing mountaineers to their bearings, the third when applicable (for there are many clans on the border who would not care about a blockade) is perhaps the most effective and satisfactory; but it requires great seal and sagacity in the young officers in charge of outposts, and judgment in the choice of positions to be occupied.

In this sort of work it is of vital importance that outpost officers be on the best of terms with the influential men in the villages about their poets, and that they should have the gift of worming information out of natives without seeming to be doing so. They should also have the instinct of at once recognising good information from worthless, and, above all, be exempt from flurry on the receipt of exciting news. Next in point of efficiency is the first plan, which, however, demands ample means in men and material, as also a certain degree of co-operation in the chiefs of our own district, whose lands border on the tribe to be overpowered, and above all, an ample margin in time, carriage, cattle, and commissariat to meet all the unforeseen contingencies attending operations in the hills on an unexplored theatre of war, when a few projecting rocks or a narrow pathway may delay a column for hours, and the foil of a dozen camels involve a rear-guard in a night's hard fighting.

The second is the most unsatisfactory and hazardous plan, for one has to depend entirely on that broken reed "native information" for distances, numbers, etc., in fact for the basis of all those calculations which can alone secure success; and besides, it is but a half-measure at best, only to be resorted to when other circumstances Tender No. 1 operation politically inconvenient The most satisfactory way, however, to settle differences with a clan is to thrash them on No. 1 plan and apply No. 3 until they give in completely, and then leave them to their own devices. This generally has a lasting effect, while any of the other remedies may be forgotten as soon as the actors in them die off

Before starting with your corps on any expedition, look to the following points:—

1st That you have a correct route to the rendezvous, and a dear idea of where you are going.

2nd. That all superfluous baggage is left in quarters, and that only absolute necessaries are taken with yon, for both men and officers should feel that every extra load is a great hindrance to the force.

3rd. See that you have ample ammunition, and that it is well packed on your mules,

4th. That you have axes, saws, and *phowrahs* for entrenching pickets, etc.

5th. Clothing according to the season, but especially warm for night work in a hill climate, and such as affords protection against wet—a *choga* and *poshteen*, besides cloth coat. (Cloth pantaloons are useless, for the men cannot go uphill in them.)

6th. Spare tents for pickets and guards.

7th. Shoes and sandals, at least two spare sets besides the pair in wear.

8th. Good carriage for everything, as there is no use in starting with indifferent cattle to delay rear-guards and unnecessarily fatigue the troops, to say nothing of the chances of having to destroy necessaries as the camels knock up. Your regiment should be able to carry at least four days' supply for fighting men and camp followers in the *bazar*, and be provided with a proportion of spare animals, to ease sick cattle and replace casualties.

9th. The medical officer should look to his *doolies*, *dandies*, and *kajawas*, as well as a few spare *kahars*, in case of any of these useful servants falling sick or getting disabled. He should also see that he has an ample supply of the common country cloth usually in requisition for bandages, for I have known the stock in camp run out.

10th. Provision should be made for a regular supply of opium and spirits for such men as Sikhs, Goorkahs, Dogras, etc, of the regiment as habitually use stimulants.

11th. You will require sickles for cutting forage for horses and *yaboos*, and spare shoes, at least three complete sets per animal, as the boulders in the beds of torrents (which are the usual roads in the hills) make sad havoc amongst horse-shoes, especially those of the English pattern, with their narrow webs and uneven bearing. Hobbles should be provided for the mounted branch rampageous and restive horses, and no excuse admitted for their getting loose.

12th. Take care to have a supply of common *bazar* medicines for your cattle, conveniently packed, so as to be easily got at, and also material for the repair of mule gear and the stuffing of saddles in general The chief requirements are sulphur, *tarameera* oil, turpentine, opium, aloes, calomel, tartar emetic, ginger, alum, sulphate of copper, nitrate of silver, a paper of pins, some silk thread, a firing iron, *numdah*, thread, and leather, bandages, a probe fleam and scalpel and a clyster-pipe.

13th. All men and establishments should be paid up to the latest convenient date, so as to obviate the necessity of carrying treasure with your regiment, or at any rate reducing it to the smallest possible amount

14th. No women, or dogs, should be allowed to accompany the regiment, as they are apt to disturb the rest of the troops. Especially the latter, which chase loose horses and answer each other from different parts of the camp all night

In the Punjab Force it is customary to allow men on service to wear their native pyjamas, provided they are dyed the colour of their uniform; this practice eases the fatigue of working on a hill-side considerably, and is looked on as a great boon by the men.

It is a good plan to keep your regimental *puckalies* always on the reverse flank of their own particular companies; and to give the men frequent but short halts, so as to enable them to drink as they get thirsty. It prevents many a man from knocking up and eventually becoming a straggler.

Mountain Train Battery.—Mountain train guns, with their ammunition, can be conveniently carried on mules and *yaboos*, whilst camels are substituted for store carts, and if a few elephants can only be added to carry the gun and limber over difficult "*kothuls*," there is no limit to the use of such pieces, in fact their superior range and penetration make them invaluable in covering the ascent and descent of mountains. The sudden opening of a battery of mountain train guns from the top of a ridge has a great moral effect on the minds of hillmen. I think most Infantry officers are apt to expect too much from Artillery fire in general, and not to give these pieces time enough, should the first half-dozen shots not clear the front. These officers are apt to order an immediate advance of their own arm, and lose men in carrying the position with infantry, when a little more patience and allowing the Artillery to get the range and develop its fire would have cleared the ground for them. Provision, however, must be made for good, warm clothing for elephants, as they are particularly sensitive to cold, and soon knock up under its influence.

Cavalry.—Infantry is the sheet anchor in all hill work, and guns its support; but it must be borne in mind that all hillmen have an instinctive dread of cavalry, and give this arm a position in their calculations which would not always be borne out by the effect actually produced. This feeling may extensively be taken advantage of whenever an open space admits of the movement of even a small body of horsemen, and in practice it will be found that a few *sowars* sprinkled along the flanks of a column of baggage give it a security quite out of proportion to the actual value of cavalry in such a position. In the same way their superior powers of locomotion give cavalry great advantages in watching herds of camels scattered over a large tract of country at graze. The food of horses, however, is bulky, and therefore the number of cavalry to be taken on an expedition must be regulated by the amount of forage to be procured on the route, and the general character of the hills which are to be the theatre of the operations.

Advance-Guards.—On entering hills, good advance and rear-guards, as well as flanking parties, will be ordered; their constitution depends entirely on the nature of the ground to be passed over. Advance-guards seldom have much to do beyond keeping their eyes and ears open and taking care of themselves until the main column is formed for action.

Flankers.—Flanking parties are generally left from the main column, at commanding points, right and left of a pass, to hold the ground till the arrival of the rear-guard, and protect the flanks of the baggage. The officer in command of each should have a slip of paper given him with his name, corps, and strength of his party noted on it, which he will deliver to the officer commanding the rear-guard on joining him. These parties should not, except on an emergency, be kept with the rear-guard, but be ordered after making their report to rejoin their own corps. Thus a constant succession of parties will be found patrolling the whole length of the column of baggage, ready to succour any point which may be threatened. The posting of these flanking parties requires practice and judgement, so as not to detach more than necessary, and at the same time ensure perfect safety along the whole line.

Rear-Guards.—Rear-guards are the real trial in the hills, for they are pretty sure to be more or less engaged daily, and the handling of them is often a delicate operation, the first starting off from the old ground being usually the most difficult part of the day's work, as the enemy has had time to make himself acquainted with the position of each of the pickets around camp which are withdrawn to form a rear-guard. From my own experience I should say that the best plan is to cover the descent of your pickets with either long-range rifles or artillery, withdrawing the more distant ones gradually as the baggage clears off the encamping ground, and not being in a hurry to gather them in before you are quite ready to move off It is better to let the baggage get away half a mile or so before you more, and then be off after it, making your next stand when you come on eligible ground close up with the rear camels.

Every rear-guard should have a proportion of spare cattle to bring on the loads of knocked up animals, as well as *doolies* and *kajawas* for wounded or sick men who fall to the rear. Most rear-guards have some Artillery with them, but care must be taken not to destroy the moral effect of this arm by firing at small parties of the enemy, when the best of shots does not ensure any result; a few long-range rifles-are here most useful in keeping the enemy at a respectful distance. In retiring along a ridge, when the enemy presses sharply on, occupying your positions the instant you leave them, it is often a good plan (when you have time) to bury a few pounds of powder or a live shell connected with a slow match left smouldering under a stone or two, and then to hold your next position until you hear the explosion; one man of the enemy blown up in this way has a great moral effect, and makes the rest very suspicious and careful where they are running to.

Firing a volley from the crest of a ridge and starting off as if down-hill, but in reality going but a few paces to reload, and creep back to your original position, or just below it, there to wait the arrival of the leading files of the enemy, and then meet them with a well-delivered volley, often produces satisfactory results. Care must be taken, however, to prevent your men creeping up the ridge so far as to try and peep over, for their heads are sure to be seen by the lynx-eyed mountain-eers, and your project spoiled.

Retiring firing, both ranks together, loading on the march (as laid down in the new drill-book) is simply impossible with our rifles and ammunition; and retiring by alternate ranks (according to the old method of skirmishing) would in many instances degenerate into a run to the rear with native troops when closely followed up. It's an ugly lookout for wounded men. The best plan, in my opinion, is to extend the supports, and retire by alternate lines of skirmishers passing through each other, and selecting your ground carefully as you retire. The great difficulty is to get neatly off the long slope of a bare hill, with good shots pegging at you from behind the crest The best plan is to bring your first line right down to the bottom before you give up the crest, and let the second line run clear off the hill at one run. You should always come down a spur of the hill in preference to such a slope, as there is generally cover under one side or other of the crest of the spur, and usually a succession of knolls from behind which to check an enemy.

In threading a pass, sometimes a few horsemen hid behind a pro-jecting rock or corner, rushing suddenly out and sabring the men following the rear-guard in the pass, and then galloping on to join the rear-guard before the enemy on the hills can outflank them, is calcu-lated to make the enemy cautious. The most awkward position for a rear-guard to find itself in is when a long march has been made with indifferent cattle, and night overtakes it still a considerable distance from camp. Here an enterprising enemy, acquainted with the ground, should have a chance of doing infinite mischief with comparative impunity; but mountaineers are generally found to have had enough of following up all day, and leave off just when they should be commencing their pranks. The best thing to be done under such circumstances is, I think, to send on an intelligent officer to reconnoitre the ground between you and camp before darkness sets in, to order all flanking parties to stand fast, and to collect the baggage as much as possible in knots under the protection of these parties, looking out for strong ground to be occupied by the rear-guard itself, and reporting these arrangements, and the cause of them, to the officer commanding in camp, and working in quietly as the cattle get on to camp. Of course, these arrangements would only be necessary where a rear-guard is followed in considerable strength.

The Attack.—In attacking positions on the hills, where the movements of troops are considerably cramped, and their general super-vision difficult, it is a good rule to have as strong a line of skirmishers as possible to cover the front A few loose files have little chance against a determined knot of men behind a *sungar* or breastwork, and to attack them under such circumstances in this order is to ensure the discomfiture of your own men and the consequent depression of their dash.

I would make the skirmishers advance to within sixty or seventy yards (if possible overlapping the flanks of the *sunga*, so as to get it under a cross fire), and lie down till the supports pass them with fixed swords and storm the *sunga*—the reserve dosing up and taking the place of the supports for the moment.

Supports.—It has been well said that "contending without reserves is desperate risk in struggles of all kinds, civil and military." In such predicaments, if fortune frowns, well-nigh all is lost The supports should therefore always be at hand, but especially when an attack on a breastwork is impending, for it may possibly devolve on them to carry this particular point. The mere fact of a portion of a line of skirmishers being checked, or even driven in, can never have much effect either on the general results of the particular operation going on, or on the reputation of the corps to which the skirmishers belong, provided that the supports of the same regiment are in hand, and ready to retrieve matters on the spot It should be remembered by all "that skirmishing is not, as generally supposed, a prowling wolf-like proceeding, but sheer hard, open fighting, in which, indeed, the parties engaged make the best of any cover that presents itself."

But still ground must be gained, held, or given up, according to orders, hanging in cover and slinking in open ground when it has to be crossed being equally reprehensible in a skirmish as in closed ranks. Very often a heavy breastwork may be taken with but comparatively little loss by threatening its front with supports whilst the skirmishers push round its flanks; and should the enemy continue in it a moment too long, this movement is sure to inflict heavy loss on him while retiring through the cross-fire of the skirmishers and closely pursued by the supports.

Reserves.—Your best troops should be in reserve, for good reserves powerfully influence the moral courage of a soldier, who does not fear facing danger when he feels himself well supported. Reserves therefore should be particularly alert and well up while an attack on a breastwork is taking place. The wisest combination must frequently prove defective in hill warfare, and the commanding officer must have good troops in hand to meet all eventualities and to retrieve mishaps.

Pathan Sepoys.—Pathan skirmishers, if not narrowly watched, have a nasty trick of breaking their ranks and rushing to the front without orders when the enemy begin to give way, and the result is, as soon as they come on unexpected opposition or an unseen breastwork, they in turn as readily recoil. This propensity must be carefully guarded against, and everyone presuming to move without orders severely punished. Your men should, of course, always have a rush in them, but kept under control I have seen a whole regiment thrown into inextricable confusion and ultimate disgrace from this very failing. Another ugly trick of these hillmen is that of wandering off in twos and threes in search of what they can pick up as soon as the enemy give way and they can find a convenient ravine or cover to slink off behind. A roll call or two in the field, and heavy punishment on non-commissioned officers as well as the offending men, will be found excellent preventives.

Camps.—It is impossible to lay down even general rules for castrametation in the hills when the formation of the ground must dictate the shape of your camp, but economy of space and pickets, together with easy access to water, and a free communication from right to left, and from front to rear through camp, are the points to be looked to. It will sometimes happen that the force will be divided, and pitched in the bends and hollows in a pass; in such cases each detached portion becomes a camp, and should be so arranged as to admit of free communication through the lines of tents as above stated. All pickets about camp should be posted by daylight, so as to enable men and officers to become so familiar with objects in their immediate neighbourhood as to readily recognize them, and be able to move in any direction in the dark. Pickets, when practicable, should be protected by breastworks, which can generally be made in an hour or so from loose stones in the vicinity, and when brushwood is procurable an abattis may be thrown round the front at about thirty paces distant.

This bothers the enemy considerably in the dark, when attempting to overpower a picket by superior numbers, and affords good opportunity for inflicting heavy punishment. Pickets in the hills should always be strong, connected (when practicable) with each other by double sentries, and so posted that no body of men could slip between them without being exposed to fire. They should seldom consist of less than thirty men, and be much stronger when at any distance from camp, or so situated as not to admit of being easily reinforced, and in the two latter cases each picket should, if possible, be commanded by an European subaltern. At night many tricks are played by hillmen to bother a camp and deprive it of that rest so necessary for long-continued exertion. One is running a little slow match between the strands of a long piece of string at every two feet, lighting them all, and then two men walking up with the string stretched between them towards an outlying picket Of course, the sentries fire and turn out their picket, which in turn opens volleys upon the supposed line of matchlock men. This brings out the inlying pickets, and the whole camp is roused.

As soon as the desired hubbub has been created in camp, one man lets go his end of the string, whilst the other sits down behind a bush and winds up his precious burden, running off to react the same game in an hour or so at some other part of camp, giving an idea of numbers of the enemy having been prowling about all night, while in reality not more than three or four have been in the neighbourhood. Anyone who has watched these proceedings and once observed the steady, regular way of a string of this description cannot again be deceived, and two or three horsemen told off with carbines loaded with buckshot to ride sharply in at the end of the string and fire at anyone he may see generally spoils the amusement. Imitation jackal cries are favourite signals at night between hillmen, and when they appear to answer one another at different points round camp the circumstance should make sentries and pickets doubly vigilant

Clearing a Ridge.—In pushing hillmen off a ridge to clear the road it is always advisable to hunt them back sharply for some distance beyond the point you actually wish to occupy, as by so doing they are kept at a more respectful distance and prevented from troubling much when your party has to be withdrawn. The quicker that mountaineers are pushed when they once begin to give way, the less resistance they are capable of showing, even when passing over the strongest ground; and I have observed that these people are seldom capable of contin- ued attacks on any occasion; if their first charge does not succeed, and the slightest offensive move is made, they break up and disperse. Here and there a desperate man may turn and try to cover the rear, but the game is to all intents and purposes up if your troops are only kept in hand, but with men running wild in the excitement of victory it is not impossible that ten or twelve resolute men hid among rocks suddenly jumping up, sword in hand, in the midst of them, may cause a panic and mar all your bright prospects.

Intelligence.—I have before insisted on the importance of the cor- dial co-operation of the Chiefs of our own tribes bordering on the scene of action, and the reason is that they alone can furnish reliable guides and information, and may when so inclined save an infinite deal of harassing escort duty with supplies, etc, and for this reason officers and men should be taught to look upon them as friends and to treat them with every consideration. Refugees from across the bor- der are sometimes exceedingly useful as guides from their intimate knowledge of their own country, but should not be too implicitly trusted till they have established their claim to be so. High rewards for faithful services, with prompt and uncompromising punishment for deceit, are the surest means for obtaining information, combined with a tact not always met with, in extracting the information possessed by an individual after you have got hold of the right man. Few natives can tell a plain, unvarnished tale intelligibly, and their instinct leads them to try and discover what will be agreeable to the ear of their superior, and then to shape their story accordingly; in this lies the secret of half the falsehoods they tell.

Appendix B

A FEW NOTES ON AFGHAN FIELD-SPORTS.

By H.B.L.

It would be impossible for a stranger to live any time among Afghans and not to be struck with their passionate fondness for field-sports, especially hawking. The late Wazir Muhammad Akbar Khan spent a great part of his leisure time in this diversion, and his sons as well as many of the chief *sirdars* follow his example; his great delight was in deer-hawking.

Hawking.—The birds usually trained in Afghanistan are of two classes, distinguished, I believe, in Europe as the long and short-winged hawks, but which in the East are better known by the colour of the eyes, which are either yellow or black. The female of both varieties is the larger and more valuable bird; and the following are the native names for the different species in each of these families:—

	Females.	Males.
Yellow-eyed.	Báz (goshawks)	Jurrá.
	Báshin (sparrow-hawks)	Báshí.
	Shikrá	Chippakh.
Black-eyed.	Charúgh (falco cervialis)	Charghelah.
	Bahrí (true coursing falcon)	Bahri Bacha.
	Shahín (peregrine falcon)	Koellah.
	Lagar	Jhagar.
	Turmuti	Tuni.
	Regi (falco shuter)	Maknoni.

Peculiar Training of each Sort.—The initiatory training of all is the same, but the yellow-eyed hawk is never hooded after its education is completed, unless it be in the case of a sparrow-hawk, and she only when at rest in the house. The black-eyed birds, on the contrary, are never unhooded except at the instant when required to fly at game, or for practice; and it is wonderful to see the quickness with which these birds will at once distinguish the quarry at almost incredible distances, on being suddenly unhooded in the full glare of a tropical noonday sun. The former are short-flighted, and seldom lost; while the latter from the length of wing tower to an immense height and follow their game to any distance, circumstances which often lead to the best of hawks being frequently lost, even in experienced hands.

Age of Hawks.—The age of a bird is at once distinguishable from its plumage and the colour of the legs and beak; so much so indeed that, to an inexperienced eye, a hawk of the first year (called *chuz*) would appear of a totally different species from the same bird a year older (then called *tarenak*). Birds of the first year are always the fastest, but they are more liable to be lost than those which have been longer domesticated.

Moulting.—All the hawk species moult during spring, while the female is sitting on her eggs, and are again in full plumage about the time that their young are three parts grown. In a domesticated state the moulting season (*kurfz*) commences about March or April, when the birds are usually placed in some quiet, retired, cool corner of a room, tied by the jesses with about a yard of strong string to a low perch, and within easy reach of a large vessel of water, in which they are exceedingly fond of bathing; they are fed in the evening, but without being handled or moved. About the tenth or twelfth day the bird will be found to have shed the outer feather in each wing; in six or eight more the two next feathers will be shed, and so the process (which is much slower in the domesticated bird) goes on till the principal feathers of the wings have been renewed, when the two outer ones of the tail are shed; as soon as the tail is also renewed all the smaller feathers are thrown off in handfuls daily.

Should the hawk, however, be handled in the least, or even moved from one corner of the room to another, the moulting stops short for twelve or fourteen days at least, and sometimes is not recommenced, so that the bird has to work on for a second season with the old feathers. During the moulting, butter is given in considerable quantities with the food of the bird.

Haunts of Hawks.—The Báz and Jurrá breed in the loftiest mountains, and are only captured in such localities; it is said by natives that the higher the range from which they are taken the better will the birds prove. These are considered by the Afghans as the most valuable of the hawk tribes, and fetch when trained from 40 to 100 Company's *rupees* each. The smaller yellow-eyed hawks frequent low hills and the banks of deep, precipitous ravines (known in this country as "*alguds*"). Charughs build on low mounds in any moderate climate like that of Candahar, Balkh, etc., etc, while Shahíns and Lagars make their nests on the face of precipitous cliffs. The Bahrí is only found along the banks of rivulets or near marshes abounding with waterfowl; and the smaller varieties of the black-eyed hawks frequent deep ravines and low hills.

Modes of Catching Hawks to Train.—In Afghanistan there are four methods usually adopted to procure hawks for training.

First—Charughs and Bahries, intended for coursing deer, and Shahíns are taken from the nest when just about to leave it, and brought up by hand; the longer they are left with their parents the better, provided they do not learn to hunt on their own account.

Second—A net, called a *dogazza*, made of fine but very strong silk thread (with large open meshes), about six feet by four deep, is suspended in a perpendicular position on two slender reeds, and a pigeon or some smaller bird is tied by the foot to a peg on the ground in front of and within about a foot and a half or two feet of, the bottom of the net, in such a position that it may flutter about and attract the attention of the wild hawk, the falconer of course concealing himself at some little distance. The hawk stoops at the bird, which is too near the net to admit of her rising again high enough from the ground to avoid it, and the velocity at which she strikes is so great as to carry off the net from the slender reeds, enveloping the hawk under the net; the falconer, instantly rushing up, secures the hawk by thrusting it head foremost into a piece of cloth sewn in the shape of a cone, with just an aperture sufficient to admit of the head passing out at the apex. The bird's eyes are now closed, either by having a hood placed on the head, or more frequently by a thread being passed through each under-eyelid, and the two twisted together on the top of the head.

Third method—First catch a Jhaggar or Shikrá in a *dogazza*, as above described; half close his eyes, fasten his beak so that he cannot peck, and then tie a bunch of feathers thickly interspersed with strong horsehair nooses on to his legs, which are tied together (a bird so prepared is called a "*Bairak*"). As soon as a Charugh, Bahrí, Shahín, or Lagar is seen coursing in the air, on the lookout for game, the falconer seeking shelter in the nearest bush, tosses the Bairak up as high as he can into the air; the Jhaggar thus set free, soars off, while the wild hawk, mistaking the feathers on his feet for a captured bird in his talons, dashes at and seizes them, entangles his own claws in the nooses, and the two birds roll together to the ground, where they are secured.

The fourth method is nothing more nor less than four *dogazzas*, set back to back in the form of a square, in the midst of which is pegged down a partridge or *chakor*. This sort of trap is used exclusively for Bázes and Jurrás, and is generally set on some high and open hill; the nets are, however, much larger in every way than the one I have described, though acting on the same principle.

Points of Hawks.—The chief points looked to in the selection of hawks besides species and age are great length from crown of head to tip of tail, breadth of chest, and extreme span of talons, with a bright, clear eye. Besides these, each falconer has his own fanciful ideas of particular spots and shades of colour, but these latter will be found contradicted in every day's experience and in each new district

Training.—To train Charughs and Bahries to course deer it is necessary to give the food of each bird daily on the stuffed head of a gazelle (Chikarrah or Ahu Dashtí), the crust being placed in the eyeholes, and when the young birds can fly they are called to this lure. When full grown and obedient, they are shown a young fawn or kid of the same colour, and if they seize it, the animal is killed for them and a little of the warm blood given to the birds. A greyhound is next set after the fawn, and the hawk flown at it If the latter strikes, all that is required in the way of training has been accomplished, and the birds may be taken in quest of wild game; but if not, a few more kids are sacrificed as above, in order to give the hawks confidence. It is usual to train hawks to fly in pairs for this sort of sport

The greatest care, however, is necessary not to allow these hawks ever to see other falcons flown at birds, though they may, when first brought out *the second year*, be allowed to kill a hare or two to get them into wind. Charughs cannot, as a rule, kill deer without the assistance of greyhounds, although there are instances on record of their having done so. The best falconers in this line are Turkistanis.

Shahíns taken from the nest are always fed on a lure made from the dried wings of the middle-sized bustard, "ubara"; and when old enough, and perfectly obedient, large fowls and a snared bustard or two are turned down for them to kill, which finishes their education. These birds are, however, always most useful when trained in pairs, and should be made to soar high before they are fed, for a want of such training makes them low-flighted and spiritless.

As soon as a newly-captured bird of any other description is brought home it is laid on the floor and allowed to roll about, being occasionally touched with a stick until it gives over all attempts to claw and peck. Its eyes are now opened and a hood put on, the cloth also being opened sufficiently to admit of the bird's standing up. Jesses or small leather straps, about eighteen inches long, are fastened, one on each leg, just above the claws, and a pair of small bells fixed immediately above the jesses, which completes the dressing of black-eyed hawks; the yellow-eyed species require a strong silk loop adjusted very loosely round the neck, with an end about eight or nine inches long left hanging down the breast. This string is held under the middle finger of the right hand, to balance the bird while in the act of being thrown off, for there is a great art in casting off all short-flighted hawks, so as to give them as good a start as possible; while the others are merely unhooded, and start of their own accord as soon as they see their game.

In a very short time the cloth is removed from the body, and the hawk made to sit on the gloved hand. About the second day of its captivity the hawk will usually take a little food, although some refuse it for three or four days. As a general rule, the sooner a bird feeds and the longer she takes to subdue, the more valuable she will turn out.

In training yellow-eyed hawks a small hole is next bored in the hood for the bird to peep through, and daily enlarged. The hawk is constantly handled, carried about in bazaars and crowded places to accustom it to people, and kept awake day and night. For black-eyed hawks the hood is constantly removed and replaced (at first in the dark, and by degrees in daylight) for the same purpose. As soon as the bird has become perfectly quiet and tame in hand, a pair of dried wings of the quarry to which it is to be trained are tied together, and the food always given on this lure, the bird being induced to come a short distance (from one hand to the other) for it.

When a greater distance becomes necessary, a long string with a ring in it, to which is attached about four feet of strong light string tied to the jesses of the hawk, is used, an assistant holding the bird and one end of the long string, while the falconer goes to the other with the food on the lure, and calls the hawk. On the hood being removed the hawk flies to the lure, while the ring traversing along the string enables her to reach it, where she is fed. This practice is continued for several days, after which the hawk is kept very hungry and let fly at large, the lure being now and then shown to keep her within bounds; and after a short flight she is fed.

A few days of this practice, and the hawk is ready for a "*bowli.*" This is generally a specimen of the quarry the hawk is to hunt hereafter, turned down alive for her to kill; but if the bird cannot be had conveniently, the largest fowls are used as *bowlies*. When the hawk has struck it, she is allowed a full meal (the first she has had since she was caught) on the flesh and blood; and after this she is ready for the field. It must be always borne in mind in training hawks that it is easy to bring any bird to kill small game after she has been broken in to large, but that the reverse is almost impossible.

Any of these hawks can be easily trained to kill small game, such as partridges, *chakor*, teal, quail, and snipe; but the following is a list of the quarry to which each sort is generally broken in:—

Báz, for ducks, *ubara*, jungle-fowl, peafowl, pheasants, and hares.

Jurrá: ducks, pheasants, jungle-fowl, and partridges of sorts.

Charughs: to deer, herons, cranes, bustard, *ubara*, curlew, hares and kites.

Bahries: deer, ducks, herons, cranes, *ubara*, geese, curlew, and hares. The male of these two last can only kill partridges, plover, and rooks.

Shahíns in pairs: bustard, ducks, hares, pheasants, jungle-fowl, partridges, and rooks. Male as above mentioned in the case of Bahri-bachas.

A most murderous practice is to take a brace of Shahíns and let them fly over a small *jhil*[1] covered with ducks, while the fowler shoots the ducks on the water. The hawks will not allow a single duck to leave the water, and the last one of the flock may be thus secured, provided that care be taken not to shoot one on dry land. If this occurs, the hawks will instantly fasten on the dead bird, and allow the remainder of the ducks to escape.

---

1. Pond or marsh.

The Lagar: is chiefly kept for hares, crows, partridges, and the like, and the male bird for catching larger falcons, as I have already shown. All the smaller varieties of hawks are kept for quail and partridges, except the Regi, which is usually trained to hunt in couples, and kills larks and small birds after a long chase.

For an Englishman to follow this sport enjoyably, the best of trainers and first-rate horses are absolutely necessary; for without the assistance of the first his falcons will never be in trim for long flights, while the want of the latter will invariably lead to the loss of his finest hawks; for even with all appliances of the very best description, it will frequently happen that a strong *ubara*, or black curlew, and a good *bahri* will so far outstrip the speed of a first-rate horse as to get completely out of sight, and if not found at once she will soon gorge herself; and when in this state these black-eyed birds will seldom look at a lure or obey anything but the dictates of their own wild natures, although one or two rare instances are on record of their having gone home to the spot where they were trained. Colonel Coke had a *charugh* which got away in the neighbourhood of Nilab, on the left bank of the Indus, and was found again on the top of his residence at Kohai

Food and Physic—The feeding and physicking of hawks, and a knowledge of all their various disorders, is in itself the study of a lifetime, and the latter a subject on which each falconer professes to have, as a matter of course, some very dark secrets, so that I cannot pretend to give even an outline of their practice; suffice it to say that when a yellow-eyed hawk is too high in flesh a small dose of white sugar is given as a purgative, while charughs and black-eyed birds have a pinch of borax, tied up in a piece of soft, thin flannel, shoved down their throats, which in half an hour acts as an emetic.

The great art in falconry is so nicely to adjust the feeding of each bird that it shall be in the very highest condition and flesh compatible with hard work and wind, but at the same time to have it so sharp-set with hunger as to be extremely keen after its quarry, and at all times obedient to the call and lure. All hawks must have a certain portion of fur, bones, and feathers given them with their food, which will be all rolled up into a ball and thrown out of the mouth some ten or twelve hours after they have been given. This ball is called in England, I believe, the casting of a hawk, and in Afghanistan "*parmorah.*" If this process is not gone through, the bird soon sickens and dies. A sure sign of poor or improper feeding is a peculiar fine worm-eaten looking line, carried across the web of each of the larger feathers of a hawk, which will not disappear till the next moulting season. When a bird is too fat it will not hunt, and if too thin it cannot do so; in the first instance the meat is well soaked in water before given to the hawk, and in the latter more flesh, mixed with a little blood, will soon fatten the bird.

Almost the worst accident which can happen to a hawk, short of breaking a limb, is to get loose with its hood on; for it will then frequently soar into the air, with a peculiar hovering fluttering stroke of the wing, until it is completely lost in the sky, and at last falls down exhausted to die; the only chance in such cases being for the falconer, before the bird has got to any great height, to keep striking the palms of his hands sharply together, the noise of which some-times attracts the poor bird's notice and brings it downwards within reach.

Should any of the principal feathers of a hawk's wing or tail get broken, from dashing against a bush or on the ground while she is in the act of killing her quarry, the feather should be spliced; and for this purpose all the good feathers thrown off at the time of moulting, or those of a dead hawk, should be carefully preserved in a book, or other convenient place. The splice is made by cutting the feather in the bird's wing diagonally across, and adjusting another feather cut exactly to fit it; a needle is then pushed head-first into the pith of the stump in the hawk's wing, and the portion of the new feather passed down over the point of the needle till the splice is almost closed; a little good glue is now painted over both edges of the splice, and the feathers pressed firmly together. If the operation is neatly done the mended feather is just as useful as the original one, and will last till the moulting season.

Natives generally prefer the yellow-eyed hawks, as they are never lost, and give no trouble in following, while they will kill any number of partridges, etc., that can be found in a day. But for real sport there is nothing to equal the charugh or bahrí, and deer-hawking is the cream of this sort of sport.

Shooting.—An Afghan has not the slightest idea of shooting moving objects, nor indeed are the huge, cumbrous weapons generally in use in the country adapted for such practice. This class of field-sports is therefore more circumscribed than with us. Deer-stalking in the hills is only practised by the enthusiastic professional *shikáries* of the mountain ranges, whose whole lives are spent among the haunts of ibex, "*markhore,*" *thar*, and wild sheep; *sirdars* and men of substance have neither the physical energy nor perseverance required for such sport, so that the only hill-shooting in which they indulge is carried on by "*hankwa*," or as it is called here "*Jirgha Shikar*," and consists in having the shooters placed in some pass or well-known run of the game, while the game is driven towards them by a host of *shikáries* and other attendants.

Ahu Gardani—*Ahu Gardani*, or deer-stalking in the open plain, however, is a very favourite amusement of the *sirdars*, and is conducted in the following manner.

Three or four sportsmen, with their attendants, resort to the sandy, open plains, where ravine deer abound, and the shooters, having scattered out to the distance of about two gunshots from each other, lie down flat on the ground, the flatter the better. The *shikáries* and attendants move off in quest of a herd of deer, and endeavour, by keeping at a very long distance from them, not to frighten the animals, but by cautious and exceedingly quiet approaches to make them quietly browse towards the shooters, and generally (nine times out of ten) succeed so well that standing shots are made at from forty to eighty yards, seldom over the latter distance.

Practice on the part of the *shikáries* and attendants, together with extreme patience in the shooters, is all that is required to secure ten or a dozen deer a day in this way, but it is at best but poor sport. Wild hog are mobbed with dogs, cut down with *talwars*, shot, and in fact murdered in every possible way, the poor animal never being allowed the slightest chance for his life. As for spearing a boar in the open plain, an Afghan cannot see the fun of such sport, but, on the contrary, considers the whole proceeding as a tempting of Providence and an unnecessary exposure of both men and horses.

Wild Fowl Shooting.—Wild fowl shooting is practised by almost every person in the Kohistan, at Cabul, and in the Kandahar district. The usual mode of proceeding is to build a small hut with loopholed walls on the margin of some *jhil* or pond of water, and at about some twenty yards from it a whole flock of stuffed ducks of all sorts is placed out on the water to attract passing birds; these decoy-ducks, or "Units" as they are called, are merely the skins of ducks stuffed with a little straw, and fastened on the top of a stick, which is pushed into the soft mud at the bottom of the *jhil*, till the bird appears to float naturally on the water. Whole flocks of ducks are thus allured down and shot On a good day, after a shower of rain, a single Afghan will frequently secure forty or fifty ducks. The wings of cranes are also stretched on a stick, and placed standing separately and upright in the water, and attract passing flocks of cranes from almost incredible distances.

All the common modes of taking wild fowl practised in Hindustan are also resorted to here, but do not require explanation. A novel method, however, which I have not heard of elsewhere, is adopted in the Kohistan. An artificial tank is formed by damming up some small stream or rill, and a small hut built at a sluice gate made in the dam, through the middle of which the cut carrying off the water is carried. A few decoy or tame ducks are placed on the pond, and wild fowl allowed to visit the spot unmolested for several days, till they get quite accustomed to all around them. The fowler now gets into the hut, and remains perfectly quiet till he sees a large flock of ducks sleeping on the water; he then opens the sluice gate, and the water gently running out floats down the ducks quietly into the house by ones and twos, where they are secured without those outside being any the wiser. I am told that two men will thus capture over a hundred ducks in twenty-four hours. Sometimes the middle of the day is best for this sort of wholesale murder, and at others night.

The *chakor* and *seesee*[2] are shot in flocks at springs in the hills during the hot season, and from behind a sort of shield made of two sticks, tied across each other and covered with cloth dyed a dirty yellow colour, having black eyes painted all over it; this strange object so astonishes the birds that they all huddle into a small space, and by degrees approach closer and closer till they arrive within easy range, and are knocked over six and seven at a shot. Another form of this screen is made of two short sticks stock into the sportsman's turban, with a piece of the same sort of yellow cloth fastened between them, and allowed to hang down well over the face like a mask, having two holes to peep through. The man's body is hid behind a rock, and this strange face presented to the birds while they are at some considerable distance off, which makes them pack close and come up to be shot, as in the last instance. Both these methods of killing birds are most strongly condemned by all orthodox Muhammadans, who say that the poor birds mistake the rags covered with eyes for the face of the great prophet, and come up to pay their respects; and that all those which are killed under such circumstances become martyrs.

Netting.—Quails are usually netted, first by a net being thrown

---

2. Small French partridges.

over a corner of a corn-field, and two poles, on which are hung several cages with calling quail in them being stuck up immediately behind the net. This arrangement is usually made very early in the morning, and when the sun is up a long rope is stretched across the other end of the field by two persons, who work it backwards and forwards, so as to make a gentle rustling sound, and gradually carried forwards towards the net; when close to the latter, the fowlers rush up and secure the quails which have been driven under the net; hundreds are thus caught of a morning in the height of the season.

The second method, also a most successful one, is for several men to carry the net over the fields, two men holding the corners of the net in front, and keeping it up by stretching, while the remainder of the party form a line along the back of the net and act as beaters; when a quail is put up under the net, all let go, and the bird is at once secured; this is more generally practised in the evening.

Another form of net is called a *dogazza*, and consists of a tri-angular piece of net stretched between two long and strong reeds, which is carried by a single individual before him through the fields, and secures a quail as it rises.

Dogs.—The dogs of Afghanistan, used for sporting purposes, are of three sorts—the greyhound, pointer, and "*khundi.*" The first are not famed for speed, and would have little chance in a fair course with a second-rate English dog, but they are said to have some endurance, and when trained are used to assist charughs in catching deer, to mob wild hog, and to course hares, foxes, etc., etc. Afghans, however, run everything to kill; and it is not an uncommon sight to see half a dozen of these dogs after a single hare. The pointers are obtained from the hills in the Jalalabad district and the Kohistan; they are large, heavy, slow hunting, but very fine-nosed animals, and staunch to a fault. Their heads are heavy and very square, and altogether the dog reminds one very strongly of the old double-nosed Spanish pointer. "*Khundis*" are the most useful, and at the same time the most cross-bred animals in the country; they have an undoubted cross of the pointer in them, but the rest of their parentage is beyond conjecture; but for working out game from thick cover, there is no breed of dog that I have ever seen like them.

The training of a "*khundi*" commences from the day that it can eat meat. Small pieces of flesh are roasted and trailed along the ground in every direction, and at last thrust under thick bushes of thorns and buried in holes; the young *"khundi"* is then called, and has to hunt up each separate morsel of its food; this sort of practice every day makes them most determined hunters, and accustoms them to work their way through the thickest bushes. They are chiefly used for turning up quail, and partridges to hawks; and it is a beautiful sight to see a good khundi work out a black partridge which has been frightened by a hawk, from the middle of a thick vineyard; and their endurance is such that they can work *through* the whole of a hot day without showing the slightest signs of fatigue.

Afghan *sirdars* have of late taken a great fancy to English dogs of every description, and frequently amuse themselves baiting jackals, badgers, etc with animals which they call *"sag-i-tiger,"* but which are really nothing more or less than the various crosses of the bulldog which are always to be found about the barracks of any European regiment. These *sirdars*, however, will never have a good breed of dogs, as they do not take the slightest trouble about them, but allow all to cross just as it may happen. Were it not for this carelessness, the climate of Afghanistan is so exceedingly favourable to the development of the canine race, that I am quite confident dogs equal to the best imported English could be bred from really good stock with the most ordinary care.

Wolves, jackals, foxes, and vermin of all sorts are hunted and trapped for their skins, which are made up into clothing for the cold season; but this is more in the way of trade than sport. Wolves are taken in deep trenches cut in the form of a circle, leaving a large island, as it were, in the middle, on which the carcase of some dead animal is placed as a bait These trenches are about ten feet deep, four feet wide at top, and not more than one and a half at bottom. The wolf naturally drops into the trench instead of taking it at a bound, and when once in it continues to run round and round the circle, but owing to the narrowness of the trench, has not a chance of working his way up the bank.

The wolves during winter pack together, and while the snow is on the ground are so sharp-set with hunger that they frequently attack single travellers on the main roads, or even horsemen.

In conclusion I may remark that Afghanistan affords a splendid field to its native sportsmen, for on its mountains are to be found *markhore*, ibex, *thar*, wild sheep, and most of the deer common to the Himalaya ranges; while in the plains, ravine, deer, *"yeire"* (a species of leopard), wild hog, and black lynx, together with ducks, woodcock, partridges, etc., etc., are most abundant; but the people of the country are so extremely bigoted and jealous of foreigners that a stranger in these countries runs a much greater chance of being stalked himself than of stalking anything worth the trouble of taking home.

Appendix C

To show the happy-go-lucky way of doing things in those days, Lumsden relates:—

I have only to mention that the man we depended on for supplies of every sort on this long march through foreign country was an old drunken *havildar* (sergeant) of Runjit Sing's army told off for the purpose, who used to come to our tent and drink gin out of our hands, so long as anyone would pour any into them. Yet such was the good order and respect for authority maintained by the old Lion of the Punjab in those days, that this one drunken old soldier of his was enough for all our requirements, and got in all we wanted. I have often thought in later days, after we had discovered of what metal these Seikhs were made, what would have been the fate of the 33rd Native Infantry and many other corps sent in the same scrambling way through the country if the Maharaja Runjit Sing had turned against us. The indignities those proud Seikhs, who felt themselves to be in every way superior as soldiers to our overbearing "Poorbeah Sepoys" of those days, created heart-burnings which nothing but the orders of their own chiefs restrained, and which can be easier felt than described.
We reached Peshawur on the 3rd April and joined General Pollock's force on the 4th. We were encamped within four miles of the mouth of the Khyber Pass and were told off into brigades. Each regiment received orders for its particular position in the attack to come off before daybreak next morning. On retiring from our mess tent on that starlight evening, we could see the heights on either side of the pass brilliantly illuminated by the cooking fires of the various tribes who were to defend them, affording the most heart-stirring display imaginable, especially to

lads on the eve before a soldier's first introduction to the more serious part of his work—the first contact with real warfare.

At two in the morning of the 5th April, 1842, the several corps took up their allotted stations without a bugle-sound, and moved off so as to reach the foot of the hills and commence the attack as the daylight developed. The skirmishers covering the front had not got more than a few hundred yards up the steep incline before they were received with a dropping fire of matchlocks from behind breastworks prepared at every advantageous spot by the Khyberies; but discipline and consequent order proved too much for the courage of even mountaineers on their own chosen ground, and our men soon worked their way from point to point to the crest of the ridge, the enemy retiring before them. Our loss was considerable, of course, but slight when compared with the advantage gained.

We arrived at Ali Musjid about 3 p.m., posted picquets for the protection of our camp during the night, and made the best arrangements we could to secure rest before our early start for next day.

The enemy had evidently been severely punished, they left us unmolested during the night, and in fact offered but little resistance to our further progress to Jellalabad, where General Sale and his brave little garrison triumphantly awaited our arrival, having themselves turned out and administered a disastrous defeat to Muhammad Akbur and his army, which had been besieging them in their trumpery little fort for the last two months.

We halted a long time in the neighbourhood of Jellalabad, re-organising preparatory to our advance on Cabal.

During the interval some Shinwari tribes in the Sungoo Khel Valley made themselves conspicuous by attacking our convoys on the line of communication with Peshawur, cutting off our posts, plundering cattle and cutting up followers sent out on the neighbouring grazing grounds; and at last roused General Pollock's anger to that pitch that he determined to make an example of them and ordered out a lightly equipped column under Brigadier-General Monteith for the purpose.

The 33rd formed part of this force, which entered the beautiful Sungoo Khel Valley by its southernmost end, opposed by the whole of the Shinwari tribes, who at first made a most obstinate resistance, disputing every inch of ground along the spurs of the ridges which commanded the valley on either side. But though they knocked over many of our skirmishers and occasionally obliged the supports to be pushed forward, they could not altogether stop our steady advance, and as soon as we gained the crest of the range they were obliged to abandon it altogether, leaving their valley and villages at our mercy.

It was necessary to make a lasting example of these Shinwaris, who had proved themselves to be the most bloodthirsty of freebooters. Working parties were detailed to undermine the foundations of the walls of the houses and of their surrounding fortified enclosures, and the water of the irrigation canals was led in to sap and destroy them. The trees were cut down and the elephants dragged all the useful timber to the banks of the Cabul River to be floated down to Jellalabad, whilst the sappers blew up the reservoirs and the troops returned to Jellalabad.

ALSO FROM LEONAUR

THE 9TH—THE KING'S (LIVERPOOL REGIMENT) IN THE GREAT WAR 1914 - 1918 *by Enos H. G. Roberts*—Mersey to mud—war and Liverpool men.

THE GAMBARDIER *by Mark Severn*—The experiences of a battery of Heavy artillery on the Western Front during the First World War.

FROM MESSINES TO THIRD YPRES *by Thomas Floyd*—A personal account of the First World War on the Western front by a 2/5th Lancashire Fusilier.

THE IRISH GUARDS IN THE GREAT WAR - VOLUME 1 *by Rudyard Kipling*—Edited and Compiled from Their Diaries and Papers—The First Battalion.

THE IRISH GUARDS IN THE GREAT WAR - VOLUME 1 *by Rudyard Kipling*—Edited and Compiled from Their Diaries and Papers—The Second Battalion.

ARMOURED CARS IN EDEN *by K. Roosevelt*—An American President's son serving in Rolls Royce armoured cars with the British in Mesopatamia & with the American Artillery in France during the First World War.

CHASSEUR OF 1914 *by Marcel Dupont*—Experiences of the twilight of the French Light Cavalry by a young officer during the early battles of the great war in Europe.

TROOP HORSE & TRENCH *by R.A. Lloyd*—The experiences of a British Lifeguardsman of the household cavalry fighting on the western front during the First World War 1914-18.

THE EAST AFRICAN MOUNTED RIFLES *by C.J. Wilson*—Experiences of the campaign in the East African bush during the First World War.

THE LONG PATROL *by George Berrie*—A Novel of Light Horsemen from Gallipoli to the Palestine campaign of the First World War.

THE FIGHTING CAMELIERS *by Frank Reid*—The exploits of the Imperial Camel Corps in the desert and Palestine campaigns of the First World War.

STEEL CHARIOTS IN THE DESERT *by S. C. Rolls*—The first world war experiences of a Rolls Royce armoured car driver with the Duke of Westminster in Libya and in Arabia with T.E. Lawrence.

WITH THE IMPERIAL CAMEL CORPS IN THE GREAT WAR *by Geoffrey Inchbald*—The story of a serving officer with the British 2nd battalion against the Senussi and during the Palestine campaign.